SOCIAL AND COMMUNITY PAEDIATRICS
IN DEVELOPING COUNTRIES

Other titles by G. J. Ebrahim include:

Breast Feeding: the Biological Option
Child Care in the Tropics
Child Health in a Changing Environment
Practical Mother and Child Health in Developing Countries
Handbook of Tropical Paediatrics
Paediatric Practice in Developing Countries
Maternal and Child Health Around the World (with Helen Wallace)
Care of the Newborn in Developing Countries
Nutrition in Mother and Child Health
District Health Care (with R. Amonoo-Lartson, H. J. Lovel and J. P. Ranken)

The authors and publishers wish to thank SIDA (The Swedish International Development Agency) for generously subsidising the paperback edition of this book.

Social and Community Paediatrics in Developing Countries

Caring for the Rural and Urban Poor

G. J. EBRAHIM

MACMILLAN

First published 1985

Published by
Higher and Further Education Division
MACMILLAN PUBLISHERS LTD
Houndmills, Basingstoke, Hampshire RG21 2XS
and London
Companies and representatives
throughout the world

Filmsetting by Vantage Photosetting Co. Ltd,
Eastleigh and London
Printed in Hong Kong

British Library Cataloguing in Publication Data
Ebrahim, G. J.
Social and community paediatrics in developing
countries: caring for the rural and urban poor.
1. Child health services —— Developing countries
I. Title
362.1′9892′00091724   RJ101
ISBN 0-333-39570-0
ISBN 0-333-39571-9 Pbk

Contents

Preface

Lack of adequate coverage continues to remain the most pernicious health problem in many developing countries. The reasons are partly intrinsic and related to the nature of the health services which, being based on an implanted foreign model, largely exist in the form of hospitals and referral centres. National *élites* who adopted the system have tended to opt for a type of health care utilising high technology in prestigious institutions instead of non-institutionalised basic services employing simple interventions which can be assimilated into the existing health traditions. The cost of high technology makes it impossible to provide wide national coverage. Thus, whilst costs have escalated over the last two decades, there has been very little improvement in the health status of the population in many countries.

Another reason for a disappointing record in health coverage is a socio-political one. It is generally agreed that improvement in the physical environment within the home, the neighbourhood and in the community is essential to break the poverty-related interaction between undernutrition and infection. The impressive decline in mortality since the beginning of the century in the more developed countries has been achieved largely through environmental improvements, through hygiene, safe water, sanitation, adequate nutrition and control of communicable diseases. But in many of the less-developed countries, services like education, health, water and sanitation are not justly distributed. The socio-political *milieu* determines the distribution of these services in accordance with the distribution of power in the society. In most developing countries between 40 and 50 per cent of the population subsist below the poverty line. They have no voice in decision-making, and can exercise very little political power. In such societies health and social planning is more responsive to the demands of the rich than to the needs of the poor. The prevalence of preventable diseases indicates the extent to which basic health needs are not being provided in these countries.

At present paediatric care in most developing countries consists largely of hospital care for those fortunate few who can afford it or are within reach of it. But total child care extends beyond acute medical care into preventive and promotive care. These are even more necessary in the case of the disadvantaged. Providing such communities and societal groups with basic needs and services to ensure optimal growth and development of their children is the

main concern of social paediatrics. But health, like socio-economic development, cannot be imposed from above. In community medicine all interventions must be agreed upon with the people and implemented with their active
understanding and support. There is no other way. Failure to act with the
community has often been blamed for the poor impact of a number of
community health programmes in the past. Thus, health planners everywhere
face the daunting challenge of breaking loose from conventional models and
replacing them with community-based programmes aimed at the provision of
basic needs and services for the disadvantaged. The new approach calls for co-
ordination between different government departments and professions.

Experience of the past two decades has shown that poverty is the single most
powerful obstacle to national development. People who are underfed,
illiterate and repeatedly ill can only be passive partners in development. The
creation of human capital is as much the objective as it is the driving force of
development. Thus health has come to occupy an increasingly significant
place in national planning.

Many of the strategies and technologies described here were first set out in
the form of a prize-winning essay on the occasion of the fiftieth anniversary
of SIMAVI (Succurrens in Mundo Afflictis Viribus Iunctis), a voluntary
organisation in The Netherlands. They stress the point that health and other
social services do not necessarily have to be capital intensive and administered
through a highly specialised and complex bureaucracy. A number of simple,
low-cost and decentralised technologies are possible. Since the publication of
the essay, a number of its proposals have been implemented in a district health
programme in Tanzania, and several have come to be adopted within the
national health service of the country. The publication of the book, which
marks the sixtieth anniversary of SIMAVI, is intended to make the experience
available as a text for the training of health and other related professionals.

London, 1985   G.J.E.

1 Community and Social Aspects of Child Care

Growth and development are the two fundamental biological processes of childhood. Growth implies increase in size and development the acquisition of function. But growth and development are more complex than these definitions convey. For example, growth has been compared to the weaving of a tapestry with rich colours and patterns in which each thread is fed into the weaving with specific rates at specific times. Biologically speaking, growth requires a whole set of traffic in different nutrients, energy and biological mediators for controlling cellular differentiation and increase in size and numbers. In order to achieve the full genetic potential of growth the individual needs a balanced interaction between the environment and the genetic endowment. But the environment is never consistently ideal and from time to time growth suffers so that 'catch-up' is necessary in order to recover lost ground. Thus the 'velocity of growth' varies from time to time—partly on account of biological rhythms, e.g. the growth spurt of puberty, and partly on account of the needs for 'catch-up'. Where the environment is inadequate, the needs for catch-up are larger and more frequent, and often individuals end up without achieving the full potential of growth.

The most important environmental influence is that of nutrition. For a number of years classic teaching in nutrition emphasised the importance of protein, especially that of animal origin. Since the early 1960s there has been a growing disquiet concerning the undue emphasis on animal protein, culminating in the present view that a mixture of vegetable proteins is equally adequate, that the early recommended allowances for protein were too high, and that the energy density of the diet is a crucial factor. For supplying the nutritional needs of children, this new understanding raises two important issues. First, the general level of awareness and knowledge amongst parents and the community about nutritional requirements of children, and skills in preparing suitable diets from locally available foods. Secondly, the availability of adequate material resources within the family unit for obtaining food. In a number of countries up to 40 per cent of the rural population have an annual per capita consumer expenditure below the estimated breadline. A great deal of such low levels of living is caused by landlessness in rural areas and

1

unemployment in the cities, especially in Asia and Latin America. In much of tropical Africa it is due to poor techniques of agriculture though landlessness is progressively increasing in several countries. These are then the social origins of undernutrition and underachievement of the growth potential.

Critical period of growth

Growth of body organs occurs in two stages. First is the stage of hyperplasia when cell nuclei divide and subdivide. Next is the stage of hypertrophy during which each newly formed nucleus acquires cytoplasm and becomes a mature cell. Several animal studies have shown that whereas a growing organ can recover from nutritional or other insults if they occur during the stage of hypertrophy, full recovery is rare if the organ happens to be in the stage of hyperplasia at the time of the insult. The stage of hyperplasia is the critical period of growth for the organ. Studies in humans tend to support the concept of 'critical period of growth'. When the growth of the kidney, the heart and the liver in the human fetus was studied, several phases could be identified, as follows:

(1) Between the 14th and 25th weeks of intrauterine life the cells in all the three organs are dividing rapidly and approximately double in number each week.
(2) Between the 30th and 40th weeks there is a rapid growth in cell size. The cells still increase in number but more slowly than before.
(3) At term all three organs still have less than 20 per cent of the numbers of cells characteristic of the adult indicating that further increase in cell number occurs after birth.

In the case of babies who were small-for-dates, the total cell content tended to be low.

However, the body organ most vulnerable to environmental influences in early life is the brain, and the vulnerability of the growing brain to periods of malnutrition is now widely accepted. The period of growth of the human brain corresponding to a 'vulnerable period' in animal experiments would seem to extend from mid-pregnancy to the second birthday. The timetable of brain development is such that many of the events have possibly only a single opportunity to occur. If conditions are not optimal at a given time, that opportunity is lost and compensation may be difficult.

The above discussion brings into proper perspective what is loosely termed 'underachievement of growth'. By looking at the biological phases in which organ growth occurs it identifies the dangers of undernutrition and other adverse environmental influences at critical periods of growth. If the undernutrition and environmental inadequacy are persistent or recurrent, no catch-up may be possible and growth potential may be lost permanently. This may be one way in which disadvantaged groups build up a permanent underclass of second-rate citizens unable to break out of poverty.

Undernutrition is just one of the symptoms of disadvantage. The same inadequate environment and lack of material resources lead to poor and overcrowded housing, lack of sanitation and hygiene, lack of education and a life style in which gross contamination occurs routinely. Infective and parasitic diseases are common and are both the result as well as the cause of poverty by inducing weakness and inability to work. In the case of growing children, infective illnesses like measles, whooping cough and diarrhoea are as important as inadequate diet in the causation of malnutrition.

Many of these causative factors of disturbances in growth also affect development. As the infant grows into a child, cognitive mechanisms also develop. Several studies have shown the importance of environmental stimulation in the development of children. A sense of well-being arising from good health and vigour together with a stimulating home environment in which to apply the natural curiosity of childhood are essential for adequate development. In the disadvantaged home all these are lacking and children often grow up without reaching their full developmental potential. They are often unable to derive the benefits of education and training, go into menial and low-paid jobs and into a life style of poverty thereby perpetuating the intergenerational cycle of disadvantage (see figure 1.1).

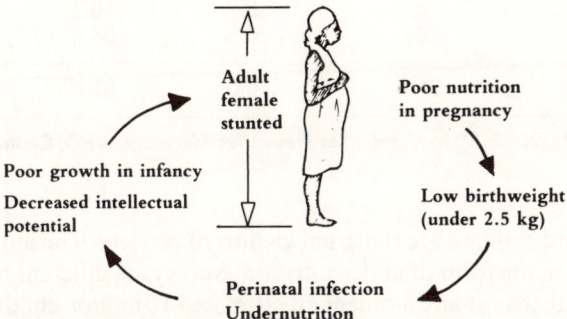

Figure 1.1   The cycle of undernutrition.

The world's one billion 'absolute poor'

A disturbingly large proportion of the world's children are growing up in circumstances of extreme poverty. Life can only hold out experiences of hunger, illness, lack of education, chronic unemployment and lack of opportunities for them. Many of them, if they survive the vulnerable period of childhood, will become driftwood on the social and economic currents of their countries (see table 1.1).

Table 1.1 **The world's poor—1975 to the year 2000**

| | Population (millions) | | | |
| | 1975 | | | 2000 |
	Total population	Absolute poor	Under-nourished	Total population (estimated)
Low-income countries (per capita income US$ 300)	1300	700–800	400–640	2000 +
Middle-income countries (per capita income US$ 300 +)	800	150–200	80–120	1200 +
High-income countries (per capita income US$ 2000 +)	700	50–70	20–35	800 +

Table 1.2 **Total number of children affected by malnutrition**

| Area | Population aged 0–5 years | No. with malnutrition (millions) | | |
		Severe	Moderate	Total
Latin America	46	0.7	8.8	9.5
Africa	61	2.7	16.3	19.0
Asia	206	6.6	64.4	71.0
Grand Total	314	10.0	89.5	99.5

Source: De Maeyer, E. M. In *Nutrition in Preventive Medicine.* WHO, Geneva. 1976. p. 28.

Women and children are the usual victims of poverty. The most immediate effect is seen in the form of undernutrition. Surveys in different regions of the world indicate that at any moment an estimated 10 million children are in the grip of severe malnutrition and a further 200 million are inadequately nourished (see table 1.2). As a result, about half of the 15 million children who die each year in the developing world are killed by malnutrition or by diseases, usually infections, that malnutrition makes fatal.

Who are the world's poor?

As table 1.1 indicates, 'absolute poverty' is concentrated among the low-income countries and so is malnutrition. About 40 per cent of the poor are concentrated in India, Bangladesh, Pakistan, the Philippines and other south Asian countries. About 20 per cent are in China though China's food security as well as basic health and education services blunts the impact of poverty. Nevertheless, it is estimated by the World Bank that approximately 150 million in China have living standards similar to the absolute poor. Fifteen per cent of the absolute poor are to be found in sub-Saharan Africa and another 15 per cent in Indonesia and Indo-China. Latin America, north Africa and the Middle East have about 3–4 per cent each of the world's absolute poor.

The greatest majority of the absolute poor are the rural poor who provide agricultural labour or non-farm work dependent on agriculture. More than half are either small farmers themselves or lease land. The remaining 20–25 per cent are landless with precarious livelihoods. It is the landless labourer who is more likely to see his job disappear in a crisis and is less able to fall back on reserves including the final option of selling or mortgaging land. Most landless labourers are to be found in countries with high population densities like Bangladesh, India and Pakistan. In some Latin American countries over half the rural dwellers are agricultural labourers, e.g. Chile, 66 per cent; Mexico, 49 per cent; Brazil, 26 per cent. It is also worth bearing in mind that up to 25 per cent of the labour force in rural areas is involved in non-agricultural pursuits like handicrafts, food processing, service and repair, leather work, tailoring, metalwork, carpentry, etc. Their work is threatened by industrial mass production and consumer goods arriving from the cities.

The needs of children

These facts indicate the need to identify certain basic needs of children to achieve the optimum in growth and development. When the needs are not fully met, growth deficits arise from which recovery may be possible to a certain extent. But if the deficits are prolonged or recurrent, as amongst the children of the absolute poor, the ground is set for a vicious cycle of undernutrition, interacting with adverse environmental influences and pathogens leading to further deterioration of growth. The poor do not possess the knowledge, economic strength nor political power to bring about improvements in their physical and social environments. Overcrowding, lack of hygiene, inadequate water and sanitation, contaminated food, vermin and pests are all the accompaniments of poverty.

In the circumstances of an average developing country growth failure in children carries connotations that extend beyond the medical diagnosis. It indicates unmet needs and deficiencies in the environment. In some cases it also points to the fact that serious troubles lie ahead since the same adverse influences can lead on to a variety of undesirable consequences. In a study of 3000 children aged 1–36 months in the Punjab, it was observed that child mortality doubled with each 10 per cent decline in body weight below 80 per cent of Harvard median for weight. A similar study in Bangladesh of 2019 children aged 13–23 months showed that weight for age and arm circumference were strong indicators of mortality risk. Children whose weights were less than 65 per cent of the Harvard median experienced a three-fold higher death rate in the next 2 years compared with those whose weights were above this level. By the arm circumference measurement the worst 10 per cent of the children were found to have five times higher mortality risk compared with the

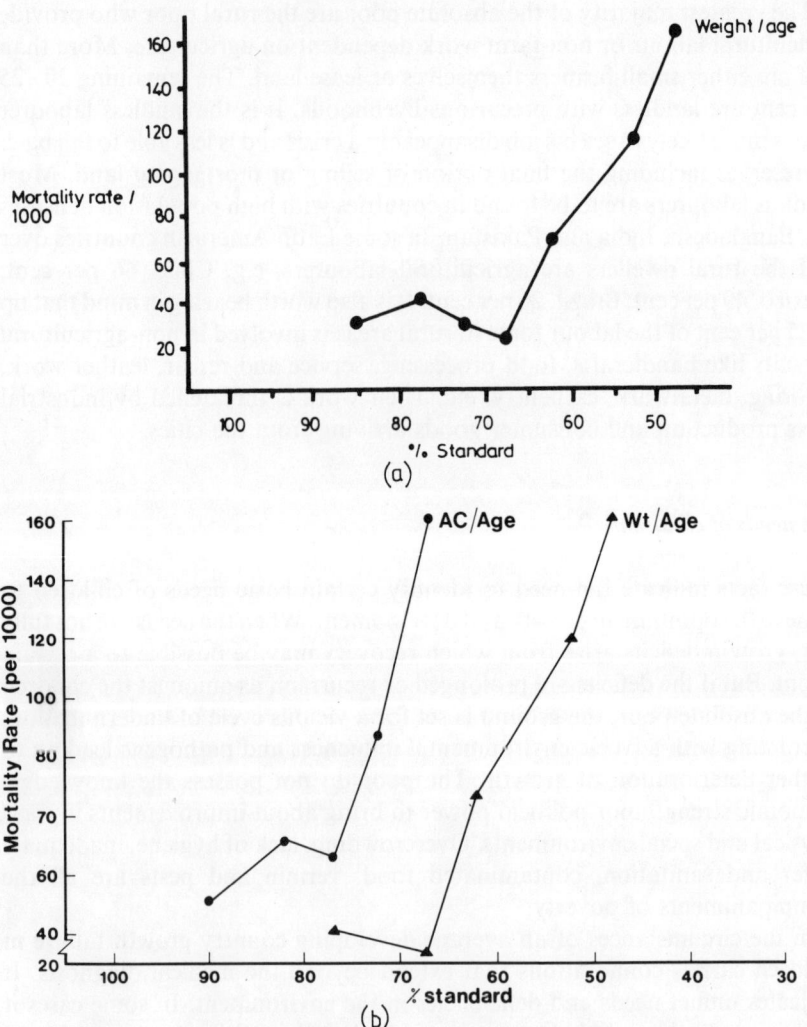

Figure 1.2   Malnutrition and mortality. (a) Punjab. (b) Bangladesh. AC = Arm circumference.

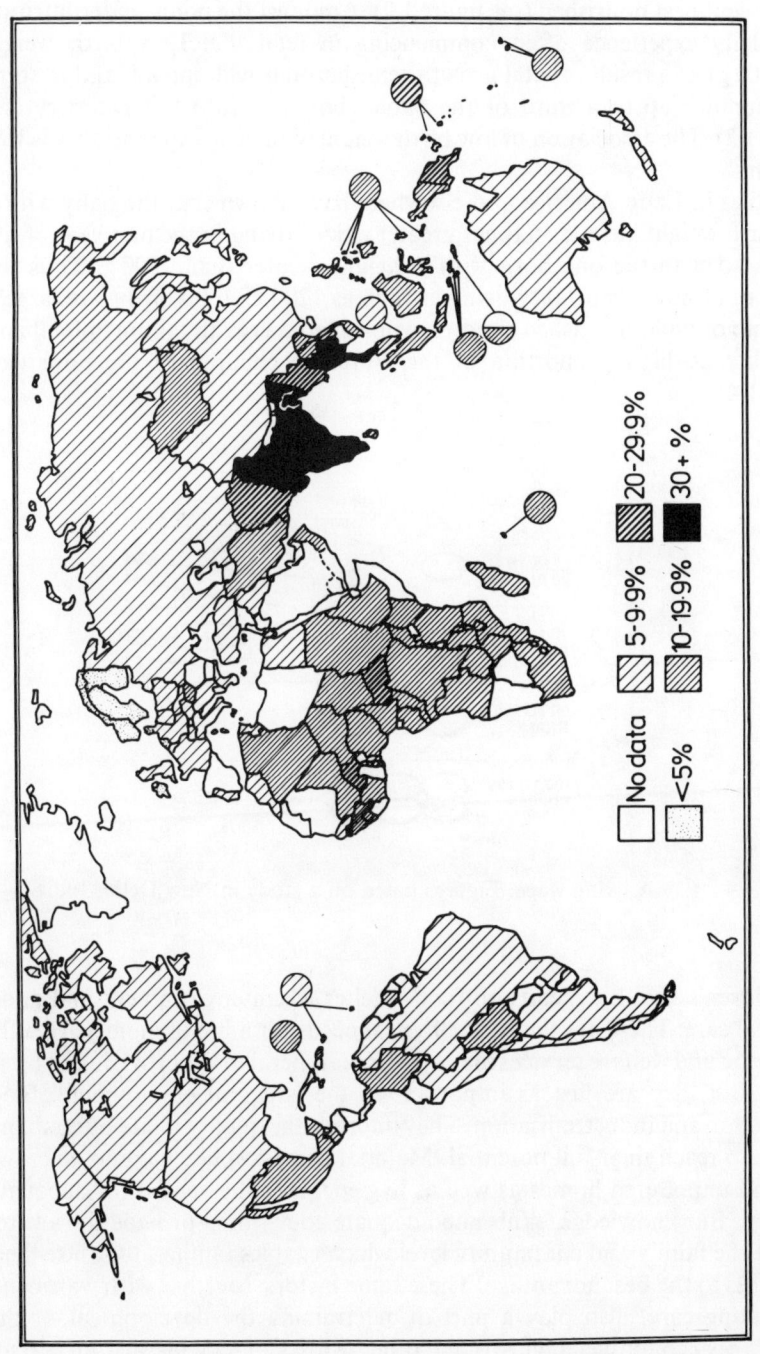

Figure 1.3   Prevalence of low birth weight.

10 per cent best nourished (see figure 1.2). Amongst the poor, undernutrition is a daily experience often commencing in fetal life. Low birth weight (<2500 g) as a result of fetal growth retardation is widespread, and in some communities up to a third of the babies born fall into this category (see figure 1.3). The association of low birth weight with neonatal mortality is well known.

Studies in Latin America and elsewhere have shown that the baby with a low birth weight has a 5–6 times greater risk of dying in the first year of life compared with the one born with a weight greater than 2500 g. Thus the statistics of infant mortality being as high as 120 per 1000 births are largely made up of undernourished children who suffered growth failure in fetal and early life. A high proportion of these are the children of the poor (see figure 1.4).

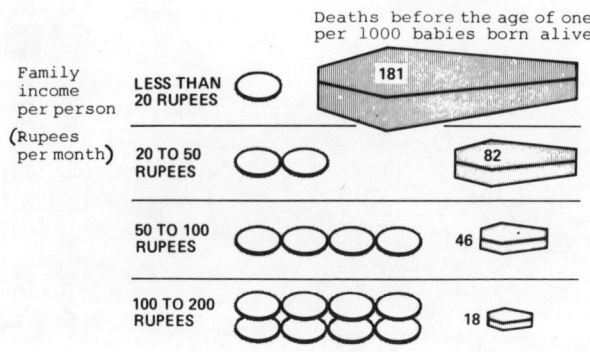

Figure 1.4   A living wage. Figures based on a study in New Delhi, India.

Children's health depends on food, shelter, clean environment and good parental care. These are the basic physical needs for a life of dignity. Health, education and welfare services may appear peripheral to the provision of basic needs. But they are just as important as the issues of employment, food production and industrialisation. They improve the quality of life by enabling people to reach their full potential. Material provision like income, uncrowded and unpolluted homes as well as hygiene, are all essential for adequate survival. But knowledge, skills and adequate counselling provide the awareness at the family and community level which enables families to utilise their resources to the best advantage. These same factors, together with warm and stimulating care, also play a part in determining the development of the infant's own cognitive, linguistic and other skills. Competence acquired at an early stage in life can profoundly influence later intellectual achievement.

The place of health services in the basic needs approach

Faced with the enormous problems of poverty-related diseases, health workers often ask whether the services they provide can have any effect on the determinants of disease. Preventive and promotive services can undoubtedly produce a measurable impact. For the poor, freedom from ill health means availability for work. Literacy for them means awareness of their rights, e.g. basic wages. Counselling through service contacts helps them utilise their scarce resources. The crucial question for health workers is making their services available to all, including those families who do not or cannot come to the health facilities because they feel excluded and unwanted. In all societies the upper social classes have the skills, economic strength and political power to divert all available resources including services to their own best advantage. Providing adequate and regular coverage with basic health care to the disadvantaged groups in the community continues to remain the major challenge in health planning this century. When the distribution of health care in a society is governed largely by the market forces, then its availability to families will be no different from that of cars, refrigerators and television sets. Removal of the élitist element and instilling the egalitarian outlook with focus on disadvantaged groups can be one way in which health services can respond to the challenge of poverty. It has been the experience in several countries that when health care is being provided through auxiliaries, village health workers (VHW) and trained traditional birth attendants (TBA), over 80–90 per cent of the clients tend to be families from the poor and low-status groups. A second approach will be to make the health services more relevant to the problems. This will mean shifting the emphasis to preventive and promotive aspects of health care from the predominantly curative care to which most health workers have been conditioned by their training.

A core bundle of basic needs identifies the minimum requirements of a family. In addition to the obvious needs for adequate food, shelter, clothing and household equipment, basic needs also include essential services like health, education, safe drinking water, and sanitation. Several of these services are to be considered in detail further in the book.

Family resources and child health

The majority of the world's poor live in countries that are so poor that provision of basic needs for the people even at relatively elementary levels can only be achieved by a much more egalitarian distribution of income and communal services than is currently the case. In most developing countries the richest 10 per cent of the households receive about 40 per cent of national personal income whereas the poorest 40 per cent of the households receive 15 per cent or less (see table 1.3).

Table 1.3 **Income to the poorest 60 per cent and the wealthiest 5 per cent of the population of various countries***

Country	Poorest 60%	Wealthiest 5%
Argentina	30	29
Brazil	23	38
Chile	27	23
Colombia	16	40
Mexico	22	29
Peru	17	48
India	36	20
Iraq	16	34
Philippines	25	28
Sri Lanka	27	18
Burma	36	28
Ivory Coast	30	29
Malagasy	23	37
Nigeria	23	38
Niger	35	23
Senegal	20	36
Sierra Leone	19	24
Sudan	29	17

* Incomes are expressed as percentages.
Source: Adapted from Adelman, I. and Morris, L.T. *Economic Growth and Social Equity in Developing Countries*. Stanford University Press, 1973.

Distribution of wealth not only determines the availability of family resources but also the distribution of services, since economic strength determines political power and controls the decision-making process. Hence services like health, education, water and sanitation are not always justly distributed. The socio-political systems of a society determines the distribution of these services in accordance with the distribution of power in the society. Hence services in rural areas are often non-existent or of inferior quality. Child and family health in all countries are related to the availability, accessibility and utilisation of services. To the family with poor means, the importance of preventive and promotive services is even greater because they help to supplement the scarce resources at home for the care of children.

Environmental influences

The family and home provide the immediate physical, social and cultural environments of the child. Through the family the child receives his nurture, his upbringing and protection from the external physical environment. The child will receive his status in society from his family and kinship network. Thus the family is not only his first environment, but also the one by which he is surrounded all his life. It is through the family that the wider issues of the community and society determine the life experiences of the child. The prevalent customs will mould the child's habits and the beliefs and values of the community become part of his make-up. As the child grows into an adult, he becomes an integral part of the network of relationships of the family. The family's social status or class is the initial status of the child. The family's educational and economic status determines the nutrition, physique and material well-being of its children (see figure 1.5).

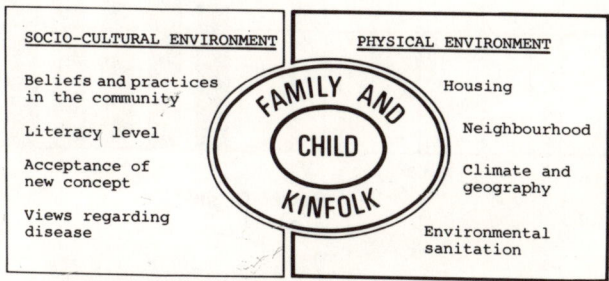

Figure 1.5   The family: an immediate environment.

The qualities of the society ranging from harmony and stability to change and conflict, as well as its concern for the general well-being of *all* its members will influence the type and quality of services made available to its members. The social system is often a major determinant of health and disease, since by determining the social, physical and cultural environments it influences the interaction between the genes and the environment. There is ample evidence from several countries to show the association between insufficient material resources and high child mortality. In Britain a commission appointed to look into inequalities in health came to the conclusion that 'occupational class differences are *real* sources of difference in the risk of infant mortality' (see figure 1.6).

What evidence is there to show that availability of services reduces the incidence of disease or death and improves the general welfare? Standards of living are determined not only by material wealth but also through the availability of such amenities as water and sanitation, education and cultural facilities, social welfare, nutrition programmes, communicable disease control and similar services. There is now growing evidence from several countries that rapid improvements in morbidity and mortality figures occur when such services are being delivered to the majority of the population. They blunt the effects of a poverty-related environment. In Sri Lanka the institution of the food coupon system which catered for all families with incomes less than

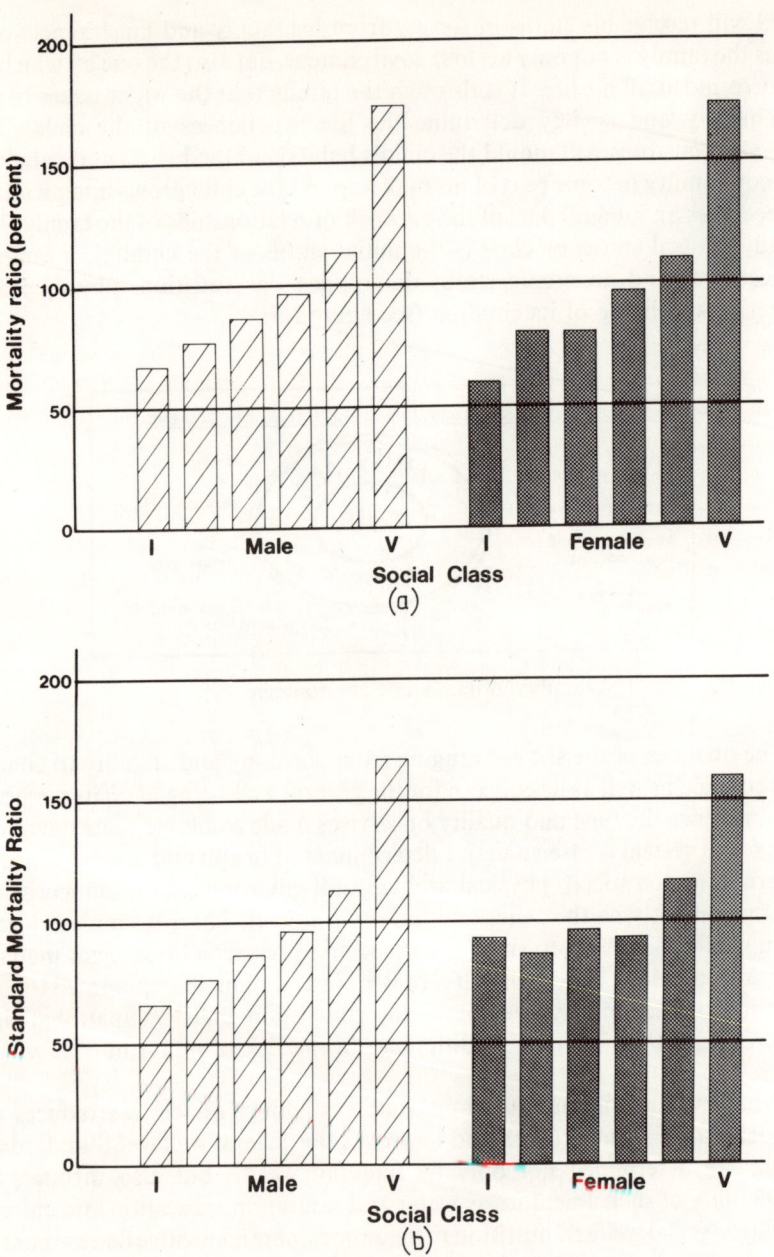

Figure 1.6   Mortality by occupational class of parents. (a) Infants (aged under 1 year). (b) Children (aged 1–14 years).

Source: Occupational Mortality 1970–72. HMSO, London. 1978. p. 196.

US$ 10 (Rs. 300) per month marked the beginning of improvements in the quality of life. The system carried a choice of nine major food commodities and influenced 20 per cent calorie consumption and 14 per cent income of poor families. Together with free education and health services, and a good nationwide coverage of both, there has been a marked effect on infant mortality and life expectancy. In Kerala, one of the poorest states in India, mass literacy and universal primary education together with a more equitable distribution of health services as well as the availability of food at controlled prices through government shops have jointly produced a similar effect on health. Kerala has one of the lowest infant mortality rates and highest life expectancy and literacy rates amongst all the states of India. In both Sri Lanka and Kerala the processes of social development which have brought about the improvements in health have also had the 'domino effect' of initiating improvements in other aspects of life, e.g. fertility decline, improved status of women, reduction of social disparity and so on.

Similar improvements in the quality of life have been documented from China and Cuba where remarkable progress has been achieved in a short span of 20 years or so. In both countries the provision of services and a good nationwide coverage have been underpinned by socialist ideology. Such rapid improvements are also possible in non-socialist communities as demonstrated in Jamkhed, India, where within less than 10 years after a severe famine there has been a decline in infant mortality reaching a low of a third of the national average. Three main lessons have been identified from these experiences:

(1) Urban areas in many countries systematically exploit the villages. Expenditure on urban hospitals diverts financial and other resources from the countryside.
(2) A highly bureaucratised administration in which the worker is not responsible to the immediate community but to a distant supervisor can have very little effect on health.
(3) A political system where the village-level politician looks to the city-based party machine and does not represent the wishes of the people cannot fuel the engines of development.

Community care of children: What services are needed?

Since community services play such an important role in satisfying basic needs it is necessary to consider their design, organisation, content and methods of delivery. At the time of independence, several countries inherited a medical service largely based on a network of hospitals situated in the larger towns and cities together with the rudiments of a rural health service operating through health centres and sub-centres. A characteristic feature of the health system

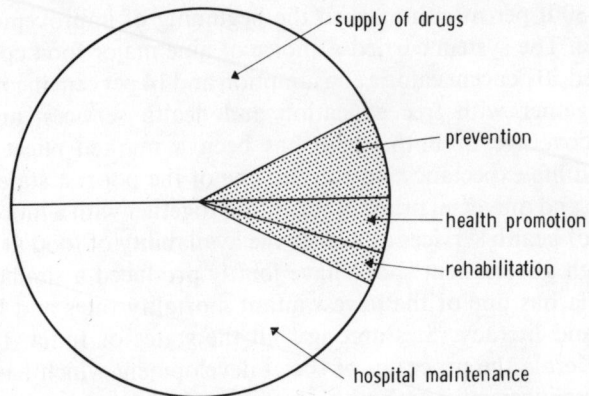

Figure 1.7   Allocation of health resources in the average developing country.

was that being an alien system developed primarily to look after the expatriate administrator, it did not get assimilated into the national consciousness, and the vast majority of the population continued to be served by the existing indigenous systems of care. After independence the hospital services continued to look after the Western-educated upper classes, who constitute the powerful élite, in a way that reinforces the prestige of the medical specialist. Allocation of health resources in many countries has consequently remained skewed in favour of secondary and tertiary care which consume up to 80 per cent or more of the health budget for the benefit of mostly the urban élite (see figure 1.7). The result is that not more than 20 per cent of the rural population receive health care on a regular basis, and the position of the urban poor is no better in spite of their proximity to the centres of excellence (see figure 1.8). This state of affairs has introduced a number of disparities in health care organisation, as follows:

NUTRITION

At least one child in three in the poorest countries is unhealthy because of inadequate nutrition.

WATER AND SANITATION

Four children out of every five in the rural areas of the Third World do not have adequate water supply or safe sanitation.

HEALTH CARE

Nine children out of every ten born in the less priviledged parts of the world are never seen by health workers.

Figure 1.8   The challenge of health care in the developing world.

(1) There is the disparity between expenditure and need. Most of the health expenditure, as described above, is on hospitals which are urban institutions by their very nature. The real health needs are for prevention, improved nutrition, water and sanitation and improvement of the environment.

(2) As a corollary of the above, doctors trained for many years in modern hospitals prefer to work in an environment similar to the medical centres where they trained. Even though several medical schools have developed field practice areas, the bulk of the training continues to be curative and oriented towards hospital practice. Furthermore, acute care is rapidly sliding into intensive care demanding ever-more expenditure on curative care.

(3) There is a disparity between growth of population and expansion of services. The real growth in numbers is occurring in rural areas where 80 per cent of the population reside. But rural services are not growing at the same rate. The overcrowded hospitals and maternity wards in the cities are more obvious and carry the added threat of commissions of inquiry. Thus the tendency is for more and more resources to be directed to urban areas.

The result of these trends is for health services to drift away from the basic issues of rural development. Curative care has become a substitute for environmental improvement at which it is proving ineffectual, and tertiary care services are used to provide rudimentary primary care which is wasteful of resources.

Environmental influences on health

Several studies in the industrialised countries have shown that the marked decline in infant and child mortality and improvement in family health have been the result of improvements in the environment. There is a need for the shift of effort from the hospital ward and the laboratory to epidemiology and community studies. Modification of the conditions that lead to disease is likely to be more fruitful than intervention in the mechanism of disease after it has occurred. The technologies and approaches for improving the physical environment are not necessarily fixed and finite. Capital-intensive and highly centralised systems have evolved in the Western countries but low-cost, simpler and decentralised technologies suitable for the small village population are also possible and have rapidly developed during the last decade or so. Improvements in the environment are normally effected through a number of services like health, education, housing, water and sanitation as well as through mechanisms like community awareness and mobilisation. Experience in all countries teaches an important lesson: in community health all interventions can only be undertaken with the people and through the people. There is no other way (see figure 1.9).

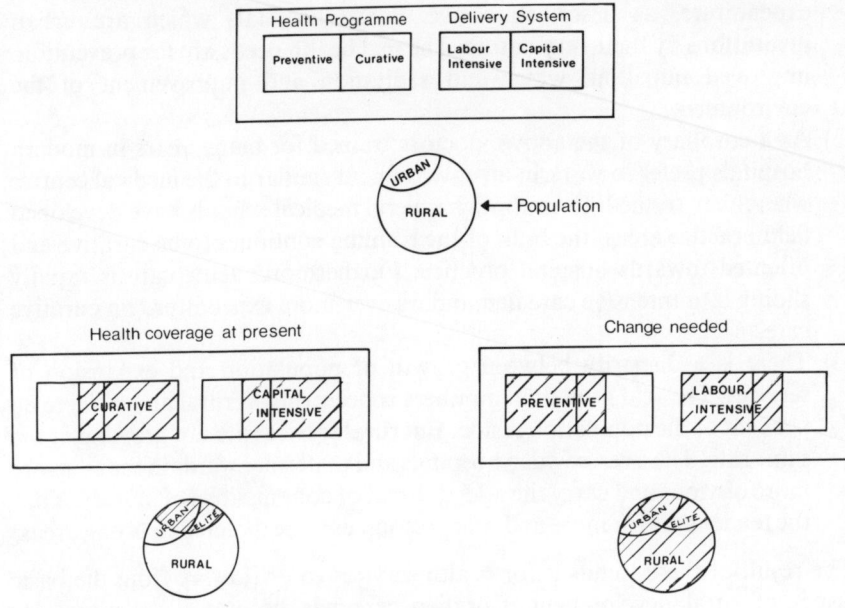

Figure 1.9   Changes needed in the health care system.

Primary Health Care approach for environmental improvement

The primary health care approach has been developed as a result of the recognition of the inappropriateness of the present hospital-based curative services focused largely on the urban élite. Such services have assumed that with modernisation and economic growth health status will improve; and that with improved means of transport, rural populations will become linked with modern hospitals in the cities. The course of events in many countries since independence has provided ample evidence that such an assumption is false. The basic mistake is to believe that the determinants of health and disease are predominantly biological and the solutions to health problems are to be sought within the framework of modern medicine. Secondly, modern medicine is being wrongly conceived of as a 'science' not to be tainted by wider cultural social and economic considerations. Thirdly, the concept that social problems are solved only through economic growth is naïve, and a reformulation of the conceptual framework on which to base medical services and medical education has been found necessary.

The characteristic features of primary health care are coverage, especially of the neediest, and its suitability for community action. Community initiative for improving health must include housing, water and sanitation as well as medical care; literacy and health-related awareness as well as immunisation; improvements in the social and cultural environment as well as preventative mental health; community development as well as community health services. Thus primary health care forms part of the overall development process and is closely linked to the general distribution of productive resources including land, education and employment as well as to the productive process (see figure 1.10).

The development process in health requires a continuous input of information for creating awareness within the community. There is the need for *epidemiological data* like demography, births and deaths, morbidity,

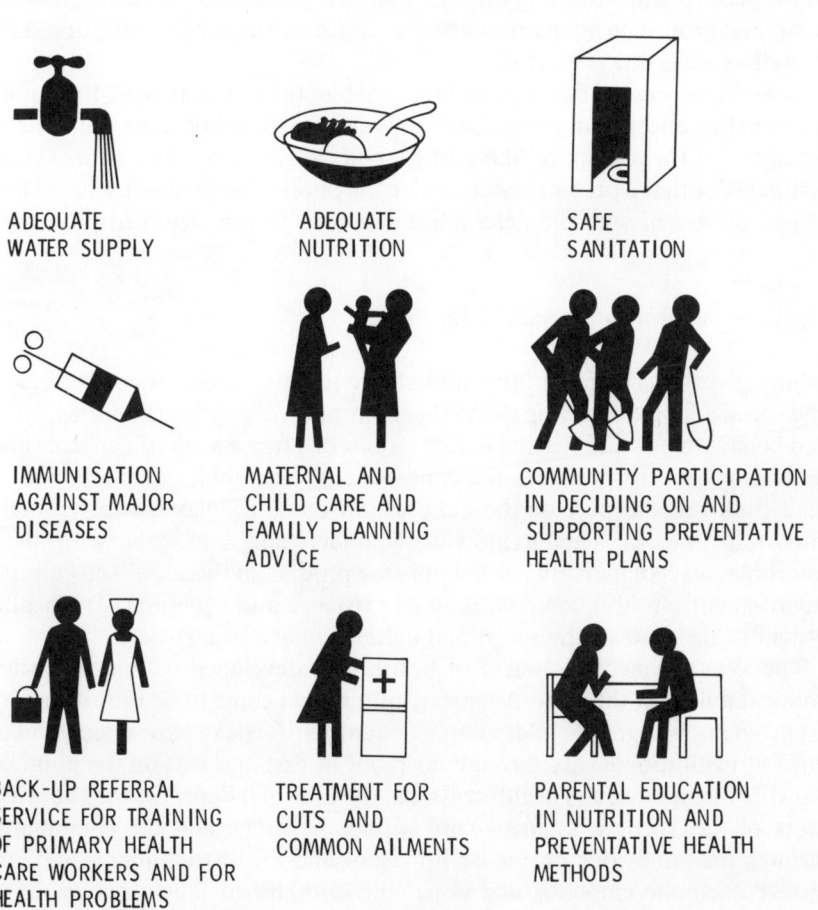

ADEQUATE
WATER SUPPLY

ADEQUATE
NUTRITION

SAFE
SANITATION

IMMUNISATION
AGAINST MAJOR
DISEASES

MATERNAL AND
CHILD CARE AND
FAMILY PLANNING
ADVICE

COMMUNITY PARTICIPATION
IN DECIDING ON AND
SUPPORTING PREVENTATIVE
HEALTH PLANS

BACK-UP REFERRAL
SERVICE FOR TRAINING
OF PRIMARY HEALTH
CARE WORKERS AND FOR
HEALTH PROBLEMS
REQUIRING MORE
QUALIFIED CARE

TREATMENT FOR
CUTS AND
COMMON AILMENTS

PARENTAL EDUCATION
IN NUTRITION AND
PREVENTATIVE HEALTH
METHODS

Figure 1.10   The elements of primary health care.

nutritional status, infections and infestations; *environmental data* like food and water supply, housing and sanitation as well as life style; and *health service data* based on utilisation of services. All such information requires wider dissemination and discussions in meetings and in small groups, followed by an action plan which is generally acceptable and is put into action. One of the problems is that in many communities health services are imposed from above with little awareness in the community about the common health problems and the circumstances that lead to ill health. The health process requires one or more community structures consisting of elected groups or councils who will work as mobilisers and equal partners with the health personnel. In countries where the social divide is large, care must be taken to ensure the involvement of the poorest and women in order to ensure that the traditional élite and the wealthiest groups do not monopolise the service and thereby acquire new skills as well as access to resources.

A health process of development that enables the disadvantaged to identify their health concerns, organise for actions around those concerns and develop solutions to them is more likely to generate self-reliance and cohesiveness compared with the present system where the poorest are largely excluded and at best presented with pre-determined solutions to pre-identified problems.

The socio-cultural milieu and child health

In any given environment human existence involves a process of biological and social adaptation giving rise to the elaboration of a system of norms, ideas and behaviours. Child rearing occurs within this framework of concepts and behaviours. As the practices and concepts acquire stability over a period of time they become part of the culture and come to play an increasingly important role in helping individuals understand and cope with their environments. An individual is not only the product of the social and cultural environment but also contributes to its existence and evolution. The health system is also part of the social and cultural milieu of a society.

The Western medical system of health care developed within the socio-political milieu of the Euro-American culture and came to be introduced by expatriate power groups in developing countries It took shape mainly in the form of institutional care through hospitals at first and was on the point of growing further through health centres at the time of independence. The grass roots of the Western system—care within the home and the community through the family doctor, the health visitor and the district nurse—did not receive adequate emphasis and is patchily established. Such services have come to play a lowly subordinate role. Non-institutionalised basic care utilising simple technologies that can be adapted and assimilated within the existing traditional systems received only scant attention. Training programmes have also developed along a similar line.

The high cost of hospital care makes it impossible to free resources for developing health services and provide adequate national coverage. Thus while the cost of health care has increased, there have been virtually no improvements in health.

In all countries where gains in health have occurred they are through promotive programmes reaching out to the maximum number of people rather than through curative activities meeting the needs of the few. Most improvements in health statistics are the result of better nutrition, water and sanitation, a widespread understanding of the benefits of a healthy life style, and promotive care for the health surveillance of the vulnerable groups. Social consciousness within the society in general and the professions in particular has contributed to wider coverage with such promotive activities. Hence the need for low-cost innovative approaches in developing countries aimed at improving the quality of life of the weaker sections of the society.

If promotive services are to have any impact on the child's environment, they must be sensitive to the socio-economic circumstances (i.e. housing and general material resources of the family), the home (physical environment including sanitation and hygiene) and the family (the emotional environment including education levels of the parents and stimulation provided to children; see figure 1.11). The main factors affecting the health (and deaths) of children are most often to be found in the child's environment, especially the home and the family. Thus most opportunities for prevention lie within the home and the community, and depend on the provision of easily available, accessible and competent care and advice with ease of referral to more skilled care when required. There is more to child care than curative hospital care. Sadly it is the only type of care in which most paediatricians in developing countries have

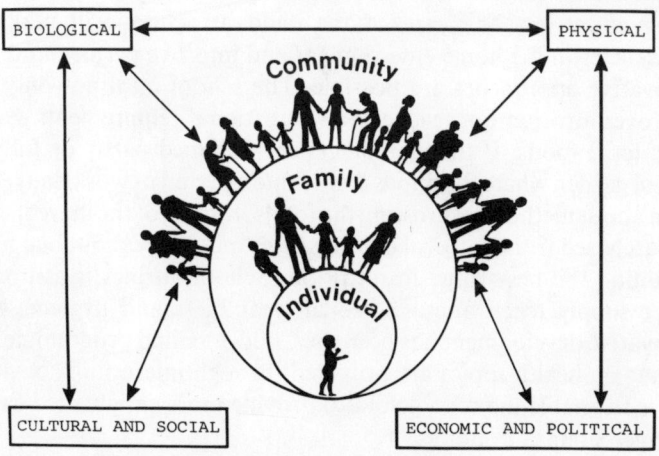

Figure 1.11   The environmental influences in child health.

been hitherto trained. There is a need for intensive care to recede from its dominant position and make way for the following forms of paediatric care:

(1) *Paediatrics of life style and habit*: The need for good counselling and care with regard to feeding, immunisation, care during common illnesses like malaria, fever, diarrhoea, and for family planning. Such counselling is best provided through an individual in the neighbourhood who is well known to the family and acts as a link with the health service. The disadvantaged and the alienated can respond best to one of their own group whom they can trust, and not to cultured voices from a distance.

(2) *Paediatrics of prevention*: Infection and malnutrition form a formidable combination, and both are preventable. Control of measles, whooping cough and diarrhoea together with regular health surveillance and nutrition advice can bring about a marked decline in mortality in a relatively short time. The under-5s and antenatal clinics are the two services well suited for such interventions.

(3) *Paediatrics of public health*: The child and the family are part of the general community, and their environment can be improved through a number of measures that improve the general environment of the community. Improvements of water supply, sanitation, disposal of refuse and the level of hygiene are examples of environmental interventions. Equally important is community organisation with a continuing dialogue about the common health problems, developing plans to deal with them and evaluating the degree of success. A rise in the general level of awareness about the social and environmental determinants of health and of the available technologies to deal with them can be a major step towards improvement in the quality of life.

(4) *Paediatrics of education*: School health services have not yet developed in many countries. The care of the child at school will make up for deficiencies in the home environment and improve performance. Several innovative approaches are possible. The school meal not only helps to improve nutrition but teaches how nutritional requirements can be met from local foods. If the ingredients are obtained partly or fully from a school garden where the pupils contribute a period of work daily, they also learn about methods of growing the foods. If some of the ingredients are to be purchased from the local market, the pupils learn about budgeting and obtaining the best value in nutrition. School latrines, washrooms and water supply teach about personal cleanliness and hygiene. A recent innovative development has been the Child-to-Child programme in which lessons on health topics are provided through interesting activities. The aim is to enable the schoolchild to provide more enlightened care of the younger siblings at home.

(5) *Paediatrics of developement—care of the handicapped child*: Physical or mental handicap, hearing and vision defects, speech and learning

disability and similar other defects are known to affect on average one in ten children. Many of these are preventable, e.g. blinding malnutrition (xerophthalmia), polio paralysis, partial deafness following otitis media. Services for prevention and remedial help can become part of the overall child care in the community.

(6) *Paediatrics of mental health*: Improved nutrition, community cohesion, improved quality of family life through counselling and support during family crises will help reduce anti-social behaviour and delinquency. In many countries the rural and the urban poor are the abandoned people with no hope and no one to turn to in crisis. Community services, however elementary, will replace despair with hope and help families develop strategies to cope with their problems.

The above six types of services form the main body of community and social paediatrics. They represent the awareness amongst paediatricians and health workers in several countries of their responsibility towards not only those who come seeking their help in the hospitals but also towards those who do not or cannot. It is largely through historical circumstances that curative care has come to occupy a dominant central position. It should in fact be the seventh service in the above list, and together with the others help the healthy child to achieve an optimum in growth and developement.

Further reading

Aaron, A., Hawes, H. and Gayton, J. (1979). *Child-to-Child*. Macmillan Press, Basingstoke and London.

Chen, L. C., Chowdhury, A. K. M. A. and Huttman, S. L. (1980). Anthropometric assessment of energy–protein malnutrition and subsequent risk of mortality among pre-school age children. *Am. J. Clin. Nutr.* **33**: 1836–45.

Dobbing, J. (1981). The later development of the brain and its vulnerability. In David, J. A. and Dobbing, J. (eds) *Scientific Foundations of Paediatrics*. 2nd edn. Heinemann, London.

Ebrahim, G. J. (1982). *Child Health in a Changing Environment*. Macmillan Press, Basingstoke and London.

Kielman, A. A. and McCord, C. (1978). Weight-for-age as an index of risk of death in children. *Lancet* **i**: 1247–50.

Korten, D. C. and Alfonso, F. B. (1983). *Bureaucracy and the Poor. Closing the Gap*. Kumarian Press, Connecticut.

Krishnaji, N. (1975). In *Poverty, Unemployment and Development of Policy: A Case Study of Selected Issues with Reference to Kerala*. Document ST/ESA/29. United Nations, New York.

Lipton, M. (1977). *Why Poor People Stay Poor. A Study of Urban Bias in World Development.* Temple Smith, London.

Maitrayee, M. (1983). Human development through primary health care: case studies from India. In Morley, D., Rohde, J. and William, G. (eds) *Practising Health for All.* Oxford University Press, Oxford. pp. 133–144.

Mata, L. J. (1978). *The Children of Santa Maria Cauque: A Prospective Field Study of Health and Growth.* MIT Press, Cambridge (Ma.) and London.

Mountjoy, A. B. (ed.) (1978). *The Third World: Problems and Perspectives.* Macmillan Press, Basingstoke and London.

Myrdal, G. (1970). *The Challenge of World Poverty.* Penguin Books, Harmondsworth.

Townsend, P. and Davidson, N. (1982). *Inequalities in Health.* Penguin Books, Harmondsworth.

Wallace, H. and Ebrahim, G. J. (eds) (1981). *Maternal and Child Health Around the World.* Macmillan Press, Basingstoke and London.

2 Health in the Context of Development

Economic thinking in the past has been concerned largely with the process of development as being a matter of factories, roads, transport, power lines, the gross national product, and so on. The emphasis has been mainly on the means of production, the creation of wealth and on the indices for measuring economic activity. Use of terminology like 'pre-industrial society' synonymously with 'developing countries' is an example of such thinking. But there is more to the process of development than the setting up of light and heavy industry, or the use of technology in agriculture. In the past two decades many developing societies have experienced the setting up of large industrial complexes. Many of these are functioning as islands of advanced technology with no supporting base of knowledge, technical skills and experience extending into the community. On the other hand, the economic reconstruction of Western Europe and Japan after the Second World War has demonstrated that when this base of scientific knowledge and experience in the community has remained intact and only the tip of the pyramid in the form of factories and communications has been demolished, the process of reconstruction is not difficult. Out of such experiences has come the second view of development: that development comes from the processes of growth occurring within a society and not from erecting structures. True development can occur only through the development of man. Human capital is the most productive force of all. Physical capital and the so-called infrastructure of industry are only the tools of development.

Development of man implies universal education, knowledge and skills. It implies health and vitality of the population, and a climate of social justice within which the drives of the people are channelled to exploit the natural resources for common good. All these factors are lacking in the Third World countries. Almost 80 per cent of the population of the developing world is rural. The life styles of these rural communities without adequate health and educational facilities, lack of sufficient potable water (or water that is heavily contaminated when available), poor nutrition causing debility and a succession of illnesses leave no doubt that the main tool of development, man, is lacking in the vitality and skills required to master his environment (see figure

23

2.1). The prevailing philosophy of the national development programmes of many of these countries did not place emphasis on genuine reforms and new approaches in the matter of health and education—both of them basic to the development of man. Instead, there has been an overriding stress on physical investment, most of it based on urban areas where capital, technical and managerial skills, and power and electricity are easily available. Thus most economic activity has bypassed the rural poor. It is assumed all along that the profits of these investments will enable the governments to spend more on

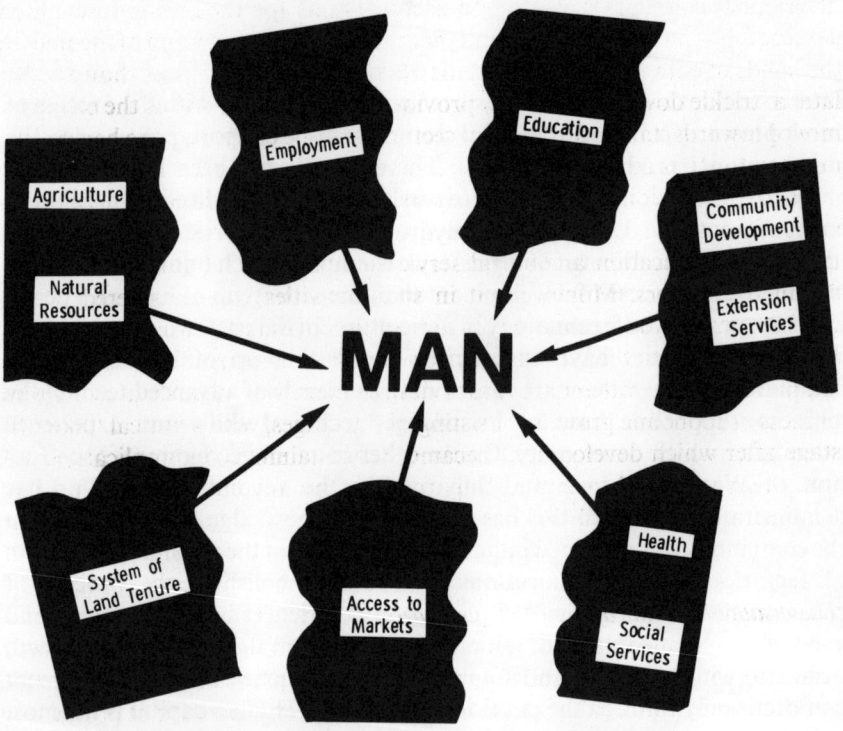

Figure 2.1   The development puzzle.

improving the quality of rural life. But this is not always true. Perhaps a rethinking in planning is necessary, based on the premise that improvement in the quality of life is a *pre-condition* to productivity, and not a *consequence*. What is required is a new economic theory of human capital which accounts for economic growth in terms of changes in the quality of human beings in a society. It stands to reason that economic growth stems from the capacity of a community to create wealth, and that human skills, imagination, drive and vitality are basic factors in development.

The Western industrial model of development

The development models of the 1950s concentrated on raising national incomes through industrial expansion accompanied by shifts in national economies from being predominantly rural–agricultural to urban–industrial. This model assumed that industrial productivity will continue to rise through the use of new technologies and increasing scientific knowledge which will enable countries to exploit their natural resources. There were also other rather naïve assumptions. It was thought that the experiences of the Western 'developed' countries can provide useful lessons for the non-industrialised developing countries to follow, and that the initial concentration of incomes in the hands of entrepreneurs was an inevitable price to pay. It was thought that later a 'trickle down' process will provide benefits for all, and as the economy moved towards 'take-off' the rural sector would be carried on the back of the urban industrial sector.

The overriding importance given to the physical attributes of development—industry, roads, railways, hydroelectric projects and so on—meant that health, education and social services came to be looked upon as non-productive sectors. Money spent in such activities was considered as not contributing to the general good and a form of waste. Proponents of this approach analysed the Western developmental experience and came up with a theoretical model wherein national development was described as a linear process of economic growth consisting of five stages, with a critical 'take-off' stage after which development became self-sustaining. The implication was that this path could be successfully followed by any country with a sound administrative, political and fiscal system.

The disappointments of the 1960s and early 1970s

It was not long before the above approach began to prove unworkable, and led to polarisation of incomes. In the agricultural sector expansion of production according to this model meant mechanisation and costly inputs. Government departments providing investments, credit and supplies concentrated on the best-endowed areas. Within these areas larger farmers were favoured because of their political influence so that they began to increase their holdings by buying out the smaller farmers, making them landless. Thus in India the number of landless increased from 28 million in 1951 to 48 million in 1971. In Brazil, the bottom 50 per cent of landowners account for 3 per cent of the land while the top 5 per cent hold about 68 per cent of the land. In Indonesia, two-thirds of the rural households own less than half a hectare of land; in Bangladesh a third of the rural households are landless, and another 45 per cent own less than half a hectare of land each. Such statistics can be quoted for a large number of countries. What is more important, however, is that national development plans have brought about hardly any change at all. In Brazil especially the pattern of land holding has remained unaltered since 1920.

Industrialisation policies also failed to produce the hoped-for industrial revolution. It produced a few small centres of growth utilising advanced technology and often unable to work at full capacity. The idea that new technological advances bought 'off the shelf' will transform industry was proven to be as ill conceived as that of trickle-down of benefits to the masses.

A number of unforeseen outcomes of these policies came to light in the late seventies. A great deal of the new technology being obtained from the developed countries was through large multinational companies, and so the development strategies of many poor countries in fact opened their markets to multinationals resulting in exploitative commercial relationships. The rapidly expanding modern urban sector formed technical, commercial and scientific linkages abroad and has become increasingly alienated from the rural masses in most developing countries. Urbanisation in many countries has become unhinged from national economic advancement. Borrowing of foreign technology meant that the growth of local and appropriate technology was smothered, local innovativeness and reasearch capabilities did not receive the needed encouragement and a dependent relationship came to be perpetuated. The 'modernisation' strategy of development was based on the assumption that external aid from developed countries would help to bridge the savings or foreign exchange gap. The aid was never enough and whatever was made available came with commercial strings. The most crippling outcome of the modernisation strategy of development was the size of the external debt. Country after country saw the dream of an 'economic miracle' turn into the spectre of 'permanent debt' and bankruptcy. At the same time disparities in income also increased. In many countries urban incomes are up to ten times higher than rural incomes, and it is not unusual to find the wealthiest 5 per cent of the population receiving between a quarter to a third of the national income. Moreover, a dual economy has developed so that one or two core areas are surrounded by extensive undeveloped areas of traditional economy putting millions beyond their own trading economy. There has also been a massive increase in poverty in most developing countries.

In 1976 the International Labour Organisation estimated that almost two-thirds of the population of the developing countries was living in serious poverty, and 700 million of these were destitutes with incomes more than 50 per cent below the poverty line. Such families suffered a series of multiple deprivations adding up to a life hardly worth living: people with poor land, little or no land; people with not enough work; people with inadequate diets; perpetual illness; no basic knowledge and skills to improve the quality of life; and no services to counsel or help at times of crises. In fact, people were denied the right to develop their full potential.

The evolving new strategies for the future

Growing disillusionment with the pattern of development over the past three decades has led to the questioning of the real meaning of development. The present consensus is that the ultimate purpose of development is the development of man and the full realisation of his creative potential. Thus man is to be not only the object of the development process but also a tool for achieving it. Hence the first requirement is improvement in the material conditions of living so as to fulfil physiological, social and phychological needs. A great deal has been written about this new strategy of development but five core concepts can be identified in this new approach:

(1) Man as the focus of development.
(2) De-alienation of man so that he can evolve appropriate technologies for raising production thereby becoming both the subject and object of development.
(3) Participation as a true form of democracy.
(4) Community cohesion and organisation to use surplus labour and savings for increasing production.
(5) Self-reliance with choice of appropriate technology.

For this strategy to be put into practice there must be an emphasis on redistribution of productive resources and priority given to the meeting of basic needs like food and water, housing, clothing, as well as non-material needs like health, education and sanitation. The poor have no physical assets. Their only asset is an able body and willingness to work. The development of this resource through education and health can become a rewarding investment. There is now a growing amount of evidence to show that education and health services often make a major contribution to improving productivity compared with other forms of investments.

The influence of developmental thinking on the growth of health services

Many of the above approaches in national development are reflected in the way health services have evolved in the developing world. In the past capital-intensive hospital services utilising expensive and complex health technology have been given precedence over more basic health care reaching out to the masses. Some of the historical and social factors leading up to the present pattern of health services in the developing world and disparities arising out of such a pattern have been discussed on pages 14–15. Not very long ago a joint WHO–UNICEF study of alternative approaches to health care estimated that only about a fifth of the rural populations in developing countries received any basic health care. The situation of the urban masses is no better. Major inequalities in health are apparent between the urban and the rural populations and between the urban poor and the élite.

The Western model in planning for health services being hospital based also means a sequestration of health resources in urban areas serving largely the élite. Up to 80 per cent of the government health budget in many countries is spent on hospital services (see table 2.1).

Table 2.1   **Health budgets—UK and Tanzania**

	UK (£)	Tanzania (£)
Total health budget 1961	981 million	2 million
Hospital services	56.8%	80%
Local health authority services	9.3%	—
Public health	—	5%
Total health budget 1971	1880 million	7 million
Hospital services	61.2%	79%
Local health authority services	10.4%	—
Public health	—	8.5%

The effect of a predominantly hospital-based and curative service is that it is dominated by the specialists, who are more concerned with running their specialty services than with coverage. The inevitable over-spending on curative care each year has to be balanced by cuts in spending in the rest of the budget.

It is not always possible to correct the situation by simple administrative decisions nor by grafting a programme of community health on to a totally inappropriate health system. Planners and providers of care face impossible choices. These are the choices of reducing the gap between the 'haves' and the 'have-nots', of making preferential allocation of resources to the social periphery in order to ensure full health coverage instead of hospital-based specialist-oriented services for the élite, and of ensuring the necessary reforms in medical education so that the health profession can be more supportive of auxiliaries and village-level workers. To give an example, in Tanzania after a critical evaluation of health programmes in the early seventies (see table 2.1) the budget allocation for hospitals was reduced by 50–60 per cent in 1971–72 so that curative services came to receive 20–25 per cent of the total health expenditure compared with 80 per cent in previous years. In 1973–75, allocation for hospitals was further reduced to a low of 12–15 per cent and there was a simultaneous increase in training facilities for auxiliaries. This illustrates that the correction of past mistakes in the planning of health services is not merely a matter of issuing directives or letting loose a new cadre of health workers nor of expanding the existing services. It is more a matter of fundamental changes in identification of objectives, of identifying the weaknesses of the system and of setting up a national dialogue to generate a national will which will enable society to take a number of rather difficult decisions concerning the provision of health care.

If health services are to change their emphasis from intensive care to prevention of common illnesses, from a preoccupation with care for the élite to a concern for health services in rural areas and urban slums, then new approaches and strategies are necessary. Health planning in the past has created not only the above-mentioned disparities and maldistribution but also the following paradoxes.

There are not enough doctors and nurses available either because of their unwillingness to work in rural areas or because they are being trained in inadequate numbers. Thus in South Korea more than 80 per cent of the hospitals and 90 per cent of the beds are concentrated in large cities. Less than 30 per cent of health centre posts in rural areas and 60 per cent in urban areas have been filled. In East Africa 54 per cent of the doctors are concentrated in the cities to look after 5 per cent of the population.

The training of the doctor may not equip him for dealing with the health needs of rural communities. This is reflected in the quality of health care provided by the health centre. In a comparison of daily service contacts in health centres in the north and south of India it was found that more than 90 per cent were for illness care and the remainder for maternity care, child health services and family planning. The potential of the health centre for preventive and promotive work has not been fully utilised. The teaching hospitals are obviously concentrating on the training of a good medical scientist capable of performing well as regards the diagnosis and treatment of disease in the individual, but failing to grasp the issues involved in the delivery of health care to communities within a limited budget.

All systems of health care at present operate only in institutions–With such an approach it is possible to provide services to only a small number of people within a radius of 5 miles from the health centre or dispensary. The total number of people that can be covered depends upon the population density. Thus an average health centre in India is expected to serve a community of 80 000–100 000 people, but with the traditional institutional approach ends up by serving only about 10 000–20 000 individuals.

The university-trained graduate is far removed socio-culturally from the rural masses–Entry to medical schools and other training institutions is based on academic grades, and since most secondary schools and pre-medical training institutions are in urban areas the large majority of entrants to professional training institutions come from urban families and the higher socio-economic groups. It is little wonder then than the doctor finds himself far removed socially, culturally and intellectually from the peasant or the urban poor. The lack of identification with the masses leads to an attitude of non-involvement, resulting in lack of communication and non-utilisation of services. In a study of unmet health needs in 8000 episodes of illness in rural Punjab, it was found that in more than half the cases where service was required the need was not met, and that the health centre met only 10 per cent of the total service needs. In another study covering 13 villages, seven of which were the headquarter villages of the primary health centre in four different regions of India, it was found that the overall image of the auxiliary nurse–midwife and the lady health visitor was that they were remote people whose services were available only to those who could pay for them. Except for very overt medical care needs, services like MCH, nutrition, immunisation, environmental sanitation and water supply were not met, and the health workers were mainly concerned with supplying the needs of the politically influential upper-class families.

Inequalities in health care are greatest and most worrying in the case of preventive services. Even though ignorance is commonly blamed, recent research indicates that under-utilisation of preventive services by the poor is often due to under-provision, the social, financial and psychological costs of attendance and the alienation created by the insensitivity of an élitist health system. Simple services like the under-5's clinics and antenatal clinics are not adequately provided so that in many countries not more than a third of the pregnant women receive care during pregnancy, with even fewer being delivered under medical supervision, and not more than 7–11 per cent of the children are immunised. The results of such skewed planning and distorted development of health services are reflected in the poor health status of people in the developing world (see table 2.2).

Table 2.2 **Health-related indicators in developing countries**

	Developed	Least developed	Other developing
Number of countries	37	29	90
Population (millions)	1131	283	3001
Infant mortality rate	15	160	94
Life expectancy	72	50	60
Death rate of children 1–5 years/1000	1	30	20
Percentage of newborn with a birth weight of 2500 g or more	93	70	83
Coverage by safe water supply (%)	100	31	41
Adult literacy (%)	98	28	55
Deaths of children under 5 years as percentage of all deaths	3	55	21

Source: WHO. 1981.

In the backlog of health problems arising out of past neglect, the major tropical diseases also need to be included. In fact in some regions the situation may be getting worse. Table 2.3 stresses the enormous dimensions of the threat to health due to tropical diseases.

Table 2.3   **Tropical diseases as a public-health problem**

	Prevalence (millions)	*Exposed (millions)*
Malaria	250	1800
Schistosomiasis	200	600
Leprosy	11	2000
Leishmaniasis	400 000	?
Filariasis	300	600
Trypanosomiasis:		
African	?	45
Chaga's disease	24	65

The development of new health strategies of Primary Health Care

Many of the above-mentioned failures and disillusionments have led to a reappraisal of health strategies. An impetus for such rethinking has come from the recent reports of successes in health improvement reported by China, Cuba, Tanzania, Sri Lanka, Costa Rica and by a number of small-scale pilot projects in several countries. A major ingredient of success has been the creation of services that were available to all, regardless of the ability to pay for them, besides being accessible from the point of view of their geographical distribution as well as culturally acceptable. The expansion in coverage was achieved through reliance on simple structures like health posts and sub-centres, from where auxiliaries, health aides and other lesser trained community level health workers provided health care utilising technologies which were appropriate to the resources and the needs of the community. It is becoming increasingly obvious that many of the disease problems of the developing world are related to poverty and as such have no purely 'medical' solutions. Instead, social, educational, economic and political solutions have to be sought. Medical technologies evolving in the affluent societies of the industrial West have very little relevance for the disease problems of the peasant communities and for the urban poor in the developing world. In fact, such technologies led in the past to monopoly of knowledge by the specialist and an élitist attitude which did not engender the community's responsibility for its own health care. Hence community participation in planning, implementation and evaluation of health services of the above type came to be recognised as a fundamental objective in health service development.

The convergence of new thinking and strategies in national development and health planning further evolved into the new approach of Primary Health Care (PHC) set out in the Alma Ata Conference in 1978. PHC was to '. . . address the main health problems in the community providing promotive, preventive, curative and rehabilitative services'. Eight activities were included as the major concerns of PHC:

(1) Promotion of proper nutrition.
(2) Provision of adequate supply of safe water.
(3) Provision of basic sanitation.
(4) Maternal and child care including family planning.
(5) Immunisation against the major infectious diseases.
(6) Prevention and control of locally endemic diseases.
(7) Education concerning the prevalent health problems and the methods of their prevention and control.
(8) Appropriate treatment for common diseases and injuries.

In the above list curative work is stated last and the traditionally non-health sector activities are amongst the first three. Thus PHC embodies the basic needs approach of the development strategies, and health comes to assume a significant role in national development—a role that becomes possible only by assuming the broader responsibilities in place of the current overemphasis on curative skills. Taken together, the new strategies stress that we must define the basic needs with regard to food, water and sanitation, shelter, clothing and other requirements that must be satisfied to give people a minimum acceptable standard of living and to guarantee survival. Having drawn such a poverty line to define the basic needs of the people, we must then proceed to produce the goods and services that are needed to satisfy the basic need standards. This would often require a reorganisation of the public services so that they become more acceptable and more relevant to the needs of the poor. In all countries the lower social classes do not enjoy easy access to services because they live in remote areas, or because they are illiterate and do not know how to make use of the public services, or because they have been put off by a traumatic previous experience. The new strategies also call for reorientation of professional training so as to create the personnel with relevant attitudes and skills. There is, however, a third and more crucial factor besides those related to a minimum standard of living and access to public services. If one really wants to attack poverty, then only the poor themselves really know how to cope with it. Decentralised planning to encourage decision-making and participation at the local level is necessary. Thus community involvement is looked upon both as a means and as an end, the objective being to raise the capacity of the people to become their own agents of change. Social institutions and structures must be so designed as to encourage community participation and to bring together both the formal scientific and informal traditional approaches to bear upon health and development activites.

The new strategies of national development look upon health not so much as the fruit and outcome of economic growth but as an integral part of it. Human capital and social factors supportive of its nurture have come to occupy the central role in the development process. But however important, for the human capital to become more productive the physical and natural resources including land, water, forests, minerals and others must also become more productive. Hence the need for several processes of change—social, political, economic, administrative and technological—to come together into an integrated approach. In practical terms this requires not only an intersectoral approach in each province and district, but also an effective combination of external resources with local resources and of outside professionally trained workers with local village and community-level workers for stimulating and sustaining local activities. By concentrating on the millions who have been bypassed by the main stream of development, the new strategies aim not only to make them more productive and to become 'included', but also to protect them from the consequences of poverty by changing the focus of health programmes. The new strategies for health recognise that what is needed most is the availability of food, sufficient knowledge of nutrition for balancing diets, immunisation, safe water supplies, efficient disposal of human waste and family planning.

A new way of measuring development progress

Hitherto it has been a common practice to measure development by calculating the Gross National Product (GNP), and maximising GNP was the aim of a number of development plans. This approach, developed in the industrial West as a basis for full employment policies, when applied to the economies of the developing world led to lop-sided development. The inclusion of health in the development process calls for other health-related parameters to be included as measures of development. The two most important indicators of health are infant mortality (reflecting the effect of the environment in the broadest sense) and life expectancy at birth (reflecting life chances including the mitigating effect of services). To these a third indicator is added, literacy rate, and together they make up the Physical Quality of Life Index (PQLI) (see figures 2.2–2.4). In Chapter 1 the gains made by Sri Lanka and Kerala in recent years were mentioned. The PQLI of these societies is compared with the average in low-income countries and a few selected low income as well as two high-income countries in table 2.4.

Table 2.4 indicates that though income and the physical quality of life show a certain degree of correlation, it is not invariably so. Both Kerala and Sri Lanka are ahead of rich oil-producing countries like Iran and Libya in spite of far lower GNP. Secondly, the political ideology along which a society is organised is not always an important factor for meeting basic human needs of

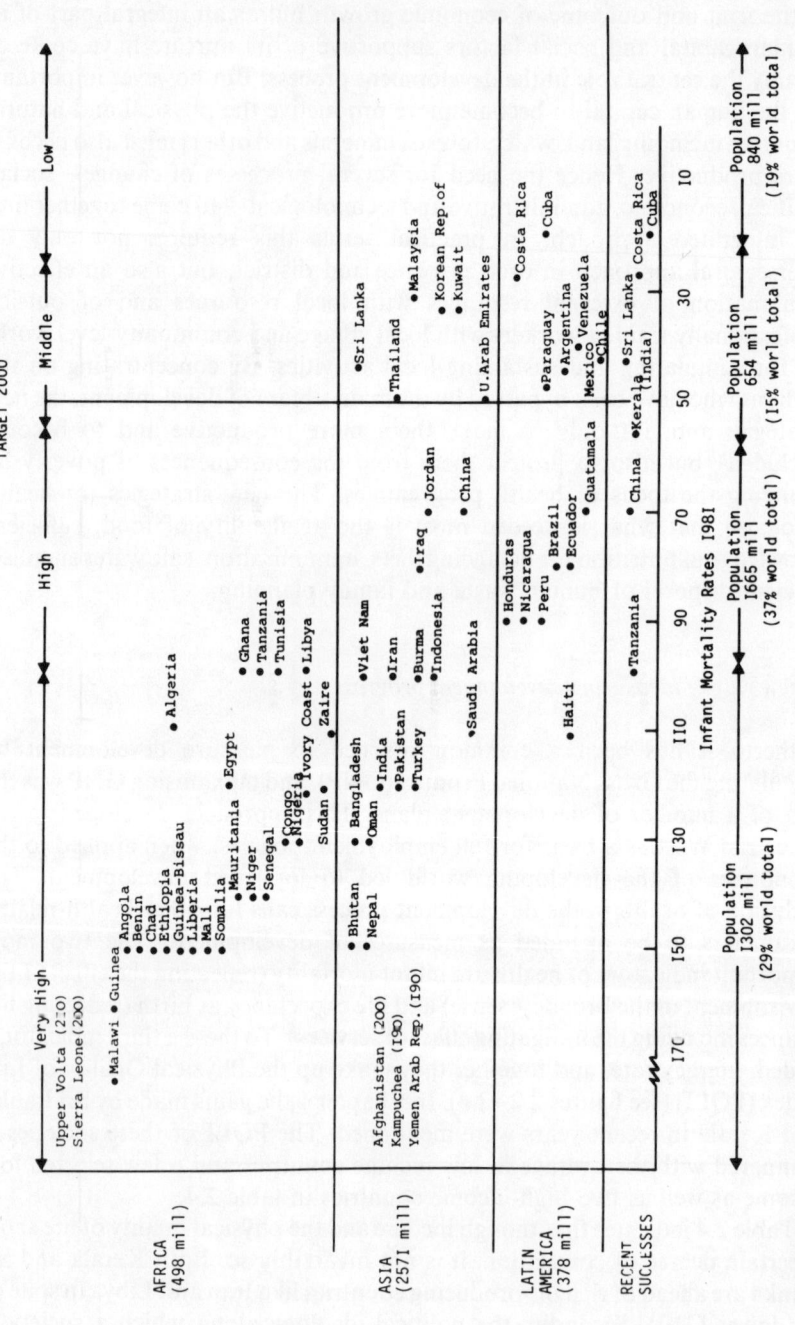

Figure 2.2   Infant mortality rate.

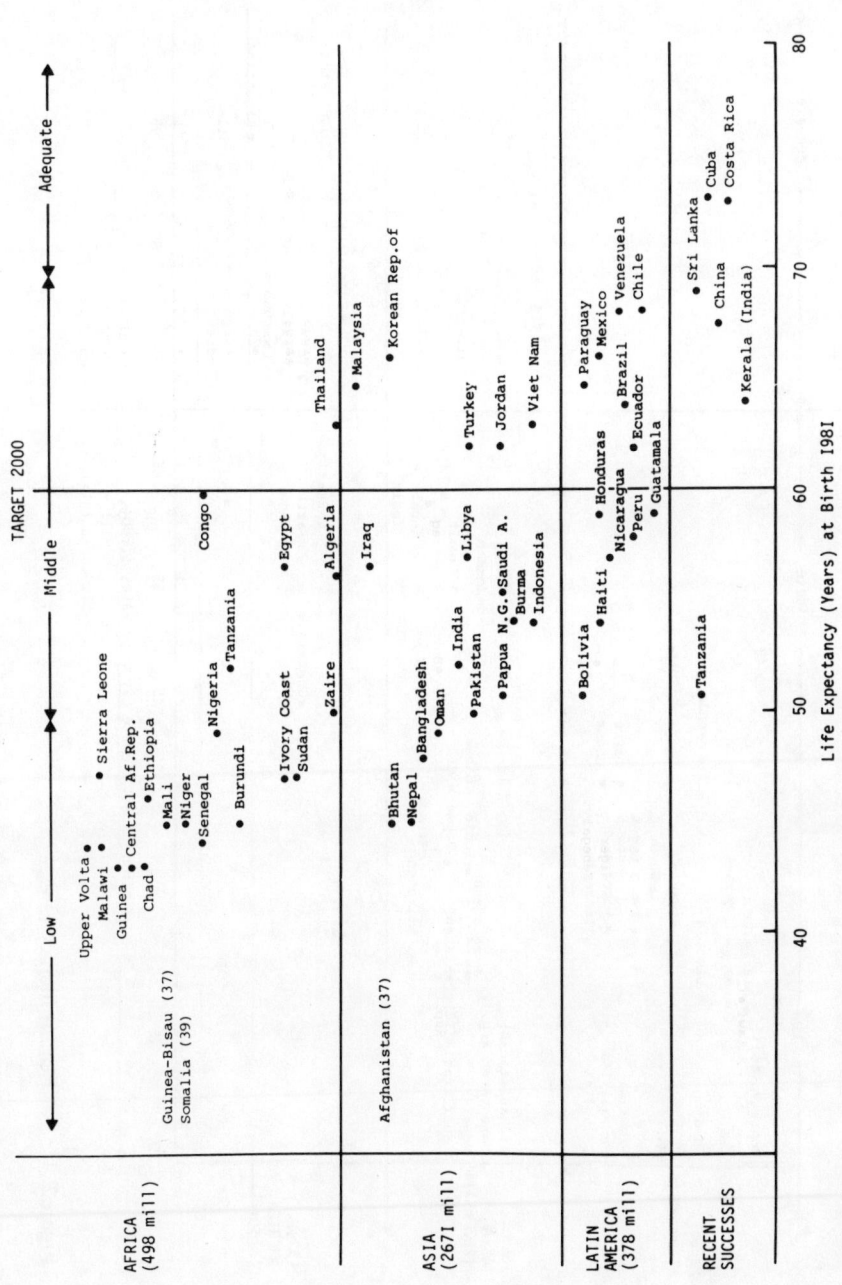

Figure 2.3   Life expectancy at birth.

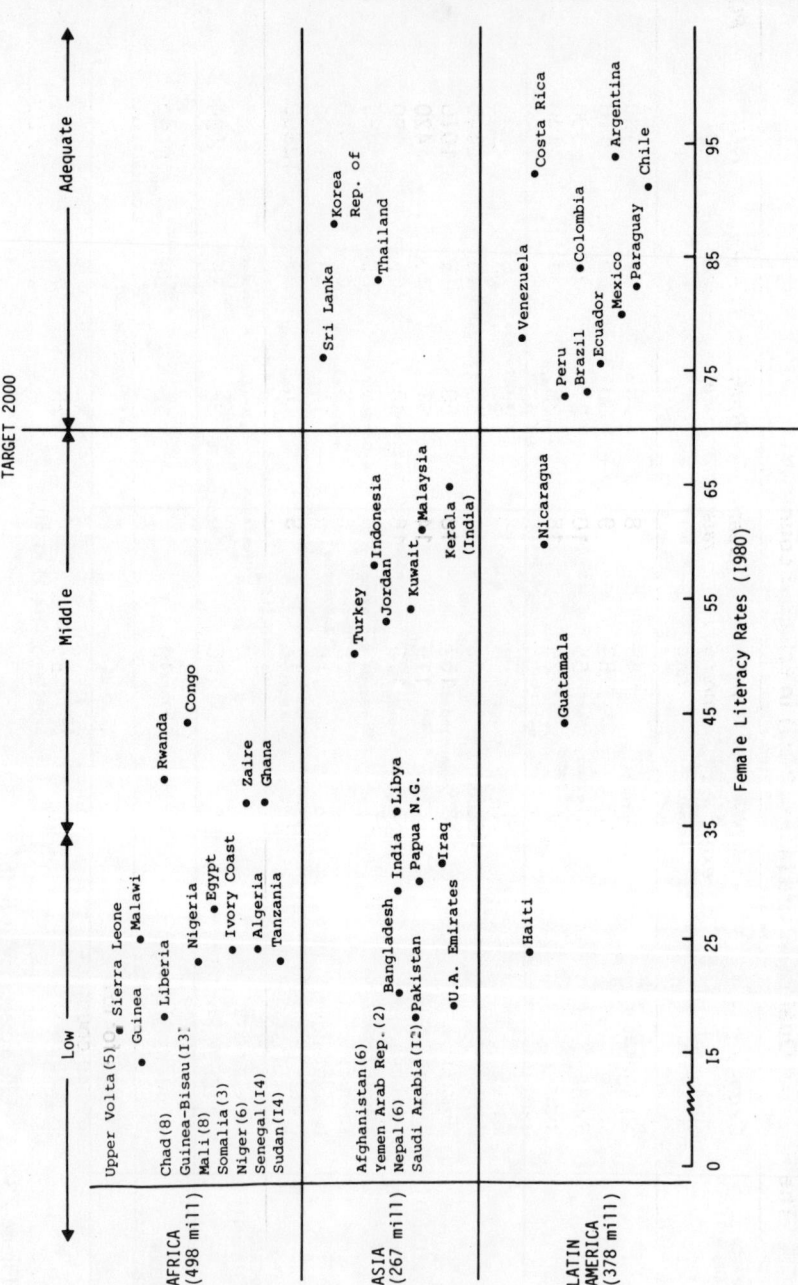

Figure 2.4   Female literacy rates.

Table 2.4 The Physical Quality of Life Index (PQLI) in selected countries

Country	Life expectancy	Infant mortality rate	Death rate	Birth rate	Literacy rate	GNP ($)	PQLI
Sri Lanka	68	45	8	28	81	130	83
Kerala	61	56	9	30	60	110	69
China	62	55	10	27	25	300	59
India	50	139	15	35	34	140	41
Iran	51	139	16	45	23	1250	38
Egypt	55	108	13	36	43	580	44
Libya	55.5	130	14	48	48	8640	43
Nigeria	47.5	157	18	50	15	1010	27
Kenya	54	119	14	51	40	420	39
Tanzania	50.5	125	16	48	66	190	30
South Korea	61	47	9	29	88	480	80
Taiwan	69	26	5	23	85	810	88
Netherlands	74	16	8	14	98	11000	99
USA	71	17	9	15	99	12800	96
Low-income countries (average)	53	108	14	38	36	680	39
High-income countries (average)	72	28	10	15	98	8130	92
Targets for low-income countries in year 2000	65	50	?	25	75	?	>50

its people. In recent years, three groups of countries have made remarkable progress in the direction of improving the physical quality of life of their people: (1) China and Cuba; (2) South Korea, Taiwan, Hong Kong and Singapore; (3) Sri Lanka and Kerala. The symptoms of poverty need not necessarily go along with low incomes nor with political ideology. Experience in different countries illustrates that two measures are crucial for improving health and productivity. Reforms for the equitable distribution of productive assets like land, education, and employment opportunities are essential to break the vicious cycle of inequality. Secondly, the availability and delivery of effective services like education, health, agricultural extension, credit, marketing etc. at low cost.

Do health services mitigate the effects of poverty?

Health workers in developing countries face this question every day. What actions can they take and what services can they organise to provide relief from the consequences of poverty and to help people get out of the web of scarcity and want? Poverty is not just a lack of money but an entire syndrome. It also means slum areas with bad housing, lack of sanitation and hygiene, poor nutrition and recurrent disease resulting in lack of regular income; and for the children inability to take advantage of educational opportunities. It also means poor family and social relationships, violence both within the home and outside, emotional and psychological stress and a feeling of hopelessness. It is true that hospitals have not been shown anywhere to influence any of the above constellation of symptoms which together make up the syndrome of poverty. But it is also true that because health systems in market economies have failed to do so and because health services in developing countries have been modelled on those of the market economies that we should continue to accept the same for developing countries. Health systems develop in response to the problems they have to face and not in accordance with some hypothetical international model. When health systems in the developing world are truly responsive to health problems and begin to tackle the determinants of disease, they can be expected to make inroads on the diseases of poverty.

Are the eight activities of PHC (see page 32) or the type of services described in Chapter 1 (see pages 20–21) likely to mitigate the effects of poverty? The advantage that all community-based services enjoy is that of nearness to a community's problems. Such services are better able to address the questions of destitution, ignorance and hardship; of identifying whose living standards are lowest and why; of inequality, discrimination and exclusion, and of creating community awakening to face these challenges. A characteristic of the health effects of disadvantage is that problems not only cluster together as described above but also reinforces each other. The clustering and reinforcement are so intertwined that causal associations are difficult to quantify. Partly because of this difficulty and partly because of the inability of curative techniques to influence them, present health systems have not come to grips with them. PHC aims to make poverty its major concern by directing the main thrust of the health programmes at common illnesses; by focusing on the major determinants of ill health like undernutrition, lack of sanitation and contaminated water; and by stressing health coverage, especially of the weaker sections of the community. There is an implied realisation that the major obstacle to socio-economic development and health is poverty, and there is a need to mount a direct attack on it at the global and national level through appropriate policies; and at the local community level through appropriate programmes.

Difficulties and constraints in the practical application of the new health strategies

In attempting to provide health coverage for the entire nation, many governments are faced with the challenge of having to expand their health services fivefold. In areas where no services have existed in the past the costs of putting up buildings, of training new personnel, of setting up administrative and logistical support, of transport and supplies, of equipment and of drugs must be met. Even though communities may bear part of the initial capital investment the recurrent expenditure, often equal to a third of the capital investment, must be found annually. This requires the transfer of resources from curative services and prestige institutions to community health at each level of the service. In the absence of such an action to back up policies PHC will exist only at the rhetoric level. The need for such a commitment is greatest at the district level. Professionals at all levels of hierarchy—from the lowliest field staff to the district and regional medical officers and on to sectional heads in the Ministry of Health—daily make decisions that affect the distribution and location of services. The decisions of those who are closest to the periphery have a greater effect on the daily lives of the people compared with those of distant officials. Paradoxically, providing promotive/preventive services to the poorest is often more expensive per head compared with the better-off areas. The poor live in the more inaccessible areas. There may be no access roads. Local resources may be meagre. They are not usually organised communities, and there may be no community structures to serve as jumping boards for programmes.

Within the profession itself there may be a number of opposing trends and vested interests. The patterns along which health services developed in the past have created their own institutions, training programmes, characteristics of professionalism, and the dynamics that propel the existing systems perpetuating their patterns. Moreover, the established administrative procedures, the general orders, the training programmes and the bureaucratic systems all underpin the existing patterns so that radical changes are resisted all along the line and only small incremental improvements are possible. Primary health care is not the implantation of a new form of health system but a means of assigning priorities and of delivering health care to those groups and areas that did not receive sufficient emphasis in the past. The infrastructure of sub-centres, aid-posts, health centres and hospitals must be linked to fundamental care within the home and in the community, and must become supportive of it.

The greatest challenge is for the health profession in its ability to develop effective approaches in preventive and promotive care for the rural and urban poor. The words of Mao Tse Tung in his directive on public health of 26 June 1965 still ring true for many developing countries:

'Tell the Ministry of Public Health that it only works for 15 per cent of the total population of the country and that this 15 per cent is mainly composed of gentlemen, while the broad masses of the peasants do not get any medical treatment. First they don't have any doctors; second they don't have any medicine. The Ministry of Public Health is not a Ministry of Public Health for the people, so why not change its name to the Ministry of Urban Health, the Ministry of Gentlemen's Health or even to the Ministry of Urban Gentlemen's Health?'

The values and attitudes of the professionals largely influence their day-to-day decisions and the functioning of the health system. The values reflect the influence of the urban institutions, opportunities for advancement, convenience, but above all that of education and training. In general, health professionals are not trained to look for and analyse the clusters of disadvantage that accompany poverty like physical weakness, vulnerability to seasonal stresses, illnesses and exploitation, physical and cultural isolation, and the inability of the poor to organise themselves for dealing with difficulties. The true dimensions of rural poverty are rarely known because of in-built biases causing blinkered vision. And the inability of the professional élite to learn from the poor, or of community health researchers to join hands with the people in addressing the problems of poverty. A great deal of PHC work will therefore involve learning by working with the people to find workable solutions for local health problems.

Main principles in implementing PHC programmes

During the last decade or so a number of programmes for the rural and urban poor have sprung up in several countries. Analyses of such programmes provide the opportunity for identifying the main principles and strategies as follows.

Getting to know the poor and learning from them—Statistics, describing demographic patterns or providing information on morbidity and mortality, however necessary, are no substitute for the intimate understanding of the daily lives of the poor that can only come through working together over a period of time and developing rapport.

An appreciation of the difficulties in organising the poor—Communities of the rural and urban poor are not homogeneous but faction ridden with all the foibles of self-interest and greed typical of human societies everywhere. There are divisions based on access to productive assets, on castes and religion, sex, family linkage and so on. In such a mixture there are difficulties in reaching the neediest. Those higher up in the pecking order get the maximum so that the benefits from all new services and programmes tend to be divided in proportion to the existing inequality. Hence the need for slanting the services specifically in the direction of the neediest families. A number of mechanisms like the use of village health workers and traditional birth attendants selected from within the neighbourhood have been shown to improve the uptake of services, and have been mentioned on page 9.

An integrated approach aimed at providing basic needs in food, water, sanitation, health and education for all. This calls for integration not only between sectors but also between the different components of each sector so that each component and each sector can complement the effects of others. Improvement in nutritional status requires not only better awareness of the nutritional needs of different age groups and of a more rational distribution of food within the family but also services like the under-5s and antenatal clinics, immunisation programmes, applied nutrition activities in schools, agricultural extension, feeding programmes and nutritional rehabilitation centres, formation of community groups like farmers' clubs, women's discussion groups and youth organisations (see page 152). Not surprisingly, the specialised governmental bureaucracies are often the main obstacles and hence the need for decentralisation. To bring about lasting change the impact of different services and programmes must come together at the home level to catalyse the new outlook. A piecemeal approach cannot be the same. On the other hand, integration is not an all-or-none phenomenon. It must grow slowly by degrees provided both the health workers and the recipient communities are aware of its necessity and work towards achieving it.

Community participation is an important element in creating self-reliance and sustained development. Part of the poverty syndrome is a disorganised community with poor leadership. One element in bringing about community awareness is the creation of care-taker groups and committees to look after specific activities and to provide a forum for dialogue. The task is not easy and often not given sufficient importance by the professional. Such participatory democracy and the creation of social institutions for discussing problems and devising solutions are necessary for underpinning democracy at the grass roots level.

The best way of making a beginning is through utilising traditional ways of community co-operation and traditional systems of government addressing locally expressed needs—working through different sub-groups formed to supervise different activities has been invariably found to be more effective than just a blanket provision of services. Front-line workers linked to different sub-groups thus take on an imporant role as agents for change, and the dialogues within the sub-groups serve the purpose of creating awareness and educating the participants. Thus health and education come to be closely linked. Such a network of linkages becomes the eventual base from which the process of development grows.

The characteristics of services in the future

The new strategies of PHC being advocated at the international level together with the above guidelines and experiences gathered from a number of projects help to define the characteristics of services required in the coming decades. There is a need for a shift of approach from activities compartmentalised into different sectors to an integrated 'people' approach. Preventive and curative services must join hands to become comprehensive care converging on the determinants of disease—availability of water, nutrition and sanitation—affecting the life chances of people, instead of concentrating on individual 'cases'. Different population groups need to be identified with varying risks of ill health depending upon socio-economic status, age, sex or occupation. Community resources including health and other services need to be slanted in their favour to provide maximum protection. This is by far more logical when the aim is to help the disadvantaged groups rather than offer a series of services without questioning which groups use them to best advantage. Services need to provide interventions that people can understand and apply in their daily lives instead of being couched in the mystifying jargon of biomedical science to be controlled by privileged professionals. In that way services will be less daunting and alienating. Communities should be encouraged to develop greater control over their services through the use of local workers, organisations and interest groups. All of these serve as the mechanism for integration to achieve defined objectives and to alter environmental and other factors affecting people's health.

Further reading

Chambers, R. (1983). *Rural Development. Putting the Last First.* Longman Group, London.

Djukanovic, V. and Mach, E. P. (eds) (1975). *Alternative Approaches to Meeting Basic Health Needs in Developing Countries.* WHO, Geneva.

Ghai, D. P., Khan, A. R., Lee, E. L. H. and Alfthan, T. (1977). *The Basic Needs Approach to Development.* International Labour Office, Geneva.

Hardiman, M. and Midgley, J. (1982). *The Social Dimensions of Development. Social Policy and Planning in the Third World.* John Wiley & Sons, Chichester.

Lakshmanan, T. R. (1982). A systems model of rural development. *World Dev.* **10**: 885–98.

McKeown, T. (1979). *The Role of Medicine—Dream, Mirage or Nemesis?* Blackwell, Oxford.

Newell, K. W. (1975). *Health by the People.* WHO, Geneva.

Streeter, P., Burke, S. J., Haq, M., Hicks, N. and Stewart, F. (1981). *First Things First. Meeting Basic Human Needs in Developing Countries.* Oxford University Press, Oxford.

Todaro, M. P. (1981). *Economic Development in the Third World.* Longman Group, London and New York. 2nd edn.

World Health Organization (1981). *Global Strategy for Health for all by the Year 2000.* WHO, Geneva.

World Health Organization. (1979). *Formulating Strategies for Health for all by the Year 2000.* WHO, Geneva.

3 Demographic and Socio-economic Characteristics of Developing Countries

The developing world comprises more than three-quarters of humanity and by the turn of the century the total population of the developing countries is expected to be equal to 80 per cent of the world population. The largest proportion of the population of the developing world is in Asia. Bangladesh, China, India, Indonesia and Pakistan together make up 43 per cent of the total world population. China alone contains one-fifth of humanity; India has more people than the Americas; the island of Java more than any African country and greater Tokyo more than Australia. The great bulk of total population increase annually is in Asia.

Obviously there is a great deal of diversity from one country to another and from one societal group to another with regard to the background of history, culture and practices, social organisations, political and economic systems and health. And yet there are certain features in common that help to distinguish the developing countries from the industrialised societies of Western Europe and North America. The most important of these features are the following.

The demographic pattern

The population of the developing countries consists predominantly of young age groups, so that as much as 40–45 per cent of the population may consist of people under the age of 15 years. If to this were added the percentage of women in the child-bearing period of life, then almost 60–70 per cent of the population would consist of individuals in the biologically vulnerable period of life. Figure 3.1 (overleaf) illustrates the demographic profiles of three developing countries.

The implications of such a demographic pattern for health planning are

44

obvious, and maternal and child health (MCH) services should feature strongly in the health programmes of the developing countries. However, historical development of health services in all pre-colonial countries has led to the establishment of largely hospital-based curative services mainly catering for the well-to-do élite. There are paediatric, obstetric and nutrition specialties at the larger centres with their counterparts at district hospitals. But the services provided are not the type of promotive, preventive and counselling care needed on a continuing basis for healthy child-bearing and child-rearing. Moreover, because of the élitist nature and poor outreach of the health services, a vast number get excluded from their benefits, especially in the rural areas and now increasingly so amongst the urban poor, as pointed out in Chapter 2.

Medical education normally follows the pattern of services and tends to train individuals for filling established posts in the services. Thus medical curricula are designed largely to train paediatricians, obstetricians and preventive medicine specialists along Western patterns to run the specialist services. Even though MCH is considered a priority, there is very little training provided in that discipline. In fact, only one or two medical schools in the developing world offer postgraduate-level training in maternal and child health. A discipline that is neither taught adequately nor practised lacks the impetus for growth normally provided by lively questioning minds.

In spite of various attempts by national authorities and international organisations to stress coverage and to make health services relevant to health needs, the above trends continue. Hospital-based curative care in the developing world is rapidly moving in the direction of intensive care utilising sophisticated technologies. The reasons are twofold. There is the growing demand of the urban élite for more sophisticated facilities. Secondly, a great deal of research and development work in medical sciences is presently taking place in the developed world which inevitably determines the 'frontiers of science'. The problems that are of interest to the researchers in the more developed countries are the ones that stem from their local socio-economic conditions. As such they are of limited use to the very different socio-economic conditions of the developing world. The technologies being evolved are the ones geared to dealing with diseases of affluence; their relevance for the diseases of poverty is minimal and the cost is prohibitive even by the standards of the rich countries.

Any proposals to reorientate as complex a system as that of health care delivery must inevitably meet with resistance both from entrenched interests within the profession and from the élite power groups. But that is no reason to assume that common sense cannot eventually prevail. Certainly many of the necessary innovations can only be accomplished in conjunction with far-reaching social, economic and political change. But very many others can be accomplished even in the absence of sweeping reforms. Here the example of Tanzania, Sri Lanka and Costa Rica is relevant.

A great deal of local initiative begins with the health providers asking
several pertinent questions. For whom are we responsible? For those who
come to the hospitals and health centres or also for those who do not or cannot
because of distance, poverty, discrimination and a process of social exclusion,
superstition and ignorance? The decision to serve all the population in a
defined geographical or administrative area (usually a district) can shape all
other health-care decisions. For only when the health team has accepted the
responsibility for the total population can their needs be analysed; those who
are most in need can be identified and those who can be most effectively served

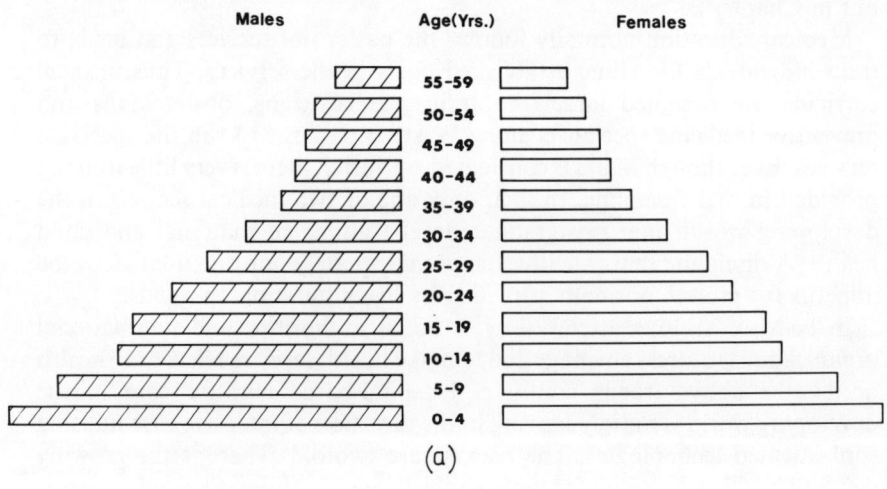

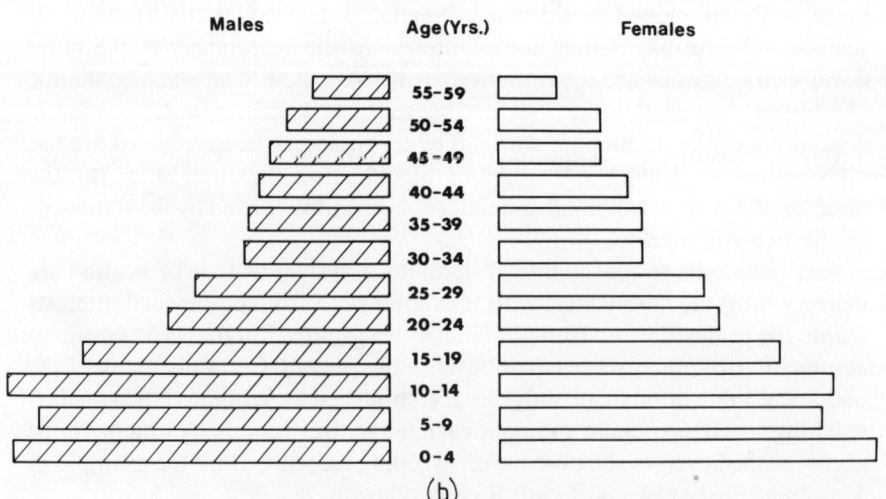

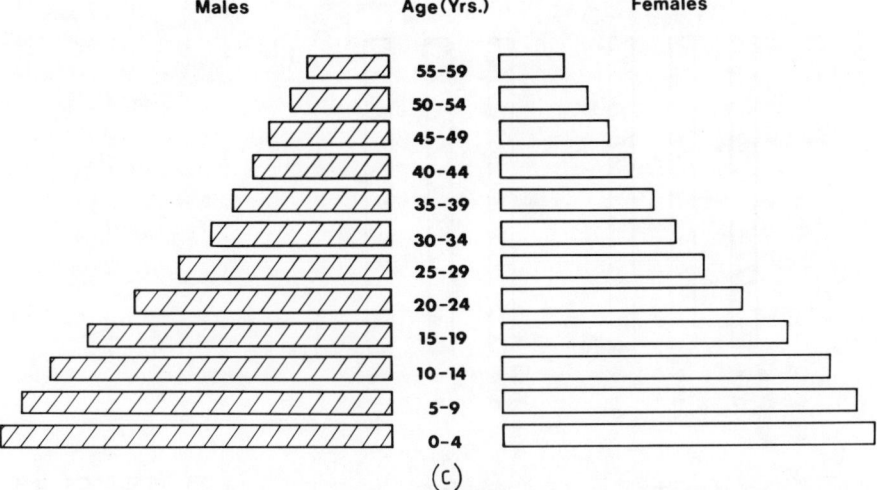

Figure 3.1   Population pyramids. (a) Brazil (123 million). (b) Egypt (36.6 million). (c) India (663 million).

by available resources can be determined. It is the responsibility of the medical training institutions to inculcate this sense of accountability for the entire population (the sick, the ambulatory sick as well as the healthy) as well as for all social groups, because only then can the teaching of disciplines like epidemiology, behavioural sciences and management studies have relevance for the true health needs.

Presently most developing countries are experiencing rapid growth of population. At the same time, improvement in life expectancy is marginal compared with the rate at which population growth is taking place. The present demographic pattern is thus likely to continue into the next century.

Rurality

Figure 3.2 shows the urban/rural distribution of population in several countries. As a rule, in Africa and Asia up to three-quarters of the population in most countries is rural, spread out in villages of 1500–2000 people each, or sometimes in smaller hamlets and scattered homesteads. Thus, three-quarters of India's 660 million people are dispersed in 580 000 villages and 80 per cent of Tanzania's 17 million population live in small villages and isolated hamlets in rural areas. Such a pattern of location of the population poses a strong challenge to the development of health care systems. There will never be sufficient numbers of doctors and nurses to be appointed to each individual

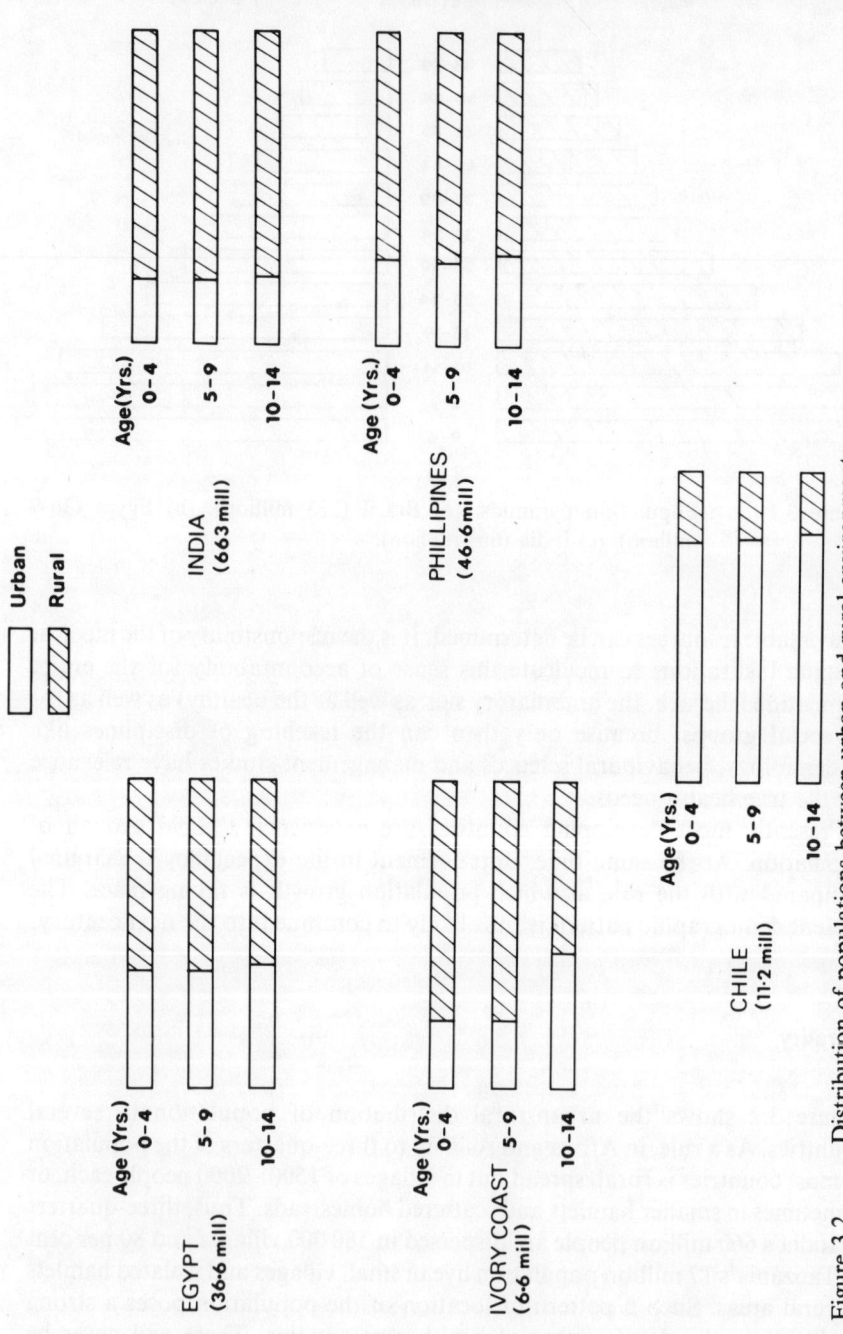

Figure 3.2   Distribution of populations between urban and rural environments.

village. Even if there were, it will never be possible to pay them nor induce them to stay in the rural areas for any length of time.

Most developing countries are attempting to meet the challenge of providing health care through a system of district hospitals, health centres and sub-centres (or dispensaries) in each administrative district. This system has failed to make any appreciable impact on the health situation in rural areas for a variety of reasons. These are given below.

In most countries 80 per cent of the hospitals and 90 per cent of the total beds are concentrated in the larger cities – This urban bias in the deployment of the health resources ends up by providing services mainly for the politically vocal urban population, and the carefully planned referral system consisting of the sub-centre/health centre/district hospital/referral hospital exists only on paper. For example, a survey of in-patients in four regional hospitals in Tanzania showed that 40 per cent came from within a radius of 5 miles (8 km) from the town, 30 per cent from 5.25 miles (8.5 km) away and only 30 per cent came from more than 25 miles (40 km). The urban population in Tanzania (6 per cent of the total) provides almost a third of all in-patients and half the total out-patients for the country's health services. Secondly, in most countries the existing system of health care delivery through the sub-centre/health centre/ hospital complex is being largely used as a conveyor belt to provide 'interesting' cases at the hospital for teaching and producing scientific papers instead of a means of extending health care to where diseases are.

The training of the doctor may not equip him for dealing with the health needs of the rural communities – This is reflected in the quality and pattern of health care provided by the health centre. In a comparison of daily service contacts in health centres in the north and south of India it was found that more than 90 per cent were for illness care, and the remainder for maternity care, child health services and family planning. Thus the potential of the health centre for dealing with the determinants of disease through preventive and promotive work has not been fully utilised.

The present system of health-care delivery is highly institutionalised, which tends to impose a certain amount of rigidity. With such an approach it is possible to provide service to a relatively small number of people, usually within a radius of 5 miles (8 km) from the health centre or sub-centre (see figure 3.3). Thus, an average health centre in India is expected to serve a population of 80 000–100 000 but, in fact, ends up by largely looking after the inhabitants of the market village in which it is situated. In many countries of tropical Africa where the population is sparse, the effective coverage is even less. For the widely scattered population of the rural areas the health services have to be mobile, flexible in outlook and culturally acceptable. Instead, the predominantly institutionalised systems of care in most countries give rise to problems of accessibility, tend to become exclusive in outlook and are often alienating.

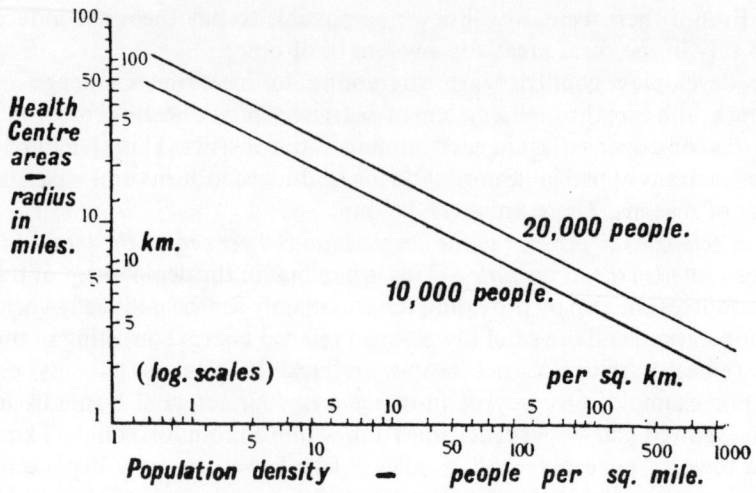

Figure 3.3   The relationship between population density and the radius of a catchment area of the health centre to serve a given population.

The university-trained medical graduate is far removed from the rural masses from the socio-cultural point of view. Since most secondary schools and pre-medical training institutions are in the urban areas, the large majority of entrants to professional training institutions come from urban families and the higher socio-economic groups. It is little wonder then that the doctor feels distant socially, culturally and intellectually from the peasant in the village. The lack of identification with the rural society leads to an attitude of non-involvement resulting in lack of communication and non-utilisation of services. An awareness of the deficiencies in one's background and training is essential to address objectively the question as to for whom is the health team responsible. Only when responsibility for a defined geographical area has been accepted by the health team can the practical aspects of coverage, costs, accountability and evaluation be considered. Such a process of analysis and rationalisation can give rise to the awareness of the need to break out of the existing patterns of care and the professionalisation of services. Alternative patterns of care which may be more cost-effective or with a lasting impact on health can then become more acceptable.

Social structure and organisation

Any programme of health development must operate within the social matrix of peasant societies and become an integral part of all existing traditional services. When this fact is ignored, programmes and services appear to be imposed by outside agencies, the community remains passive and the impact of the programme is minimal. Hence, an understanding of the social dynamics within the community is essential for the success of any service.

All village societies carry within them, like all human institutions, elements of conflict. They are very rarely homogeneous groups. Instead they are made up of factions organised around family, kinship, clan and class interests, all living together in a form of symbiotic relationship. Many activities which in a complex society will be classed as 'political', 'economic', 'educational' and so on are carried out as part of the performance of the kinship role. Being a member of a clan or a social group may give an individual the access to land and other productive assets. Membership of a kin group may require participation and loyalty in politics of intrigue against other groups. Even religion may be a matter of kinship because there are clan deities. In the absence of clearly defined social, commercial and administrative institutions like banking, insurance, local government and so on, family and kinship ties are utilised for mutual support and exchanges.

Sociologists have emphasised the role of the joint family, matri- or patri-local, as the basic social institution of the rural world. The typical social dynamics of many peasant societies can be summarised as follows:

(1) The family is the unit of social responsibility which is discharged by the family collectively. In births, marriages, deaths and illnesses the entire extended family is involved in the discharging of rites and rituals or making decisions on treatment.

(2) The political ideology compares the relation between the ruler and the ruled as that between the head of the family and its members, i.e. paternalistic. In many instances the whole character of the village chief's authority and administration is a replica of the paterfamilias' authority and administration.

(3) In the rural family the relationships between members are a result of living closely together. They work on the family farm together, share the same household and undergo the same privations. The relationships between various family members are based on a code of co-operation. The rural society bears this characteristic of the family, so that in all interactions between individuals and families there operates a code of behaviour as determined by the social law of reciprocity.

(4) The economic structure of the rural society also bears the traits of the rural family. There is family ownership of land, and the pattern of production and consumption is familistic. Exchange has often the characteristics of simple barter rather than of full-fledged monetary transactions.

(5) Religious and other ceremonies have for their object the security and prosperity of the family.

(6) Just as the family structure is hierarchical and the relationships between

individual family members are determined by tradition, so also is the social organisation, e.g. the caste system in India. In most village societies there are two legal systems: the customary law (e.g. *adat* in Malaysia) and the modern legal system. Often customary law is closely related to an all-pervasive wider cosmic order mixed up with religion.

Modernisation and political developments have brought about new trends so that in general three major components of the political and administrative system can be recognised in most rural communities. These are:

(1) The traditional institutions arising out of the local culture and consisting of the council of elders, village arbitrators, chiefs, religious leaders and so on.
(2) Statutory institutions like the village council.
(3) Peripheral elements of the government bureaucracy providing the administrative framework, maintenance of law and order, and various services like health, education, water development, etc. Together with the more wealthy farmers they constitute the main power structure of the rural society.

In most developing countries there are a number of processes at work leading to continuing change in the existing social structures. Introduction of new technology, growth of commerce, better transportation and accessibility to markets, education and spread of new ideas through the radio and other mass media, political developments, national development plans and so on affect the social structures of the traditional societies. As communities evolve and change, additional social structures are grafted on to the previously existing system based on kinship. The individual takes on additional roles besides those determined by his family and kinship alliances e.g. as a participant of the Farmers' Club, the Women's Organisations, Parents' Clubs, Youth groups and so on. Such roles call for different loyalties, allegiances and responsibilities. Thus there is a process of social differentiation as more autonomous social units are formed, and several types of economic activity become separated from family institutions. The previous practice of apprenticeship within the family declines as recruitment of labour is no longer on kinship lines. The pattern of authority gets transformed as elders lose their control. There is also a process of integration as the new social structures come together on a different basis. Political integration is no longer on kinship status or tribal membership but on a modern type of commonality of political interests. Thirdly, the evolving social structures must be capable of adaptation to new problems and to new social groups. It is this transformation in the social organisation of the peasant community which enables it to accept new concepts related to health as part of community development. Depending upon the distribution of power and of productive assets in the community these evolutionary changes either reinforce entrenched interests or reduce disparity.

The role of the health worker is to understand the social organisation within his community and enable the people to evolve social structures which would help sustain local health activities in a spirit of self-reliance. Assimilation of new concepts is facilitated through advocacy by community leaders and dialogue within the community rather than by periodic sermons from visiting experts. Thus, in Jamkhed, the farmers have increased their output and practise a better cropping pattern in villages which have established farmers' clubs, and the women were more knowledgeable about oral rehydration in villages with women's clubs (*Mahila Mandal*) compared with nearby control villages. Even though the agricultural extension programme in the project and non-project areas was identical, in the case of the control villages up to 70 per cent of the benefit went to more affluent farmers.

The rural poor including the landless, the agricultural labourers and the underemployed artisans, are mostly disorganised and fragmented groups, besides being excluded from the decision-making circles of the local élite. Getting them organised around some activity like literacy classes, cultural groups, sewing, knitting and similar income-generating activities, women's clubs and so on is one way of bringing people together to discuss their problems and to devise solutions.

Culture and world view

People's attitudes towards health and disease in peasant societies are not essentially different from those in Western societies. What really matters for many of them is not the immediate cause of an illness but the ultimate cause. That is to say, the reason why the immediate cause came to be directed towards the particular individual. This idea of intentionality is rooted in the principle of reciprocity, which considers disease as being due to a punishment for breaking taboos.

Each community has its own system of values and beliefs. Traditional attitudes and practices exist in all walks of life, and are not restricted to health alone. The use of fertilisers, irrigation water, a new variety of seeds, an improved plough, rotation of crops, cottage industry, acceptance of vaccination—these and a host of other innovations may be accepted or rejected depending upon the prevalent attitudes of the community. Into this system of beliefs and values the village improvement programme brings in new concepts and approaches through a process of education and holds the potential of commencing a process of growth. Many of the developmental activities are aimed at providing new information and skills, and change of attitudes.

Most village communities are closed communities with a characteristic outlook on life dominated by religious practices, cultural beliefs, and rites or rituals. The medical profession always refers to this as 'beliefs' and traditionally divides them into good, harmful and neutral from the disease point of view.

Such a description provides a good practical framework, but is rather narrow in meaning. Anthropologists refer to the outlook on life in traditional societies as the 'world view' or the 'cognitive map'. The world of the peasant societies consists of supernatural beings and gods of various orders, ancestral spirits and other non-human spirits, all of these being as real to them as other visible human beings in everyday life. Disease may be caused by any of them. Thus personal spirits may bring illness to a person and specific spirits of disease may cause illness of epidemic proportions to befall an entire community.

Religious practitioners act as intermediaries between men and supernatural beings. On the one hand they may communicate the wishes of their local group or political community to certain powerful gods, and on the other hand they may interpret the wishes of the gods to the people. Divinations may be made to foretell future events; ceremonies, rituals and offerings may be made to please the supernatural beings. And so religious practitioners are important members of the village society and often wield more power than the village leaders and chiefs. One of the commonest reasons for which they are consulted is to divine or determine the cause of illness.

The people's pattern of beliefs, attitudes, the life style and the behaviour stemming from it as well as the commonly accepted way in which communities organise themselves to deal with their everyday activities constitutes their culture. As new knowledge is acquired and becomes assimilated or as the environment changes, cultural practices are changed to adapt to such evolutionary developments. Concepts about health and disease also are subject to such changes. In the example of Jamkhed mentioned above, the acceptance by the women of new knowledge regarding fluid–electrolyte loss in diarrhoea has resulted in the popular use of oral rehydration therapy in preference to the previous practice of withholding all liquids. The sum total of all knowledge and practices used for diagnosis, management or prevention of physical, mental or social symptoms constitutes the health culture of the community. Thus the various systems of medicine differ not so much as to the goals but in the culture of the people who practise them. All human cultures have practised ways of looking after the sick, the injured, the chronically ill, the handicapped, pregnant women, the woman in labour and so on. This is the basis of traditional medicine. In some cultures indigenous medicine has tended to stagnate because of failing to exploit new discoveries in science and technology for its own development. In other cultures, as in China, the indigenous system has remained lively by continuing to assimilate new ideas and to evolve.

The indigenous systems of medicine have their roots in the distant past, and all are deeply rooted in the belief system of the communities where they are being practised. The traditional medicine systems of China, the Ayurvedic and the Unani systems as well as similar systems in Malaysia and Indonesia are but examples of such systems of health care. People prefer to consult different kinds of health practitioners for different illnesses as figures 3.4 and 3.5 show.

Figure 3.4   Practitioner of traditional medicine in the herb garden – Vietnam.

Figure 3.5   Traditional medicine in Bangladesh.

Often an individual may be receiving 'treatment' from practitioners of a number of different systems simultaneously.

It is essential for health workers to develop an understanding of the belief systems of the communities they serve. Any insight into how the beliefs get expressed into the different varieties of health behaviours in their communities, and people's decisions about what kind of help to seek during illnesses, will enable the health workers to make the services culturally more acceptable. Thus in Uganda it is commonly believed that kwashiorkor is caused by the heat from the womb of the mother or by the jealousy of a younger sibling and that Western medicine has no cure for either of these. Hence children with kwashiorkor may not be brought to the notice of the health worker.

The decision to consult a 'doctor' is rarely taken by the patient individually. Family groups, especially the elders in the extended family, are usually involved in such decisions. Among the Tiv in central Nigeria, the practice is to consult a diviner who may advise the sick individual to call together either the father's or the mother's kinfolk or at times both. There follows a ceremony consisting of sacrifice of a chicken or a goat, various rituals and chanting of phrases culminating in the application of medicine to various parts of the body and a meal in which all the kinsmen and spectators participate. Among the Digo of Kenya the kin group has to be present at the consultation and treatment, and the kin group assumes the responsibility for paying the practitioner. If the kin group decides to take the patient to hospital it also decides who escorts, who pays for transport and who pays for the board and lodging of the escorts.

In many communities women are particulary at risk on account of the cultural practices. Girls are married early, usually around the age of menarche. Hence child-bearing often commences before they have reached the optimum in body build and height. This is especially so if they have suffered recurrent illness and undernutrition in childhood and pubertal growth is extended into the late teens. Women also carry a heavy burden of physical work at home besides working in the field. Thus the pounding of the grain, the grinding of corn and other processing of food is part of the woman's daily chores in all societies. The fetching of water and firewood is also usually a feminine task and often requires the carrying of heavy burdens over long distances. Their nutritional status is often poor because the most nourishing foods are often consumed by the breadwinner males in the family. Such social/cultural attitudes add to the vulnerability of the women caused by the demands of repeated child-bearing especially among the disadvantaged groups. Hence the need to ensure that the promotive/preventive services like prenatal and maternity care focus on mothers in the lower socio-economic groups.

As countries respond to the challenge of providing 'Health Care for All by the Year 2000' they face the task of expanding the health services fourfold. This is not possible on the existing pattern with the available resources. There is also the question of acceptability of the Western style of a health service. On the other hand, the traditional health system reaches out to most people, besides being acceptable since it is an integral part of the people's culture. Many countries are now working towards the linking of the informal system of health care to the national health system and legitimising the traditional practitioner. In India there are 108 colleges of indigenous medicine and a statutory National Control Council directs their activities and awards recognition and registration for the graduates. In Sri Lanka where the traditional system of medicine is said to meet the basic health needs of about 70 per cent of the population, there is a governmental programme of registering the traditional practitioners.

One way of forming collaborative links with the indigenous system of medicine is to help establish training programmes and refresher courses for traditional practitioners. The present state of medical knowledge and field experiences in several countries have created the possibility of simple standardised techniques to be applied to large numbers of people utilising minimally-trained personnel. Weighing and charting the growth of children, oral rehydration, promotion of breast feeding and methods of improving the nutrient density of weaning foods, creating awareness of the importance of preventing the common childhood infections through immunisation, and family planning require no detailed bio-medical knowledge nor exhaustive training. The traditional practitioner is well suited for such training. In many situations lay individuals selected by the community are given such training

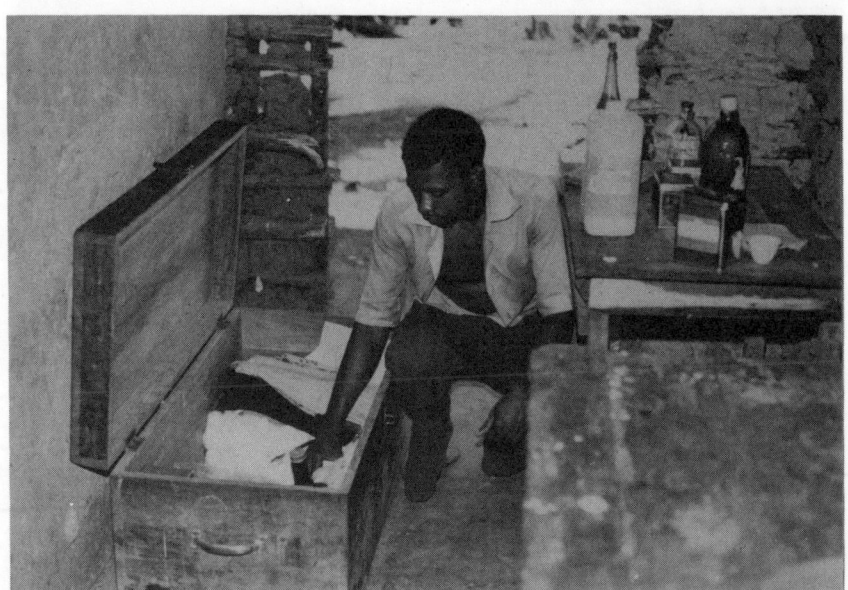

Figure 3.6   A village health worker in Tanzania.

and have been found to be effective agents of change provided they are given regular support from the formal health services (figure 3.6).

A traditional practice that needs to be urgently integrated with the formal health service is maternity care. It is estimated that as many as 80 per cent of all births in many developing countries are conducted by the traditional birth attendants (TBAs). Appropriate training of the TBAs will help spread prenatal care with emphasis on nutrition, prevention of anaemia through administration of iron and folic acid, prophylaxis of malaria and tetanus immunisation in traditional societies. Within such a basic prenatal care service early selection of high-risk pregnancies for more skilled care can be implemented and danger signals can be identified early in pregnancy. A more informed care during labour in which progress is monitored by the rate of dilatation of the cervix helps to identify difficult labour early to avoid risk to life. Several countries have mounted programmes of training the traditional birth attendants with a view to integrating them with the national health services and thereby expand coverage for maternity care several fold (see figure 3.7).

Comparable with the TBAs in efficacy of service are the multitude of spiritual healers who deal with most psychosomatic illnesses in traditional societies. Western medicine has no effective cures for such problems and by providing a culturally acceptable outlet for anxieties and neuroses through rituals, spiritual healers are taking a major workload away from the stretched resources of the formal health sector. The activities of such healers can be

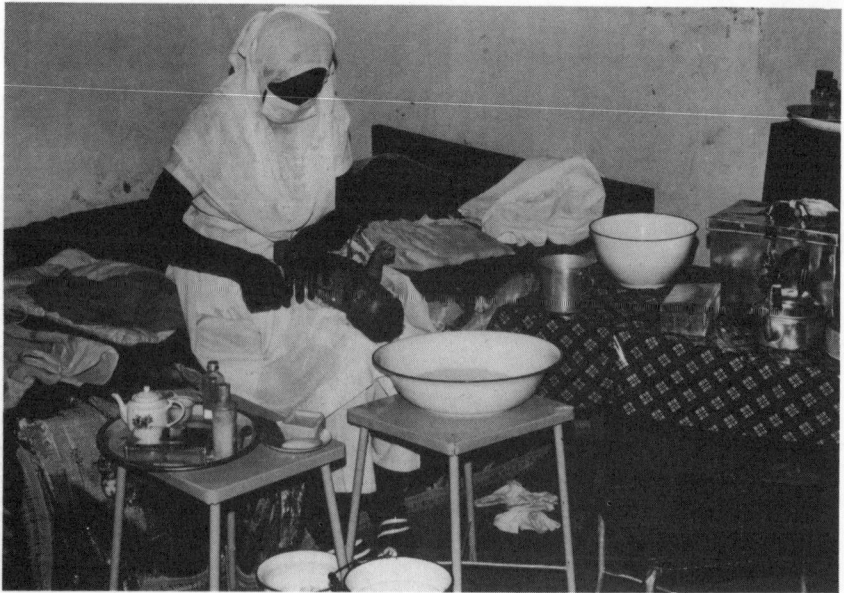

Figure 3.7   A trained village midwife in Sudan.

improved and appropriately channelled through training and seminars so as to turn them into agents of change.

The various governmental services are looked upon by the traditional society as 'external' agencies with activities based on alien concepts and to be made use of only as a last resource when indigenous remedies fail. There is a grudging acceptance of not only the health services but also of all other services like schools, agricultural extension, veterinary care and so on. As such these services are like small nuclei of modernisation surrounded by a whole world of traditional beliefs and cultural attitudes (see figure 3.8). Spread of new concepts is inhibited and slow. Change in attitude is rapid when the health worker is from amongst the community members and a long-time resident. Thus the village health worker, the trained TBA, and the trained folk practitioners when regularly supported, encouraged and supervised can be transformed into agents of change (see figure 3.8). This is necessary for two reasons. In community medicine all activities must be undertaken with and through the full participation of the people. Secondly, a great deal of improvements in health in Western countries, for which the medical profession takes unjustified credit, were in fact achieved through improved sanitation, clean water, better nutrition, spread of education, and greater awareness of hygiene. All such improvements are immediately possible in the developing countries providing an awareness can be created and communities can be mobilised to pool their resources to achieve these goals. Hence a process of increasing awareness of local problems and devising solutions through a continuing dialogue utilising community groups and health workers resident in the community is essential. Such a process is essentially one of education, of removing superstition, of opening the mind to new ideas and of creating a sense of partnership.

Resources

Lack of adequate resources is a powerful constraint on the development of health services. Even though most developing countries are spending 4–8 per cent of the general governmental expenditure on health (see table 3.1), the per capita expenditure amounts to US$1–5 as compared with the UK which spends US$200. Because the health services are modelled on those of the Western countries, this lack of resources is felt mostly in rural areas, since the bulk of the health expenditure is on curative medicine in urban areas. Allocation of resources can be faulty in more than one way. The concentration of physicians in urban centres is well known, with the result that in rural areas there may be one doctor for as many as 20 000 people.

The output of doctors may be higher than that of auxiliary personnel, e.g. in India all through the 1970s there were 2.5 doctors to 1 nurse. Furthermore, the

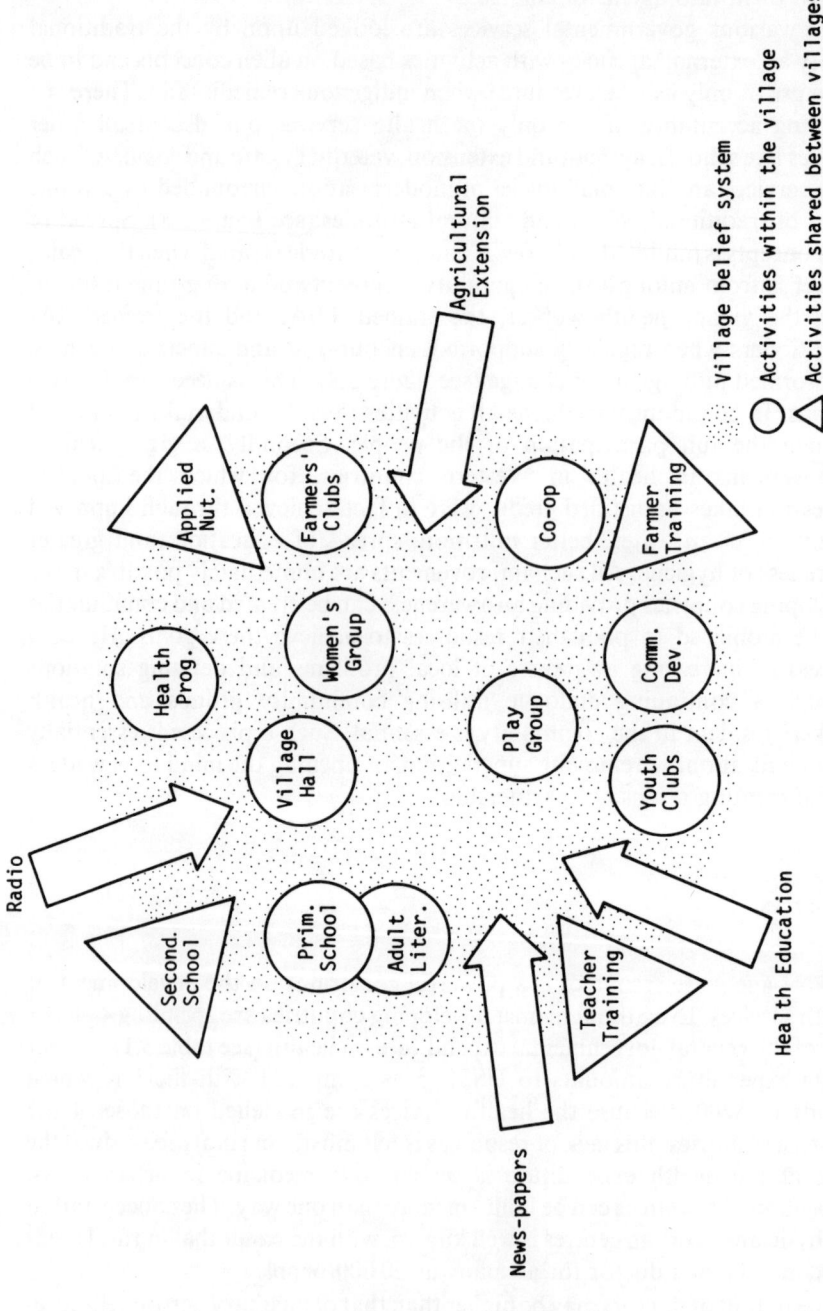

Figure 3.8   Local belief system and modernisation.

Table 3.1 **Per capita government expenditure on health and other services**

| | Per capita expenditure (US$) | | | | | | Per cent total public expenditure (1980) | | | Inflation (1970–81) (%) |
| | Health | | Education | | Defence | | Health | Education | Defence | |
Per capita GNP ($)	1972	1980	1972	1980	1972	1980				
Less than 300:										
Burma	1	1	3	2	7	5	4.84	9.7	24.2	10.7
Ghana	6	3	20	11	8	2	5.7	21.0	3.8	36.4
Sudan	2	1	3	5	8	7	1.9	9.43	13.2	15.9
400–1000:										
Bolivia	4	5	13	19	7	10	8.3	31.5	16.6	23.0
Thailand	2	4	11	16	11	17	4.8	19.4	20.6	10.0
Morocco	5	7	21	35	13	36	3.5	17.0	17.9	8.2
1000–1500:										
Dominican Republic	15	13	18	20	11	15	8.9	13.7	10.3	9.1
Tunisia	11	21	46	50	7	36	7.0	16.7	12.0	8.2
Syrian Arab Republic	2	3	19	15	64	144	0.9	4.97	47.7	12.0
1500 and more:										
Malaysia	12	15	42	50	33	38	6.6	21.8	16.6	7.4
Brazil	10	20	11	15	13	10	8.6	6.45	4.3	42.1
Korea, Republic of	1	2	14	25	22	49	1.4	17.5	34.3	19.8
UK	158	217	34	45	217	246	12.8	2.7	14.5	14.4
USA	120	193	45	49	453	392	10.4	2.65	21.2	7.2

number of medical schools is increasing progressively, whereas institutions for training auxiliary nurse midwives (ANM) are closing down. Thus, in the State of Andhra Pradesh, the number of institutions for training ANM has been reduced from 26 to four and the intake of students for the health visitor's course has been reduced from 180 to 90.

Government expenditure on health has remained static or even halved in some of the poorer countries (e.g. Ghana and Sudan) during the last decade. In those countries who have been able to increase the per capita expenditure on health, the increase has not been commensurate with the prevailing inflation so that in real terms there has been a net fall in health expenditure. For example, in Iraq the increase in health manpower between 1956 and 1975 has been between 177 per cent and 334 per cent, depending upon the category of health worker. During the same period health expenditure also increased by 226 per cent for a population which increased by 227 per cent. But because of inflation which is estimated at 250 per cent between 1956 and 1975, the per capita health expenditure in real terms declined. Most developing countries who depend on imports of essential medical supplies in the absence of a local pharmaceutical industry have experienced a 'shrinkage' of their health

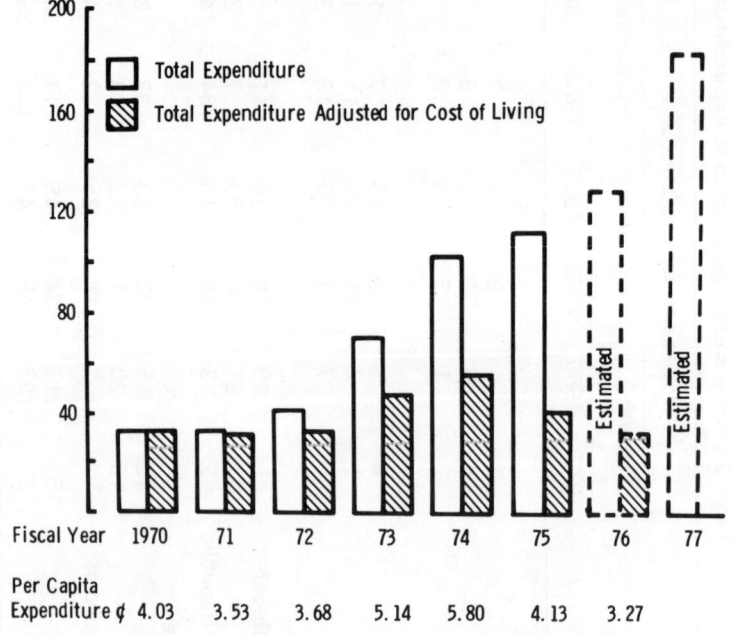

Figure 3.9   Health expenditure in Ghana adjusted for cost of living and population growth.

Source: A Primary Health Care Strategy for Ghana. Ministry of Health, Ghana. 1978.

budgets in real terms on account of the twin problems of inflation and the deteriorating foreign exchange situation. This is shown for Ghana in figure 3.9. Hence the need for spending scarce resources wisely both at the national level and at the periphery. The health planners face the same dilemma as the health workers. Should resources be spent on the more expensive 'recent' pharmaceuticals to meet the demands of the élite or on the essential drugs to supply the needs of the majority? The demands of the hospital services will have to be kept in check to provide for regular supplies of a handful of essential drugs for all villages and urban neighbourhoods, together with the setting up of primary care services. At present, in the absence of the latter, many secondary and tertiary care hospital services are swamped with providing primary care which is wasteful of resources. There is a need to change the present ambulatory care into primary care and extend health coverage to those who do not receive any (see figure 3.10). This would entail the expansion of the manpower base utilising largely the existing human resources of the community like the TBA and the folk practitioners besides training a new cadre of community health workers. Secondly, the hospital services presently providing specialist care in total isolation from the community must become supportive of and committed to the peripheral services instead of competing against them for scarce resources.

Natural disasters and political difficulties increase the demands for scarce resources. A large number of countries in tropical Africa have a problem with refugees, which now number between 10 and 18 million—enough to populate a sizeable country. Even though the international community has responded generously, the refugees still create major demands on the host country's services for distribution of supplies, maintenance of law and order, and for employment opportunities. An associated problem is that of heavy defence expenditure (see table 3.1). Since 1945 there have been 200 wars involving more than 80 states, most of them in the developing world. The Third World spent US$151 billion in military expenditure in 1976 and provides the clientele for three-quarters of the global arms trade.

World-wide recession has added yet another twist to the question of scarcity of resources in developing countries so that several nations have run up alarmingly high debts. In 1981, Third World debt was rising at the rate of 20 per cent annually and some countries were spending as much as 60 per cent of total export earning just to service the national debt.

National health expenditures must be examined in the light of the global economic picture as discussed above. In the foreseeable future growth in health services along the traditional pattern is unlikely and countries must re-examine their priorities. Patterns of health care inherited from the past have proven to be not only non-workable but also expensive, and trying to do 'more of the same' is likely to prove disastrous. Hence the need to search for innovative approaches and to share experiences between countries.

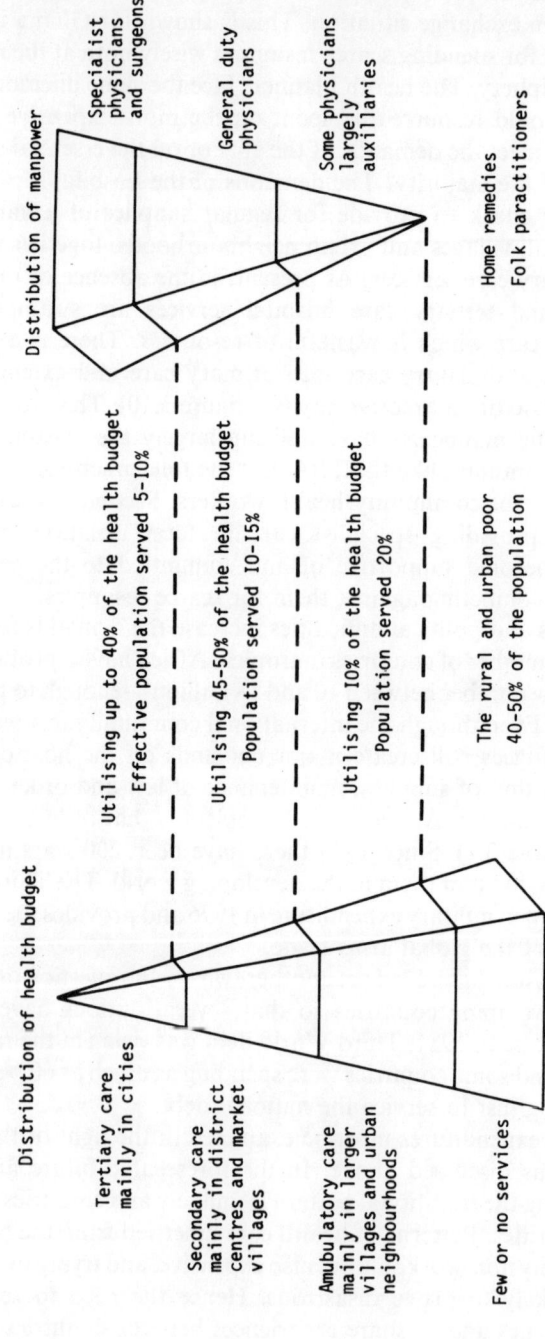

Figure 3.10   Distribution of health care resources in the average developing country.

Urban growth

By the end of the century the urban population of the developing world will have increased 20-fold since 1920 (see figure 3.11). Even though initially urban growth was largely caused by new migrants, natural increase is now playing a greater role and the process has become accelerated. The result is that whereas population growth in the average developing country is at the rate of 2 per cent per year, the urban population is increasing at twice that rate, and shanty towns are growing at four times the rate of population growth.

Rural poverty is a major factor driving people to the 'growth poles' created by the concentration of industry and commerce in the larger cities. Of the 1 billion or so absolute poor, more than 600 million are in the rural areas. They are the prime candidates for urban migration. In some instances much of rural poverty is created by unequal distribution of power and wealth, and lack of governmental control to safeguard the weak. In Mexico, for example, the number of landless peasants exploded from 1.5 million in 1950 to over 14 million by 1980. In much of Latin America 8 per cent of the population own 80

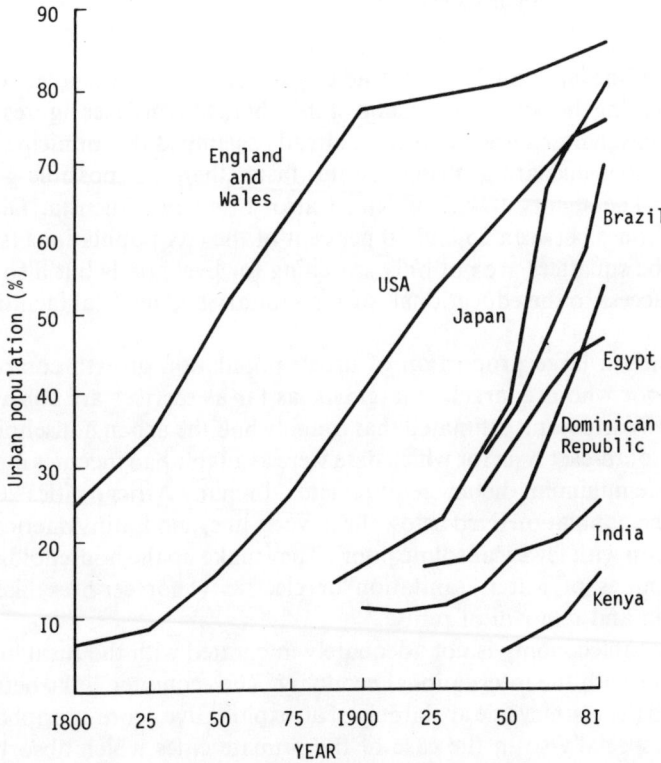

Figure 3.11   Rates of urbanisation in selected countries.

Figure 3.12   A shanty town.

per cent of the land. Such trends lead to an overflow of rural poverty into the cities, creating the new phenomenon of the 'shanty towns' (see figures 3.12 and 3.13). The squatter settlements have already swamped the municipal services in most cities and are growing at rates faster than any possible growth of services. The shanty towns of Rio, Cairo, Bombay, Calcutta, Dacca and Manila house between 25 and 30 per cent of the city populations (see figure 3.14). The squatters are not only searching for livelihoods but also demand greater access to the educational, social, sanitary and medical facilities of the cities.

Presently a large proportion of urban population growth comprises the urban poor who are largely 'marginals' as far as services are concerned. In 1976 the World Bank estimated that roughly half the urban households in the cities of south-east Asia for which data were available had incomes inadequate to provide minimum dietary requirements. In many African cities 20–40 per cent of the population lived below the poverty line, and Latin America was the only region with fewer 'absolute poor'. They make up the households without the amenities of water, sanitation or electricity nor services like health, education and removal of refuse.

The urban economy is not adequately integrated with the rural hinterland but rather with the international economy. The economic links between the cities and the countryside are largely of an exploitative, 'core–periphery' type. This is especially so in the case of the primate cities which absorb a large proportion of national investment and skilled manpower. In some countries

Figure 3.13   An urban slum in Manila.

the primate cities have grown faster than services can cope, with the result that miles of 'septic fringes' now surround these cities (see table 3.2). In some countries between a quarter to a third of the total urban population is now to be found in the primate city, largely living in slums and shanty towns.

The foregoing description of characteristics and trends in the developing countries provides an insight into the nature of social stratification and the course taken by past development activities. Health services are part of national development and are subject to the same forces and influences that

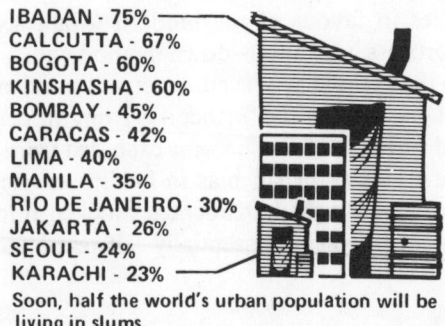

IBADAN - 75%
CALCUTTA - 67%
BOGOTA - 60%
KINSHASHA - 60%
BOMBAY - 45%
CARACAS - 42%
LIMA - 40%
MANILA - 35%
RIO DE JANEIRO - 30%
JAKARTA - 26%
SEOUL - 24%
KARACHI - 23%

Soon, half the world's urban population will be living in slums.

Figure 3.14   Life in the margin. Percentages of city populations living in slums and squatter settlements.

Table 3.2 **The primate cities**

GNP ($)	Total population (1981) (millions)	Total urban population (millions)	Population of primate city	
			No. (millions)	% total urban
300:				
Bangladesh	91	11	3	30
Sudan	19	5	1.6	31
Ghana	12	4	1.4	35
500–1500:				
Indonesia	150	32	7.3	23
Philippines	50	19	5.7	30
Nigeria	88	18	3.1	17
1500–2500:				
South Korea	39	23	2.8	12
Iran	40	20	5.6	28
Brazil	121	82	12.3	15
Mexico	71	48	15.4	32
Chile	11	9	4	44

determine the trends in other sectors. A growing disparity between the city and country and between the rich and the poor of the city can be found in most countries. Broadly speaking there is a four-layered pyramidal structure which is well established in many Latin American countries and is rapidly evolving in the newly independent nations. This pyramidal structure consists of a small wealthy urban élite group at the apex; government servants, workers in modern industries and merchants make up the second layer below them; the remainder of the urban population forming the third layer and the large mass of the rural peasant farmers and the landless are at the base. Political power is concentrated largely in the hands of the wealthy élite who influence government policies in favour of the modern urban sector. The national decision-making process is by a top–down method with a chain of command from the centre to the periphery. The administrative and executive machinery of the government gets weaker the further it is from the centre, with the result that the urban and rural poor have become excluded from the main stream of development. The resulting urban bias in health services, as also in other sectors, has led to government bureaucracies locked into a hospital-based, high-technology system which is essentially self-perpetuating.

The urban bias and development in enclaves

The class structure of most developing countries has given rise to marked inequalities, and the model of economic growth hitherto pursued has brought about an increase in inequality whilst serving class interest. The typical developing country is thus a dual economy with small modern sectors which are well provided for and large poverty-stricken areas usually practising a traditional type of agriculture with an inadequate infrastructure of services. The concentration of wealth and power has resulted in the development of enclaves—modern industry surrounded by large areas untouched by the industrial revolution. The parallel of this process in the health field is that of modern hospitals practising the most recent techniques surrounded by communities that do not have even basic health care. Just as the enclaves of modern technology have failed to usher in an industrial revolution, so also the large hospitals and 'centres of excellence' have made no impact on the health of the masses.

The unequal distribution of wealth and political power

It is not unusual in developing countries for the top 5 per cent of the population to obtain between 30 and 40 per cent of the national income, and for the top one-third to receive 60–70 per cent. The remaining two-thirds provide a source of cheap labour which helps to keep exports to the industrial world at a low price as in the case of tea, coffee, sisal, cotton, jute and minerals. These exports have largely financed the urban-biased growth of the last several decades. In the process the emerging national middle class has reproduced the dualism of the international economy. The polarisation of wealth and political power has resulted in increasing pauperisation in many societies. In a number of studies in seven countries of south-east Asia representing 70 per cent of the rural population of the non-socialist world, a decline in the real income of the rural poor was demonstrable. On the other hand, between 1960 and 1973 the GNP increased in all the seven countries and in only one of them did the population expand faster than the domestic food production. Clearly, therefore, the increase in poverty has more to do with the structure of the economy than with its rate of growth. The rural systems of Bangladesh, Brazil, Indonesia and Nigeria are characterised by concentration of productive assets in a few hands who also control the organisational structures which maintain the status quo. In Bangladesh, more than half the land is owned by 10 per cent of the landowners. In the Philippines 4 per cent of the farms are large enough to cover more than a third of the country's cropland. In the states of Bihar and Uttar Pradesh in India the poorest half of the population has less than 4 per cent of the land. In Latin America as a whole, seven per cent of the landowners own 93 per cent of the farm land. It is the families of the landless and the small farmers who have a greater incidence of malnutrition and other poverty-related diseases whilst most of the available health facilities and resources are being monopolised and controlled by the minority of the well-off. The planning and decision-making processes are

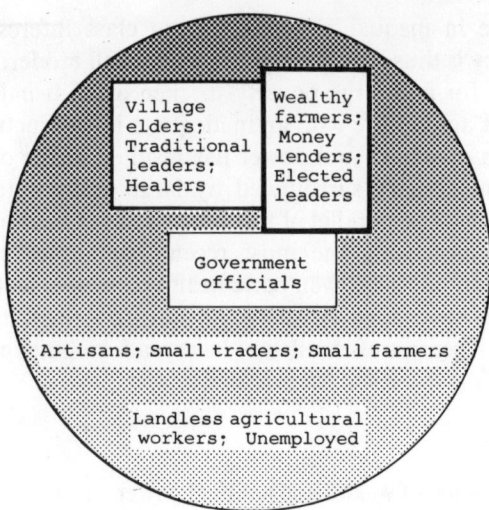

Figure 3.15   The distribution of political power.

slanted in favour of the national and rural élites who divert the major benefits of all development activities towards themselves (see figure 3.15).

The starting point of health development should be the *needs* of the bottom two-thirds of the population rather than the *demands* of the top third. This is true both nationally and also at the district level. Such a rational approach calls for minimum standards of nutrition, health and hygiene, water and sanitation as well as education, clothing and shelter for the masses. It requires a system that can mobilise the entire population utilising local knowledge and experience for solving problems. The system should be capable of absorbing modern technology but not completely taken up by it. Such participatory democracy will enable the masses to achieve true self-reliance in health, and overcome the forces that generate poverty.

Lessons of the past decades

The average life expectancy in the developing countries is 58 years, a level attained by the industrial countries only in the 1930s. During the past three decades many of the developing countries have achieved as much progress as the industrial countries did in two centuries (see table 3.3). However, such averages hide pockets of stagnation in countries, and in regions. There exist poverty groups for whom life chances have not improved at all. Studies of rural development in nine countries—Brazil, Mexico, Nigeria, Tanzania, India, Bangladesh, Indonesia, Philippines and China—indicate that the differences in the development process stem from a consistent set of factors

Table 3.3 Average trends in life expectancy at birth, child mortality and literacy

	Life expectancy (years)				Child Mortality*				Literacy rate (%)			
	1950	1960	1970	1980	1950	1960	1970	1980	1950	1960	1970	1980
Low-income countries	41	47	53	57	28	22	16	12	20	27	29	51
Middle-income countries	46	50	55	59	28	22	16	11	48	49	64	68
All developing countries	43	48	54	58	28	22	16	12	33	38	46	56
Western Europe and North America	68	70	71	74	3	2	1	1	95	97	98	99

* Deaths per thousand children aged1–4 years.

like the pattern of asset distribution, rural organisations and institutions and the set of incentives. Whether it is health, education, water development, agricultural extension, marketing or credit facilities, the cost of reaching the poor is invariably greater than that of reaching the well-off. The more glaring the inequality, the greater the cost difference and the greater is the probability of primarily serving the better-off and increasing their productivity, thereby increasing the inequality.

Hence the challenge for health workers is to go in search of those who are excluded, who do not make use of the services on a regular basis, especially the promotive/preventive services, and to ensure that the activities and benefits of the health programmes are directed largely towards the disadvantaged groups. The guidelines to follow are the following:

(1) Emphasis on making the services widely available and easily accessible for all, but with a priority for the disadvantaged and the poor. The obstacles to be overcome are the resistance of the local élite, the existing preoccupation with hospital services, weak managerial support at the periphery and the deficiencies of one's training.

(2) The services should be equipped to deal with the common health problems of the area as well as the common emergencies, and should focus on their prevention through the creation of an awareness amongst the majority rather than become monopolised by the rare clinically 'interesting' syndromes.

(3) Creation of awareness is a two-way process through a regular dialogue with community groups so that health programmes become participatory and develop compatibility with the cultural and social milieu of the community.

(4) All peripheral health services should receive adequate managerial and technical support and become integrated with the higher levels of the health system. In such a system one envisages flow of knowledge and skills from the centre to the periphery and a reverse flow of information concerning coverage, epidemiological data and trends in health indicators.

(5) Develop close collaboration with other sectors like education, agriculture, marketing and so on, both at the administrative level and also working through the process of dialogue with the relevant community groups.

(6) Health workers have an important catalytic role to perform through helping the disadvantaged within the community to organise themselves into social groups with specific responsibilities e.g.the women's clubs, the youth organisations and so on. Such groups are more effective in finding solutions to local problems like cleaning the environment, development of water resources, marketing and credit.

The poor suffer from a cluster of overlapping disadvantages, each reinforcing the other. The converse is also true. Each improvement in the well-being of a community reinforces the benefits of the others. Hence the need for an integrated approach in which new activities and developments seem to stem from within the community by a process of consensus rather than as directives from above.

The emerging trends

The experience of many countries provides ample evidence that poverty is the strongest impediment to development and also very difficult to resolve. The larger the proportion of people living in absolute poverty, the slower the development. This is as much true for nations as for regions, districts, individual villages and neighbourhoods. The 'culture of poverty' has many ramifications. It generates an attitude of hopelessness and resignation. Those caught in its web show well-defined behavioural traits like family instability, violence, alcoholism and the inability to organise themselves. Thus poverty becomes self-perpetuating. Furthermore, children brought up in this culture learn the pattern of behaviour of the majority, internalise it and grow up to become incapable of escaping their poverty. They also grow up malnourished and the whole cycle of ill health, low energy, low productivity, low incomes and the inability to improve the quality of one's life is perpetuated into a new generation. Hence the objectives of all development activities including health should be to mount a direct assult on poverty.

A variety of social, economic and political forces operate to exclude the disadvantaged. The poor have limited access to productive assets and to educational, health and other services. They have fewer opporunities for learning skills and chances of employment are limited. Hence the urgent need to change the focus of development from economic growth which at best increases inequality, to improving the qualty of life. This shift of emphasis from economic growth to direct assault on poverty marks a major turning point in the development thinking of several nations.

Recent experience has also shown that it is possible to improve the physical quality of life independently of improvements in the general economic status, and that economic growth in its narrowly defined form is not a pre-condition to development. There are, however, a number of difficulties to be overcome. First the training of the average health professional has increasingly become centred on the bio-medical aspects of disease, and the central issue of poverty as a determinant of disease rarely enters into the daily routine of diagnosis and treatment. Even for those who are sensitised to the problem of poverty its true extent and the depth of destitution often go unperceived because of insufficient scientific data, and the social and political difficulties in carrying out a detailed enquiry. Health and other statistics often hide the fact that the rates of death and a number of illnesses show several-fold differences between the social classes. Secondly, most health plans are vertically imposed, building on the existing framework at the time of independence and often taking industrial planning as a model. The danger of such a model for health planning is that in many countries the investment trends in the public sector support private sector activities, since the groups on which the government relies for support are the same which own most of the wealth of the country, supply the majority of technicians and administrators and the leadership of the army. Getting a popular movement in health going often requires skill and courage to break out of such a conventional mould of planning and thinking.

A corollary of the basic needs approach is the issue of coverage with services especially of the promotive/preventive kind. Related to coverage are the questions of availability, accessibility, acceptability and affordability of the services provided. The impact on health is better when there is full coverage with services, however basic compared with isolated 'centres of excellence' in the country. Coverage is all the more important in highly stratified societies because of the usual process of exclusion of the lower social classes in such societies.

In the past two decades a number of innovative programmes have developed in different countries. They have had a varied degree of success, but together they comprise a 'critical mass' which will accelerate the processes of change and innovative approaches for community and health development. A recent review of 10 such innovative projects, selected on the basis of availability of adequate data, stresses the benefits of health and nutrition interventions. In many instances infant and child mortality have been reduced by a third to a half within a short period of 1 – 5 years at very little cost. Care of the mother and child using low-cost health technology has been shown to be worth while. The lessons derived from the review fully support the call for developing Primary Health Care with all its essential elements listed on page 32 and further discussed in Chapter 4. It is possible to break the chain of poverty → malnutrition → inadequate development through a number of interventions, and often the most cost-effective point for breaking into the cycle is the period of pregnancy, lactation and weaning. These are the trends now evolving in many countries.

More recently, the United National Children's Fund (UNICEF) has proposed a 'minimum package of services for child survival' consisting of promotion and regular monitoring of growth, oral rehydration, breast feeding, and immunisation (GOBI). To these may be added food supplementation as indicated and family spacing. A number of low-cost standardised technologies are now available which do not require much professional expertise and can be applied in every community and neighbourhood in the developing world. It is estimated that several million lives of children can be saved each year through the following approaches.

Growth monitoring (including during pregnancy)—Growth is the central biological process throughout childhood and is a sensitive indicator of adverse environmental influences. The commonest such influence is inadequate nutrition, and amongst the disadvantaged groups undernourishment occurs from conception onwards into childhood and further extending into adulthood. Fetal malnutrition leading to intrauterine growth retardation is responsible for the high proportion of low birth weight ($<2500\,\text{g}$) in developing countries. Such infants are three times more likely to die in infancy than babies of normal weight at birth and now account for 30–40 per cent of all infant deaths in the developing world. Growth faltering during the weaning period is common, resulting from undernutrition and frank malnutrition in about 1 per cent. It is estimated that the point prevalence of growth failure (undernutrition) in an average peasant community is 10 per cent and that only 24 per cent of children show adequate growth. Approximately half of the 15 million children who die each year in the developing world do so on account of malnutrition or because of diseases that malnutrition makes worse. A great deal of growth faltering is due to poor weaning practices and because of the effects of infections like diarrhoea, measles and whooping cough.

Oral rehydration has been described as a major medical advance of the last decade. The technology is simple and eminently suited for application in every peasant home and urban neighbourhood. With an estimated 5 million deaths annually of children due to diarrhoea in the developing world, it means that approximately 1 out of every 20 children born in the developing world is likely to die of causes associated with diarrhoea. In every country where a programme of oral rehydration therapy has been introduced, marked reduction in diarrhoeal deaths has been recorded.

Breast feeding is the newborn baby's best insurance for survival in all developing countries. Recent research in human milk has identified its value as a nutrient, as a protective agent, as a mediator of metabolic patterns and responses in the newborn, and as an effective contraceptive agent. A great deal of such research has sparked new developments in the related disciplines of nutrition, immunology and child psychology. Bottle feeding in the contaminated environment of the developing world has many hazards. It is estimated that about 1 million infant deaths occur each year due to causes related directly or indirectly to bottle feeding.

Immunisation and its benefits are well known. The so-called 'common infectious diseases of childhood' are in fact all major illnesses, especially pertussis and measles. Effective vaccines are available against most and no national health service can be forgiven for not achieving adequate levels of coverage with immunisation. It is estimated that about 5 million children die each year on account of illnesses preventable by immunisation and an equivalent number suffer from the sequelae of the infection.

The above package of minimum care if applied with sensitivity and care promises to save more than 11 million infant and child deaths each year. It poses a challenge to national leaders, planners and administrators to proceed from rhetoric to immediate action. Many of the technologies are not expensive and their effectiveness has stood the test of time as well as of numerous scientific studies. However, for these activities to become permanently established within the social matrix of communities and the administrative patterns of the health services, an infrastructure of health and environmental services and appropriate training programmes as part of the primary health care approach are necessary.

An important ingredient of success in all the community-based innovative approaches is active participation by the community. People learn best by doing, and encouraging active participation by all the groups in the community is proving to be a highly successful form of health education. Moreover, the organisational patterns created for one programme–e.g. the various committees and arrangements for voluntary communal work—as well as the enthusiasm generated by one success will provide the stimulus and the experience for dealing with other problems and needs. Here again the disadvantaged have special needs since the 'more backward' communities are less organised and more fragmented compared with those nearer the centre, and hence are more likely to be left behind.

Further reading

Amonoo-Lartson, R., Ebrahim, G. J., Lovel, H. J. and Ranken, J. P. (1984). *District Health Care. Challenges for Planning Organisation and Evaluation in Developing Countries*. Macmillan Press, Basingstoke and London.

Banerji, D. (1982). *Poverty, Class and Health Culture in India*. Prachi Prakashan, New Delhi.

Coombs, P.H. (ed.) (1980). *Meeting the Basic Needs of the Rural Poor. The Integrated Community-based Approach*. Pergamon Press, New York and Oxford.

Ebrahim, G. J. (1978). *Breast Feeding—The Biological Option*. Macmillan Press, Basingstoke and London.

Ebrahim, G. J. (1983). *Nutrition in Mother and Child Health*. Macmillan Press, Basingstoke and London.

Harrison, P. (1979). *Inside the Third World*. Penguin Books, Harmondsworth.

Jelliffe, D. B. and Jelliffe, E. F. P. (1978). *Human Milk in the Modern World*. Oxford University Press, Oxford.

Korten, D. C. and Alfonso, F. B. (eds) (1983). *Bureaucracy and the Poor. Closing the Gap*. Kumarian Press, Connecticut.

Morley, D. C. (1983). *Practising Health for All*. Oxford University Press, Oxford.

4 Patterns of Morbidity and Mortality

In 1982 an estimated 122 million children were born. Of these, 9 per cent (11 million infants) died before their first birthday, and an estimated further 4 per cent will die before their fifth birthday. It is well known that many of these deaths are caused by simple preventable illnesses not requiring expensive or complex interventions. Diarrhoeal disease is largely responsible for more than half the deaths, and most of the remainder are due to measles, whooping cough, tetanus, diphtheria, acute respiratory infections, malaria, tuberculosis and polio. Similarly, the estimated half million maternal deaths annually are also avoidable, such as post-partum haemorrhage and sepsis. These deaths are not chance occurrences in unfortunate individuals, but are due to a chain of causations in disadvantaged groups within communities who are on marginal existence and without any services. Two-thirds of the population in many developing countries do not enjoy regular access to a trained health worker. An estimated 1 billion people, largely in the Third World, are malnourished; of these, 400 million are on the brink of starvation. In tropical Africa where breakdown of services has been most marked in recent years, about a third of the children are underweight, with 4 per cent suffering from clinical malnutrition. Faecal pollution of the environment resulting in endemic transmission of diarrhoeal disease, dysentery, typhoid, cholera and helminthic infection is widespread all over the developing world. In countries like Sri Lanka, Bangladesh and Venezuela a number of studies have shown that up to 90 per cent of 6 year olds were infected with worms. These living conditions provide the background for the patterns of mortality and morbidity to be described.

Not surprisingly, children under the age of 5 and women take the main brunt of the environmental hazards. In many countries deaths in children under the age of 5 years constitute more than half the total deaths (see figure 4.1). The effects are more marked in rural areas. In India the sample registration system of the Registrar General estimated that 47 per cent of all deaths in the year 1977 occurred amongst children less than 5 years old. The proportion for rural areas was 48.6 per cent. Table 4.1 shows the leading nine causes of child deaths in that year. Similar findings were obtained in the Inter-

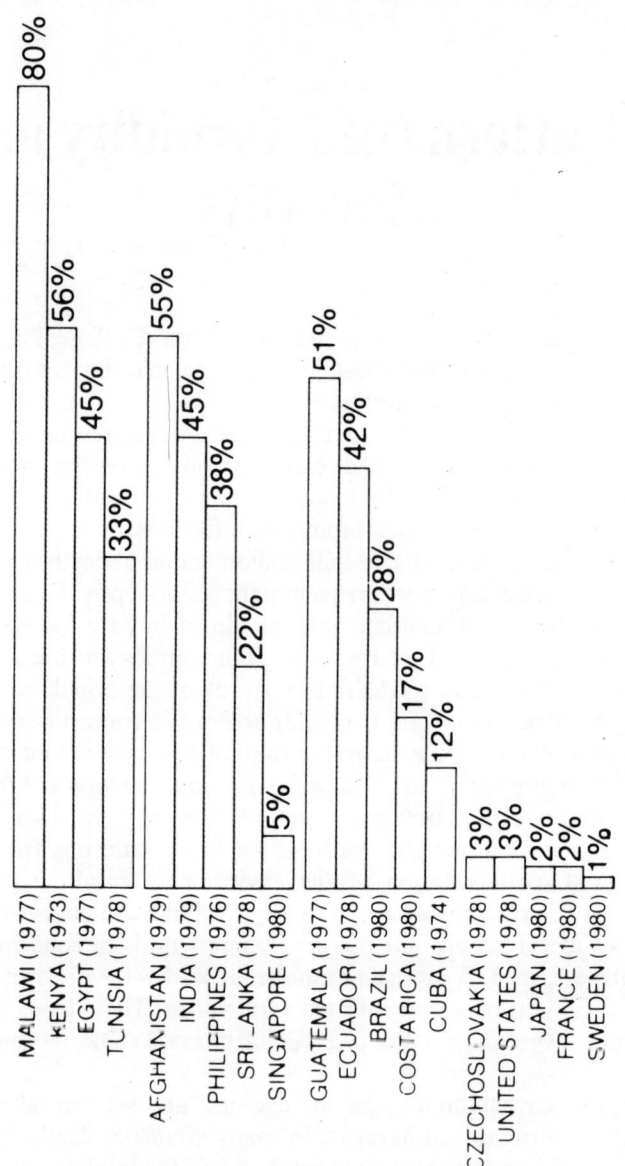

Figure 4.1   The child's share. Deaths under 5 years of age as a percentage of total number of deaths in selected countries. The figures reflect not only the differences in mortality but also the differences in age composition between the countries.

Source: United Nations Demographic Yearbook. 1981.

Table 4.1 Top nine causes of child mortality (per 100 000 population) in India, 1978

Cause	No.	(%) of deaths	Cause	No.	(%) of deaths
Rural			*Urban*		
Tetanus	2267	(17)	Prematurity	849	(12)
Prematurity	1179	(9)	Tetanus	501	(7)
Pneumonia	1015	(7)	Liver disorders	338	(5)
Influenza	729	(5)	Influenza	309	(4)
Malaria	704	(5)	Congenital malformation	281	(4)
Other respiratory system diseases	392	(3)	Malaria	180	(3)
Typhoid	573	(4)	Dysentery	408	(6)
Dysentery	906	(7)	Diarrhoea	546	(8)
Diarrhoea	437	(3)	Typhoid	250	(4)
Total	8202	(60)	Total	3662	(52)
Other causes	5398		Other causes	3338	
All causes	13600		All causes	7000	

American study of Child Mortality which analysed more than 35 000 deaths of children under the age of 5. Diarrhoeal diseases, measles and other infectious illnesses, nutritional deficiency and respiratory illness were together responsible for a large majority of deaths described in that study.

In areas with high mortality, infectious diseases were found to be responsible for more than half the deaths, and even up to two-thirds of deaths in some areas.

The social differentials in mortality rates

The rural mortality rates tend to be higher by about a third in most developing countries. Infant mortality in India is 120 per thousand live births in rural areas compared with the urban rate of 80. In a study of 12 countries in Latin America, the rural mortality rate was at least 30 per cent higher than the urban rate, indicating the better development of the health services in urban areas.

An interesting finding in the Latin American study was the important influence of maternal education on child survival. Among children born to mothers who had no education the mortality rate was 2–3 times higher compared with those born to mothers who had completed 7 years of schooling, and 3–5 times higher compared with mothers with 10 years or more of education. The rural and urban mortality rates were practically the same in children of mothers who had no education. Similar findings have been reported from Kenya, where a 36 per cent reduction in child mortality with primary education and 63 per cent decrease with secondary education compared with uneducated women was demonstrable for 1979. It may be argued that families with educated mothers are already better off since they could 'buy' education and hence enjoyed a better standard of living compared with those with uneducated mothers; or that health services will have very little impact on families with uneducated mothers since they may not be able to put the health message into practice. In Kenya, however, it has been shown that increasing poverty has a greater effect on mortality levels for women with the least education and that this effect declines with increasing education (see figure 4.2).

The lessons from the above and similar studies are obvious. Child survival is primarily determined by the social and economic resources in the child's family. There are two imporant indicators of such resources: maternal education and the economic circumstances of the household. An important function of the community health services will be to help develop the level of awareness and the information base within the household and in every neighbourhood. With greater awareness parents can look on disease and health with a rational approach instead of the current fatalistic one.

Secondly, several studies in child mortality have helped to stress the

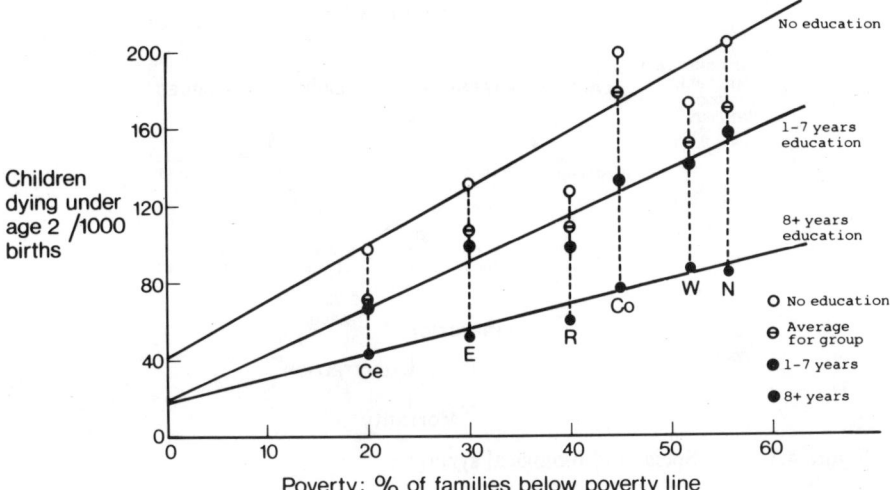

Figure 4.2   Correlation of child mortality by level of maternal education with
level of poverty in six rural provinces of Kenya. Ce = Central.
E = Eastern.   R = Rift   Valley.   Co = Coast.   W = Western.
N = Nyanza.
Source: UNICEF, *The State of the World's Children.* Oxford University
Press, Oxford, 1984.

interaction between malnutrition and infection. In the Inter-American Study
nutritional deficiency was an associated cause in 61 per cent of deaths from
infectious diseases which suggests that the deficient nutritional status of
populations is perhaps the most important cause of the high mortality in
developing countries. Such observations have helped to promote the concept
of social synergy. The same social determinant, poverty, can operate on more
than one intermediate variable to influence biological processes so that the
risk of mortality is far greater than would be expected by the simple sum of
intermediate variables (see figure 4.3). When the provision of care in a society
is also distributed in accordance with the existing social differentials the
overall effect of social synergy can be very strong. This explains why the
mortality in black infants in the United States is twice as high as the mortality
in white infants, and why in Britain perinatal mortality in social class V is twice
that in social class I and post-neonatal mortality is five times as much. Similar
data regarding inequalities in health from a number of countries show that the
majority of biological factors recognised as important determinants of child
mortality are in fact dependent variables influenced by socio-economic
factors. The most important biological determinant is food intake. In
Bangladesh a little over 10 per cent of the rural households can be considered
self-sufficient in food and more than half must make do with energy intakes

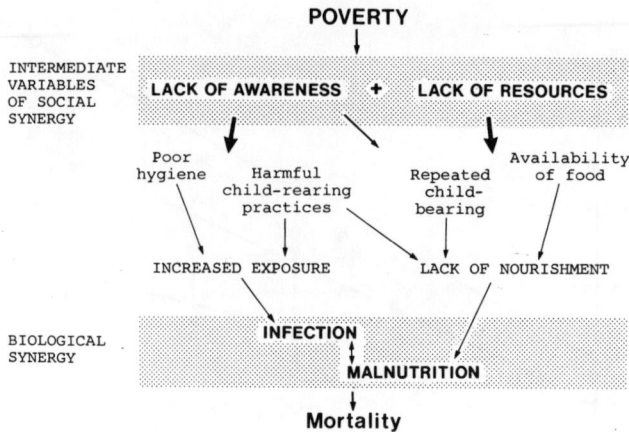

Figure 4.3   Social and biological synergy.

below acceptable levels. Many such communities experience infant mortality rates in excess of 120 per 1000 live births with two-thirds of all deaths occurring in children under the age of 4 years. Several studies in Bangladesh show that diarrhoea, gastro-intestinal diseases, helminthic and respiratory infections account for 60 per cent of the morbidity. Infections of the skin, eyes and upper respiratory tract, all indicating poor hygiene, account for another 15 per cent. Together with the common cold and general body aches and pains these illnesses make up 80 per cent of the conditions for which treatment is sought. Such observations are true for a number of communities amongst the rural and the urban poor. Community-based health programmes providing interventions within the home through awareness and using simple technologies would be more effective than expensive hospitals in the capital city in controlling these illnesses.

Low birth weight: a major contributory factor in infant and child mortality

Studies in Guatemala, India and elsewhere have helped to establish that low birth weight (<2500 g) is an important determinant of mortality not only in the newborn period but also throughout infancy. The data from a large Indian study are shown in figure 4.4. In the United States between 30 and 40 per cent of all infant deaths are associated with low birth weight. In the Inter-American Study 23% of the 35 095 deaths studied were associated with low birth weight.

Mothers who have failed to achieve the optimum in growth and physical development on account of undernutrition and recurrent illness in childhood are more likely to bear small babies. This is especially so if they also suffer nutritional inadequacies during pregnancy, are not protected against anaemia

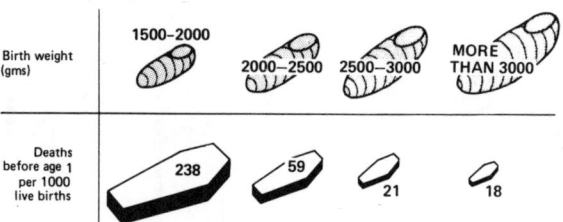

Birth weight (gms)	1500–2000	2000–2500	2500–3000	MORE THAN 3000

Figure 4.4 Birth weight and mortality risks.

and against placental infection by the malaria parasite in endemic areas, and have not had the benefit of regular prenatal care. As a consequence the growth of the fetus is affected so that between 20 and 40 per cent of the babies in many developing countries are born with a low birth weight (see figure 4.5) compared with 6 per cent or so in Western Europe.

Fetal growth is socially determined. In the United States the proportion of infants born with a low birth weight has been 6 per cent amongst the whites compared with 13 per cent in blacks for the past decade. In Britain there is an average difference of 100 g in birth weight between the upper and lower social classes. In Indonesia it is 200 g and in India 300 g. In Ludhiana, India, the neonatal death rate in scheduled castes which was three times that in the non-scheduled caste was largely related to the differences in birth weight.

Besides the broad social-class effects on fetal growth, the status of the woman in the society and within the family will influence her care, workload, food intake and freedom or otherwise from daily stresses during pregnancy. As mentioned before, in many rural and peasant communities marriages for women occur at an early age, usually around menarche. Many will have hardly completed their pubertal growth. Early and repeated pregnancy in such girls will lead to permanent stunting which explains the average short stature of the woman in developing countries. The woman also carries a heavy burden of physical work in many communities. The processing of food prior to cooking (like pounding, winnowing or grinding), the fetching of firewood, all the cooking, the fetching of water, washing clothes, tending household animals, and regular work on the farm (like sowing, weeding or harvesting), are all part of the woman's everyday chores. No special allowances are made for pregnancy or lactation. At meal times, the largest and choicest portions of food are offered to the male members of the household and the women must be content with what is left. Not surprisingly, there is a wide prevalence of underweight, anaemia and clinical signs of vitamin deficiencies amongst women which get accentuated during pregnancy. Once a woman commences child-bearing there is a continual cycle of pregnancy–lactation–pregnancy whilst subsisting on marginal nutrition, resulting in depletion of the nutrient reserves of the body. All these influences—cultural, social, nutritional and biological—work synergistically to affect fetal growth. The large incidence of low birth weight in the developing countries is a strong indication that the

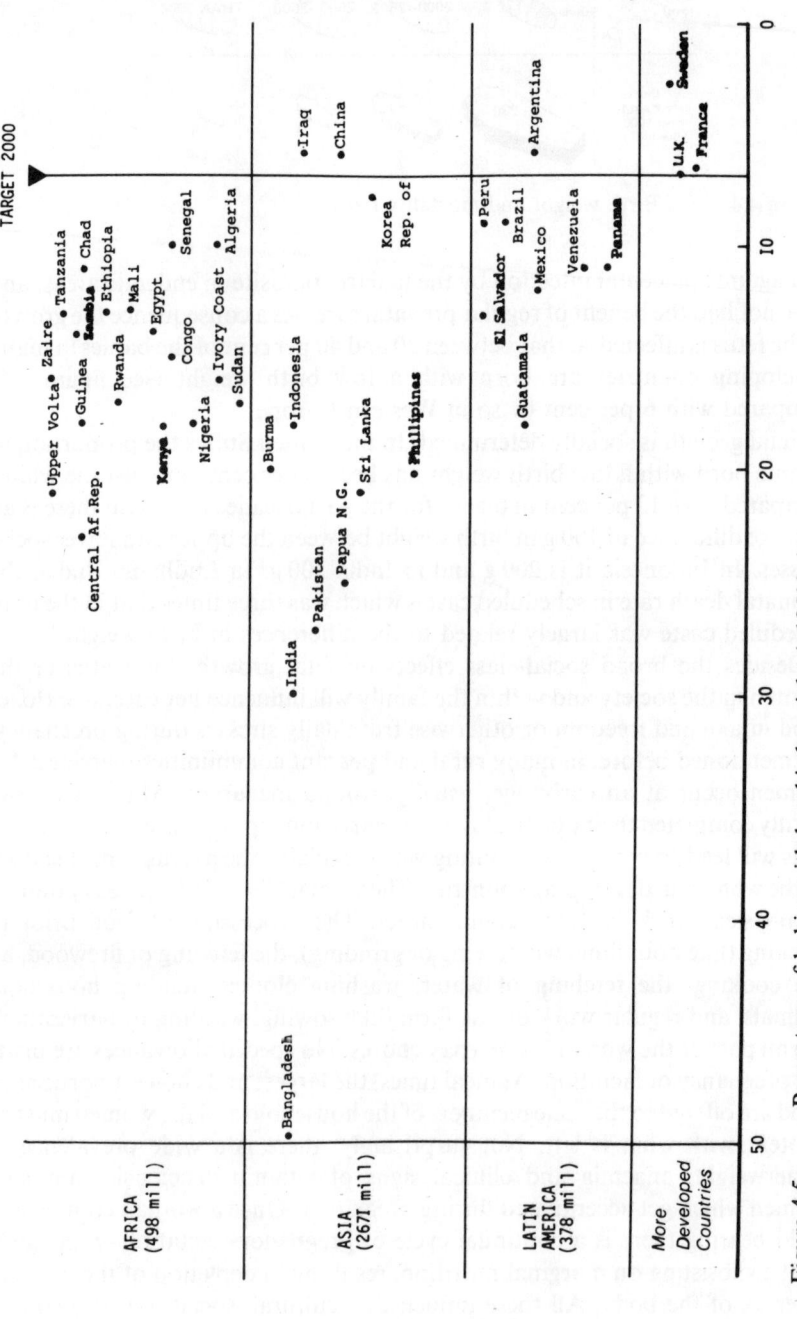

Figure 4.5   Percentage of babies with low birth weight (<2500 g).

aetiology is different from that commonly described in the more developed societies. In all likelihood fetal malnutrition plays a major role. The evidence in favour of such a hypothesis is that in those countries that have experienced recent improvements in general health and nutrition, the incidence of low birth weight has fallen. In China it has now fallen to 6 per cent and in Cuba to 10 per cent.

The 'hungry season'

In communities living on marginal nutrition, the nutritional status of the mother is the single most powerful influence on fetal nutrition and growth. During periods of food shortages or of excessive physical stress, fetal growth is likely to suffer especially if such a stress happens to occur during a period of rapid fetal growth—the latter half of pregnancy. In most peasant communities the wet season tends to be a stressful period. It is the 'hungry season' since food stores from the previous year's harvest are running low. Grain prices tend to be higher because of increased demand. In fact many peasant households tend to sell grain at a generally low price at the time of the harvest and buy back at higher rates when stocks run low. Indebtedness tends to increase and poverty is accentuated. The wet season is also characterised by long periods of physical effort on the land—clearing, ploughing or digging, and planting for the next year's crop. Illnesses like malaria, respiratory infections and diarrhoea become more prevalent, further affecting nutritional status. There is also increasing physical isolation of communities because roads become impassable or bridges are washed away and essential supplies cannot reach most of the rural areas. Studies in the Gambia, Tanzania and elsewhere have shown the seasonal effects on birth weights and breast milk outputs. In the Gambia, for example, birth weights fell by 400 g and breast milk output declined by about a third during the rainy season. Faltering in the weights of infants and older children is common and loss of weight amongst the adults, especially the women, is common. Hence provision of services for the prenatal care of pregnant women including food supplementation, and ensuring continuity of the general health services during the stressful wet season, are all important facets of a primary care programme.

Childhood malnutrition: a major determinant of mortality

The interaction between malnutrition and infection is well known. The biological synergy between the two has a devastating effect on the health and survival of children. Poor nutritional status reduces the individual's resistance to infection so that not only is infection more common but also minor illnesses progress rapidly to become life threatening. At the same time every illness brings about a further deterioration of the nutritional status because of the combined effects of the anorexia accompanying the illness, parental withholding of food because of cultural beliefs, and increased metabolic demands. It has been often said that the very high child mortality of the developing countries is not so much due to 'tropical' diseases as caused by ordinary illnesses. This observation is explained by the synergy between malnutrition and infection. It has been best demonstrated in the Inter-American study where of the 35 095 deaths recorded malnutrition was a causal or associated factor in more than half.

Recurrent infection and undernutrition are both indicators of an impoverished environment. Undernourishment amongst the poor can be extensive. Community surveys during the past 10 years in 17 different countries and including 173 000 children reveal an aggregate prevalence rate of 20 per cent. Since surveys normally take place during the dry season and usually amongst the more accessible communities, the true prevalence of malnutrition is likely to be higher, especially during the 'hungry' season. There are several anecdotal accounts of investigators coming across families during surveys who have not eaten for several days. Such accounts have come from Kenya, Upper Volta

Table 4.2   Degree of hunger in rural India (19 villages. Population 38 931). Results are expressed as percentages

Social category (%) of total population	Fully satisfied (%)	% Hungry for (months)				
		<1	1–3	3–6	+6	Irregular
Landless labourer (18)	10	2	15	59	10	6
Low caste (Harijan) (20)	18	2	15	49	8	8
Other backward castes (22)	55	1	9	28	4	4
Service & trade (10)	70	1	8	18	—	2
>3 acres wet land (13)	97	—	1	2	—	—
1–3 acres wet land (11)	90	—	1	8	1	1
>5 acres dry land (6)	69	—	6	15	4	6

Source: Banerji, D. *Poverty, Class and Health Culture in India.* Prachi Prakashan, New Delhi. 1982.

and Bangladesh. However, nationwide studies of poverty are few. In India, a recent study spread out over 19 villages and covering eight major states has shown that undernourishment largely stems from poverty and low living standards (see table 4.2). These are the social determinants of the biological processes, so carefully described in medical texts, which lead to high morbidity and mortality. Unfortunately the myopic preoccupation of the health profession with the biological processes has proven to be an obstacle leading to a neglect of the study of underlying social causes and delaying the development of effective national strategies for dealing with malnutrition. The data from India in table 4.2 indicate that a substantial proportion of the population do not get two square meals a day throughout the year. Not surprisingly many of the poor households reported a high incidence of child deaths. In this study a close correlation was found between ownership of productive assets, the satisfaction of hunger and the number of child deaths.

Diarrhoeal disease: a common indicator of poor standard of living

Diarrhoea is a leading cause of death in infants and children below the age of 5 years and one of the leading causes of mortality. In some countries up to 30 per cent of all admissions of children to hospitals are for diarrhoea. The peak incidence is during the weaning period and is obviously related to the introduction of weaning foods which are contaminated on account of the generally high level of contamination in the child's environment. The individual child in a rural or urban slum community experiences an average of four episodes of diarrhoea per year with a range of 2–12 episodes. About 10 per cent of diarrhoeal episodes tend to progress to severe dehydration with a 1 in 10 risk of mortality. It is estimated that globally there are about 4.6–5 million deaths of children under the age of 5 each year because of diarrhoea. The decline in breast feeding, especially amongst the urban poor, is a major threat to infant survival and health in many developing countries, especially in Latin America. Diarrhoea is now increasingly found in young bottle-fed infants in whom dehydration is usually accompanied by complications like shock and hypernatraemia. Moreover, many such infants are undernourished on account of over-dilution of feeds for reasons of economy. These two sequelae of bottle feeding—diarrhoea and undernutrition—are responsible for the estimated 1 million deaths annually associated with the decline in breast feeding.

In many parts of the world, diarrhoea is more often found in the undernourished child, in whom it also tends to be more protracted or life threatening (see table 4.3). Besides, each episode of diarrhoea brings about a deterioration in the nutritional status. This is largely because of the traditional practice of withholding food during diarrhoea in order to 'rest the gut', the

Table 4.3 **Incidence and severe cases of diarrhoea in children by nutritional state (Guatemala)**

Nutritional state	No. of cases	Cases/100 person-years	No. of severe cases	Severe cases/ 100 person-years
Normal (N = 25)	35	98.8	8	22.2
1° Malnutrition (N = 74)	172	164.1	65	61.9
2° Malnutrition (N = 71)	254	252.2	74	73.3
3° Malnutrition (N = 9)	35	274.5	14	107.7

Source: Scrimshaw, N. S., Taylor, C. E. and Gordon, J. E. *Interaction of Nutrition and Infection*. WHO, Geneva. 1968. p. 251.

anorexia and vomiting accompanying diarrhoea, and the metabolic losses as well as malabsorption. It has been estimated that in children an attack of diarrhoea leads to an average reduction in food intake by 20 per cent because of such causes and a negative nitrogen balance is established of the order of 0.9 g/kg daily. Tissue regeneration is a slow process because of the requirements for energy. On the traditional diets of low-energy density the recovery phase is 2–4 times longer than the duration of illness. In general, breast-fed infants are protected against nutritional deterioration during diarrhoea. In the acute phase the child with diarrhoea can still absorb up to 70 per cent of the nutrients in his diet, and so the practice of 'resting the gut' has no scientific foundation. Early institution of oral rehydration helps to cut short the length of illness so that the return of appetite is rapid. Several studies have shown that with continuation of feeding during diarrhoea, especially of breast milk, and with early treatment by oral rehydration, deterioration in nutritional status is avoidable. These observations are important since they help to overcome the present deficiencies in the medical management of diarrhoea. A great deal of clinical research in the past has over-emphasised signs of dehydration and failed to stress the nutritional consequences of diarrhoea. By promoting oral rehydration in the home at the inception of diarrhoea and by endeavouring to maintain food intake during the acute phase the nutritional consequences of diarrhoeal disease can be largely avoided.

Other communicable diseases

Amongst the poor communities in rural and peri-urban areas, infective illnesses are highly prevalent. This is especially so in children. The foremost amongst these infections is diarrhoea as described above, followed by acute respiratory infections, common infectious diseases of childhood which are preventable by immunisation, followed by malaria and parasitic diseases.

Table 4.4 **Percentage mortality from communicable diseases**

Country	Mortality
Colombia	15
Dominican Republic	15
Egypt	23
India	20
Indonesia	33
Yemen	28
Philippines	45

Together they form a web of misery from which the individual is rarely free. Studies in Guatemala, Uganda, India and Bangladesh have shown that in such communities on an average day 1 child in 5 can be ill. In Guatemala, young children were found suffering from one illness or another 15 per cent of the time, and in the Gambia 20 per cent of the time during certain seasons. Often the episodes of illness are so frequent that they overlap with hardly any period of recovery in between. In such a situation curative services by themselves can achieve nothing better than a 'recycling' effect—the *same* patients returning again and again with infective episodes, sent away with some antibiotic to the *same* environment to be predisposed to infection again. Fully 30–40 per cent of the average children's outpatient load is of this nature. Hospital mortality statistics from many countries show that between 15 and 50 per cent of all deaths are related to communicable diseases (see table 4.4). It is estimated by the United Nations Children's Fund that upwards of 2 million deaths in children occur from acute respiratory infections annually. In any given year there are 2–3 million deaths from tuberculosis amongst all age groups, and about twice that number of smear-positive cases develop. This does not include smear negative, primary and extrapulmonary forms of the disease. The need is thus not for expensive new hospitals but for the health workers to become catalysts of change—the 'enablers' who will help communities to study their problems, create awareness of the importance of hygiene and immunisation and mobilise people to participate in preventive programmes and in the improvement of their environment. In other words, such catalysts should aim to help disadvantaged communities to gain control of the forces that shape their lives.

High maternal mortality

Childbirth remains the main cause of death in females between the ages of 14 and 45 and considerably affects female life expectancy. In Bangladesh, maternal mortality accounts for more than half the deaths of women aged

15–19 and 43 per cent of deaths in women aged 20–29. Exact statistics are difficult to obtain in many countries but data gathered by the World Health Organization in 21 developing countries show that haemorrhage (50%), toxaemia (23%), abortion (16%) and sepsis (12%) are the most common causes of maternal deaths. A survey of studies reported from Nigeria revealed that severe anaemia, haemorrhage, septicaemia and haemoglobinopathy were the most common causes of maternal deaths. Eighty-nine per cent of maternal mortality in these studies occurred in 'unbooked cases' i.e. mothers who did not receive antenatal care. In Indonesia maternal mortality in such women was of the order of 78 per 1000 births.

Much of the high mortality risk associated with childbirth is an extension of the process of general neglect and discrimination against women on account of their low social status as discussed on page 83. The result is that in many countries women reach childbirth in a state of poor nutrition and vitality without the benefits of good prenatal care. Collaborative studies in several countries sponsored by the World Health Organization indicate that nutritional anaemia affects between 10 and 35 per cent of adult females and is made worse during pregnancy. Signs of vitamin deficiencies, nutritional oedema and poor weight gain are common features. In addition, food taboos are widespread, and the pregnant woman will be advised by the family elders to eat less so that with a small baby she may escape difficult labour. Items of food like eggs, meat or fried and fatty foods may be prohibited. Cultural beliefs and practices exist in many societies and extend from the practice of female circumcision to the use of herbal potions and medicaments during pregnancy, at the onset of labour or during the puerperal period. Some of the potions have a sedative effect and may cause delayed onset of respiration in the newborn; some are oxytocics and largely responsible for the high incidence of ruptured uterus, and some, like '*kanywa*' in northern Nigeria, cause excessive loading with electrolytes and precipitate post-partum cardiac failure. Such factors together with inadequate maternity services are responsible for the high maternal and perinatal mortalities in developing countries.

It is important to stress that these high risks of mortality for the mother and her infant are as much due to the socio-cultural and biological determinants-like age, parity, short birth intervals and so on—as due to obstetrical and medical complications. No one determinant can be taken in isolation. In such a situation sophisticated methods of obstetric monitoring and neonatal intensive care cannot be expected to produce lasting benefits compared with improvement of nutrition and the general health of the community, better hygiene, and prenatal care to supervise adequate fetal growth as well as for the selection of the 'at-risk' mothers.

Traditional birth attendants (TBAs) deliver between 60 and 80 per cent of babies in the developing world, and the proportion of women delivered by them amongst the poorer sections of the community is even higher. Hence one way of extending health services including prenatal care to the rural and urban poor will be through integrating the TBAs into the formal health system through improving their knowledge and skills by regular training, stressing the importance of prenatal care in their training, supplying them with the necessary kits and medicaments, and by raising their social prestige in general. In communities where women cannot freely consult a male health worker because of economic costs or religious and cultural reasons, they are left with little else than such traditional means of obtaining health care for themselves and their children. In such a situation upgrading the knowledge and skills of the traditional provider of health care is one way of improving the health status of the disadvantaged. This is especially so for countries where child mortality is significantly higher in girls than in boys, signifying lack of social investment in females from an early age in a range of activities like nutrition, health care and education.

These arguments provide a sound rationale for making primary care services cater specially for women. Their role in health is crucial, particularly amongst the poorer households. They are usually the first providers of care within the home and the family. They are also largely responsible for the family's attitude towards health, food, life style and environment. Moreover, it has been the general experience that whenever rapid improvements in health and mortality are achieved in ways that actively involve women, there is usually an accompanying reduction in birth rates. Thus they can be important allies for achieving many of the objectives of primary care.

Health trends in the industrial West

Until not very long ago the same diseases as described above were responsible for illness and death in the now industrialised societies of Western Europe and North America. The current difference in the health situation between these societies and the developing countries is due not to geographical factors or the presence of incurable tropical diseases, but is mainly ascribable to socio-economic factors and the state of development of health services. Table 4.5 shows the mortality rate in the first two years of life from 1730 to 1829 as obtained from the London Bills of Mortality and table 4.6 outlines the survival rates of children up to the age of 5 years in England and Wales.

Table 4.5 **London Bills of Mortality**

	1730–49	*1750–69*	*1770–89*	*1790–1809*	*1810–29*
Approximate mortality per 1000 births	600	500	400	300	200

Table 4.6   **England and Wales: number alive at age 5 years out of 1000 live-born males**

Years	No. surviving
1693	582
1838–1854	724
1891–1900	750
1920–1922	870
1963	972

Similar high rates of mortality and morbidity were seen in the older age groups so that the overall health picture in Western Europe and North America a century or so ago was no different from what is obtained currently in many developing countries. During the decade 1851–60 slightly over one-fifth of all deaths occurring in England and Wales were due to infectious diseases. In 1849 cholera accounted for 38 per cent of all deaths from infectious diseases and 12 per cent of total deaths. The annual number of deaths from smallpox fluctuated between 1500 and 7500 for 30 years after the outbreak of 1840 when a record 10 434 deaths were reported. Diarrhoea, respiratory infections, tuberculosis and the common infectious diseases of childhood like measles and whooping cough were recognised as major killers (see table 4.7).

As in nineteenth-century Europe, many of the major illnesses of children in the developing world are preventable. Adequate knowledge exists regarding their natural history and enough experience has been gained concerning the most appropriate means of intervention. Moreover, a number of developing countries (like Sri Lanka, Costa Rica, South Korea, Taiwan, Tanzania, Cuba and China) have succeeded in developing national strategies to deal with these diseases. The common threads running through the different national

Table 4.7   **Number of deaths from infectious disease, England and Wales, 1876**

Population	24 244 010
Infective diseases*	159 293
Smallpox	2 408
Diphtheria	3 000
Whooping cough	10 556
Tuberculosis	62 633
Influenza	203
Measles	9 971
Scarlet fever	16 893
Chickenpox	109

* Includes tuberculosis and influenza, excludes venereal and parasitic diseases.

strategies are provision of basic needs like food, water, housing and sanitation on the one hand and easy access to social services like education and health on the other. These are the very factors that have contributed to general raising of health standards in the West (see figures 4.6 and 4.7). All through the twentieth century a view has grown up that health was primarily the outcome of specific technologies made available to the population at a price through organised health services. This concept is being challenged as having failed to take account of historical realities. As figures 4.6 and 4.7 illustrate, health improvements in Britain and Sweden were not related to specific medical technologies but to improvements in living standards.

The new outlook in health

In planning strategies of health as an essential part of development it is important to step back from the profession's preoccupation with disease and think in terms of nutrition, water supply, sanitation, immunisation, child spacing and personal health behaviour. These factors determine the incidence of disease and are amenable to simple measures at the community level. The

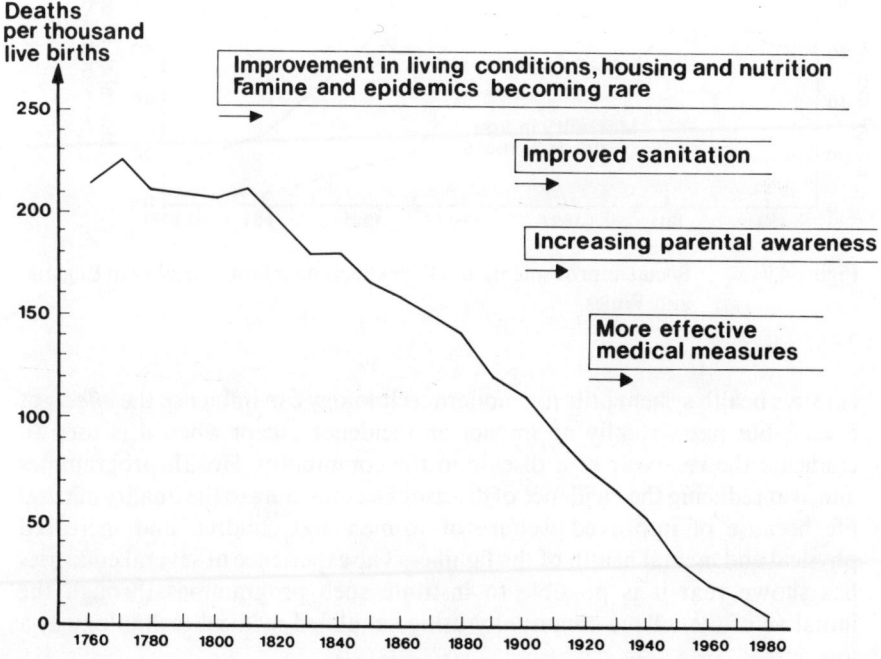

Figure 4.6   Social development and infant mortality in Sweden.

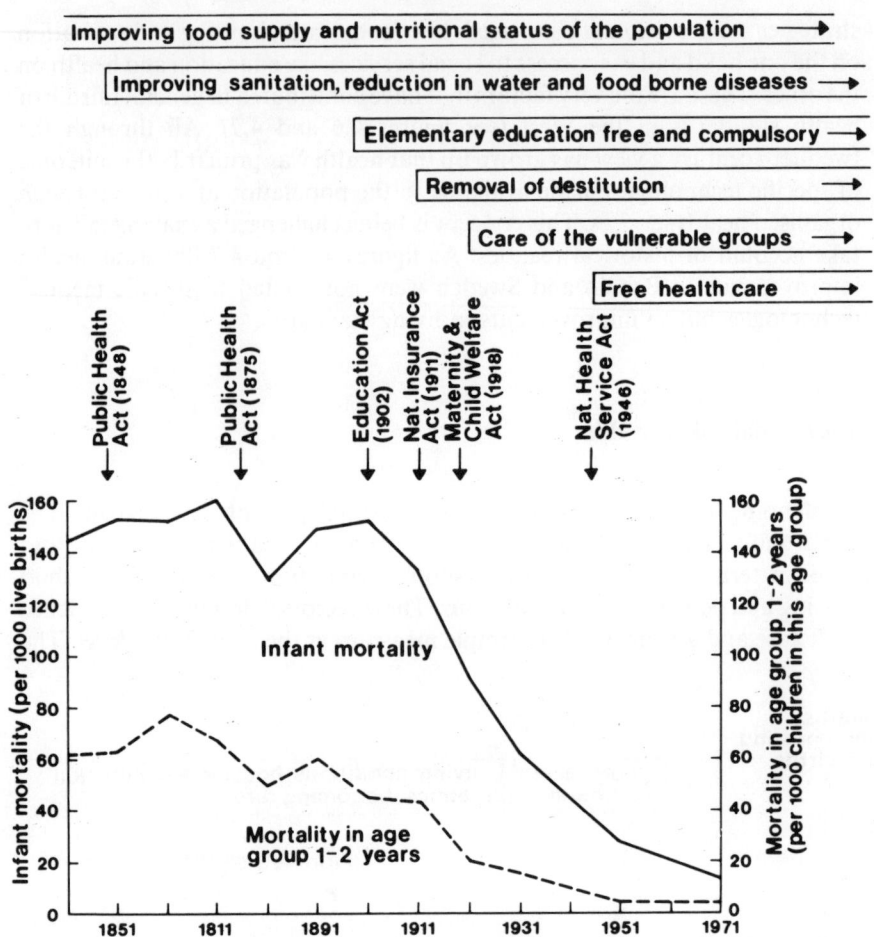

Figure 4.7   Social improvements and their effects on infant mortality in England and Wales.

curative health system utilising modern technology can influence the *effects* of disease but has virtually no impact on incidence except when it is used to eradicate the reservoir of a disease in the community. Health programmes aimed at reducing the incidence of disease can contribute to the quality of rural life because of improved welfare of women and children and increased physical and mental health of the families. The experience of several countries has shown that it is possible to institute such programmes through the initiative of the village community using simplified medical technology at a low cost.

There are also pitfalls to be avoided. In countries where the true significance of primary health care (PHC) as part of the development process has not been realised, the tendency has been to graft PHC on to an existing hospital-based health service. In such a situation the capital-intensive curative character of the established health services does not change. PHC then tends to be treated as second-class health care which must make do with what is left after the expensive running costs of the hospitals have been paid. PHC is not the question of self-care and village health worker for the poor, and hospitals staffed with specialists for the urban rich. All the eight elements of primary health care have to be established for PHC to succeed.

The lessons of the past decade show that PHC can be developed in all political systems, with a variety of social structures, traditions and existing health conditions. Its real test is the level of awareness and participation by the community. It is at its most effective when it addresses the problems of those at highest risk, and the priority health problems.

In the chapters that follow, a strategy for developing primary health care to include the rural and the urban poor is described. Some of the concepts discussed above and in the preceding chapters are further elaborated and ways in which existing knowledge can be put to work by individuals in poor households are described. A conceptual model for developing comprehensive health services is presented in which resources can be channelled preferentially to those in greatest need, bearing in mind that there is no one set model. In every situation there will exist conditions requiring adaptation and modification though the overall objectives of reaching the poor remain the same.

Further reading

Ebrahim, G. J. (1981). *Pediatric Practice in Developing Countries*. Macmillan Press, Basingstoke and London.
Grant, J. P. (1983). *The State of the World's Children 1984*. Oxford University Press, Oxford.
Morley, D. C. (1973). *Pediatric Priorities in the Developing World*. Butterworths, London.
Puffer, R. R. and Serrano, C. V. (1973). *Patterns of Mortality in Childhood*. Pan American Health Organisation, Washington.

5 Health Care for the Masses: A Model of Integrated Community Health Care

A model for health services in a given geographical area is illustrated in figure 5.1. At any point in time a community will have a certain number of ill people, a larger number of ambulatory sick and many more healthy persons. Services are needed for each of these three groups. Thus hospital beds are necessary for the ill, and out-patient services for the ambulatory sick. An assumption is usually made that those who are ill will seek out the available services and make use of them. The discussion in the preceding chapters provides evidence that such an assumption is not always true. Unless the services are easily available and accessible, both socially and geographically, their effective use is limited to the privileged few. Hence the need for creating a large number of health posts and neighbourhood health facilities. The middle diagram in figure 5.1 makes the important point that services are also needed for the healthy in order to maintain them in good health. Here two key factors determine the effectiveness of the preventive/promotive services. First, a minimum of 80 per cent of the community should receive such services on a regular basis for any noticeable impact to occur. Whether it is immunisation, antenatal care or growth surveillance of children, unless a minimum of 80 per cent of those affected receive the service, a measurable improvement is difficult to demonstrate. Secondly, in all preventive/promotive work, services need to be delivered to the people—in or near to their homes, at the place of work, in schools, in their fields and factories and other community institutions. But preventive/promotive work is usually not attractive to doctors whose training has conditioned them to dealing with the complexities of the diagnosis and management of disease problems. Experience in many countries has shown that medical and nursing auxiliaries are more suitable for the job. A recent study analysing health service 'inputs' and 'outputs' in terms of mortality in 18 industrial countries showed a positive correlation between the number of doctors and paediatricians and mortality in the younger age groups. On the other hand, a negative association was found between the prevalence of nurses and maternal, perinatal, infant and early childhood

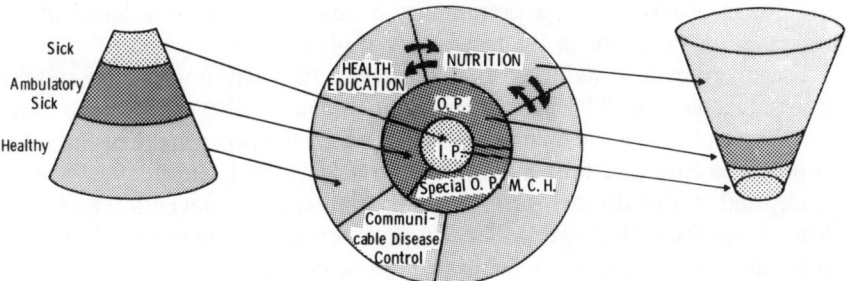

Figure 5.1   Conceptual model of a health care programme for a defined community. IP = In-patients. MCH = Maternal and child health. OP = Out-patients.

mortality. Similar correlations were demonstrable in respect of data for 1960 from the same countries, indicating that these are not chance observations. The profession's preoccupation with intensive care for acute disease has distracted its own as well as the public's attention from the inability and reluctance to prevent.

Opportunities for prevention arise at every point of contact between the health service and the community. The maternal and child health (MCH) services are particularly suitable for the purpose. They are largely concerned with important life events like pregnancy, birth, development and growth, spacing of children and so on, all of which create ample opportunities for screening, prophylactic interventions and counselling. Preventive services designed to reduce mortality nearly always reduce the corresponding morbidity as well. The MCH services are largely run by nurses and health auxiliaries and the various tasks are sufficiently simple to be performed by community health workers. Besides, these services cater for almost two-thirds of the population in the average developing country. Thus in the case of the healthy community, the MCH services provide a useful springboard for mounting preventive programmes. Because of their easy adaptability and mobility, the MCH services are also suitable for preferentially caring for the disadvantaged.

Health services as a safety net for the disadvantaged

When the three aspects of health care illustrated in the middle diagram of figure 5.1 exist, and are providing adequate and regular coverage, then and then only the diagram on the right-hand side of the figure can come true. This diagram compares the health services to a filter in which preventive and promotive care provide regular health surveillance of the population, so that any illness occurring in the community is considered to be a defect in the process of coverage or in the techniques applied.

The diagram also indicates that there is a two-way flow in the system: individuals become ill because of environmental and other reasons and move into the sick layer of the filter, with the health services exerting their influence to promote cure and thus moving them back to the healthy layer. Such a conceptual model also helps to bridge the gap between prevention and cure. When coverage with the surveillance type of services is adequate, selection of those at risk of disease is facilitated on a community-wide basis. With adequate coverage early diagnosis and treatment turns out to be an effective form of prevention. Then malaria has no chance to progress to cerebral malaria and diarrhoea does not progress to life-threatening dehydration. With adequate coverage, early identification of those at high risk makes treatment more cost-effective. Thus with such a model of health services providing comprehensive care and good coverage, the division between preventive and curative care is greatly narrowed.

The present organisation of health care in many developing countries is by a system of health centres serving sub-centres and dispensaries, and in their turn served by a district hospital. In practice the district hospital provides in-patient care for the community in its immediate neighbourhood and a limited referral service to the health centre and the dispensaries in the district. The model in figure 5.1 assumes that the in-patient beds exist to serve the whole chain of institutions and should not be considered in isolation from the rest of the system. The district hospital, in fact, should help in providing preventive and promotive services in the surrounding community on the same pattern as the other institutions in the model. Furthermore, the model applies as much to an entire district as to an isolated pocket of the community. Thus, a dispensary or health post is involved in preventive services and ambulatory care of the sick, but falls back on the health centre or the district hospital for in-patient care.

For the efficient operation of the system, co-ordination and leadership need to be provided by the senior health personnel in the administrative headquarters of the district and presumably stationed at the district hospital. Good communications and mobility in the administration of the system are provided by regular visits and interchange of personnel. Ideally, the health centre should receive a weekly visit from various staff members of the district hospital, a sub-centre (dispensary) should be visited by the officer in charge of the health centre once a week and by a staff member of the district hospital once a month. The purpose of these visits should be (1) discussions on administrative matters and problems; (2) staff meeting to discuss management of those in the 'at risk' group as identified in the MCH clinics; (3) teaching and technical discussions; and (4) consultations, in that order of priority. In addition to these visits, there should also be a staff rotation so that the auxiliary in charge of the sub-centre (dispensary) would spend 1 week at the health centre and 2 weeks at the district hospital each year, his place being taken by his counterpart at the district hospital.

Table 5.1 **The skill pyramid in the model**

		Number
District Hospital (1 or 2 in the district, each looking after 100 000–200 000 population)	Manager/Co-ordinator	1
	District Medical Officers (Medical, Surgical, Obstetrics and Gynaecology, Child Health)	4
	Medical Assistants (or equivalent auxiliaries)	4
	Ward Sisters	4
	Public Health Sister	1
	Staff Nurses	8
	Nurse Aides or equivalent auxiliaries	15
	Health Inspector	1
	Health Educator	1
	Laboratory and radiology technicians	
Rural Health Centre (1 for 50 000 population)	Medical Assistants (or equivalent auxiliaries)	2
	Rural Medical Aides (or equivalent auxiliaries)	3
	Assistant Health Inspector	1
	Nurse/midwife	1
	Community Nurse	1
	Nurse Aides	4
	Laboratory technicians	
	Other ancillary staff	
Dispensary (sub-centre) (1 for 5000 population)	Rural Medical Aide (or equivalent auxiliary)	1
	Nurse Aides	3
	MCH Aides	3
	Laboratory technician	1
Village Health Post (1 for each village, 1500–2000 population)	Village Health Worker (VHW)	1 or 2
	Trained birth attendant (TBA)	1 or more

Essential services

A number of service programmes can be generated using the skill pyramid in table 5.1 and health institutions, as follows.

Mother and child health, including family planning—These services would include:

(1) Care during pregnancy, childbirth and the postnatal period for mothers and their newborns. The main concern of such a service is the promotion of adequate nutrition in the mother, prevention and early identification of complications of pregnancy, screening for high-risk pregnancies in order to refer them for delivery where higher levels of skill and better equipment are available.

(2) Counselling for improved child-bearing and child-rearing, including the spacing of pregnancies.

(3) Studying the local patterns of child-bearing with regard to age, nutrition (including the prevalence of anaemia), and customs related to pregnancy and delivery with a view to developing local norms of prenatal care.

(4) Care and growth surveillance of infants, particularly the promotion of nutrition, immunisation, early treatment of illnesses and education of parents. Amongst the disadvantaged the mothers are often working outside the home and there is a need for organising day-care centres for their children, providing not merely custodial care but with a focus on healthy child development.

Promotion of adequate nutrition amongst the vulnerable groups and the disadvantaged—A great deal of undernutrition begins in fetal life and presents as low birth-weight. Adequate nutrition of the pregnant woman, promotion of breast feeding and of appropriate weaning through greater awareness are some of the main objectives of the MCH services. Increasing productivity through improved agricultural techniques, better methods of storage or processing of foods, and the use of backyard gardens for improving the nutrient intake of the family are examples of parallel activities which can be generated through the department of agriculture. A great deal of malnutrition arises out of infective illnesses like measles, whooping cough and diarrhoea. Their prevention and dietetic care during illness forms an important component of the drive for promoting good nutrition.

Communicable disease control—Parasitic diseases, tuberculosis, leprosy and diseases caused by contaminated food and water are responsible for a greater part of the morbidity amongst the adults. For the poor who subsist by selling the labour of the able-bodied individuals, any illness in the breadwinner can spell disaster for the entire family. Control of the prevalent communicable diseases is as much an anti-poverty programme as a health-related activity, since preservation of health means availability for gainful employment.

Environmental sanitation, including development and conservation of water resources—For the majority of the world's poor this important nutrient is in short supply. When available it is in a highly polluted form and has to be transported laboriously, usually by the women and children in the family. Its easy availability in plentiful supply will not only raise the general standard of hygiene but also reduce the incidence of many water-related illnesses. More importantly, water is recognised as an important resource and like all resources it is often jealously controlled by the dominant groups to increase their own status, which leads to a worsening of the relative position of the poor. Its easy accessibility in plentiful supplies and without undue expenditure of labour is yet another facet of an anti-poverty programme based on health development. The health services act as a catalyst by encouraging an intersectoral collaboration with the local sanitary and water engineers, in the same way as they do with agriculture and veterinary officers.

Health education—Another important area of intersectoral collaboration is education in schools to create awareness of local health problems. In traditional family life an older sibling usually has the responsibility of looking after a younger brother and sister. Improving the child-minding skills of the school-age child has an immediate effect in raising the standards of care of young children in the community. Such an approach to health education builds upon existing community structures like schools and teachers. In the same way, community resources like agricultural extension officers, women's groups and other local organisations can be encouraged and revitalised for generating health-related discussions. The mother is the family's first health care worker, and yet she often lacks access to information and simple health technology to apply within the home when the need arises.

Health supervision of vulnerable groups—The nearer the services are to the poor, both geographically and socially, and become part of their everyday life, the more relevant and responsive they will be to their needs. The major drawback of services offered through static facilities like hospitals and health centres is their tenuous connections with the daily life patterns of the populations they serve.

Gathering of health information and its wider dissemination to create awareness of health problems and of activities (see figure 5.2). For all community health activities there are three possible targets—reduction of overall ill health, sickness or disability; equitable distribution of health resources and services; achieving defined targets of coverage with services like immunisation, antenatal care, water, sanitation and so on. Of these, an equitable distribution of health resources and services is the most crucial in order to bring about a shift from the present monopolisation of services by the dominant groups. In most countries at present the national health services are neither physically accessible on a fair basis nor attuned to the most pressing needs of the poor, especially with regard to the training of the health workers. Only with a just distribution of resources can the target of achieving full coverage for the disadvantaged with acceptable standards of care be attained. Part of the process of achieving coverage is the enlightenment of the people. Their involvement in gathering information about health events occurring amongst them often paves the way for their participation in health activities.

Community organisation—Most communities are faction prone. They are organised along familial, tribal, religious, group or occupational loyalties, and live together in a fragile state of mutual dependency. In particular, the poor

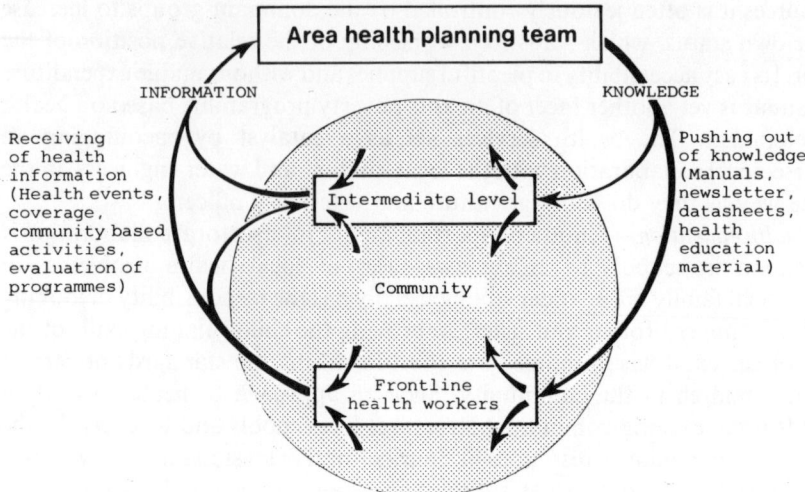

Figure 5.2   Gathering of information and dissemination of knowledge.

are less organised than the dominant groups and thereby lack the strength for demanding their basic rights. Group activities like literacy classes, income-generating activities, parents' clubs, youth groups and so on help to generate the community cohesion which is essential for informed participation in health activities.

Early diagnosis, management and prevention of the prevalent diseases in the area—For example, nutritional disorders, respiratory illnesses, diarrhoeal disease, common infectious illnesses of childhood, malaria and other parasitic illnesses, tuberculosis, minor injuries, conjunctivitis and skin sepsis.

Personal preventive services including those for promotion of mental health.

All the programmes listed above can be described as the ones required for maintaining the healthy in the community in good health. In practice, the present organisation of services and deployment of resources in most countries is such that an inordinate amount of time and resources is spent on curative work, and the preventive and promotive work is left to the individual enterprise of the auxiliaries in charge of the dispensaries or health posts. The auxiliary has no training for such work nor is he supervised adequately, and thus the full potential of the system is not realised. In the organisational model presented in figure 5.1 the emphasis is on the healthy community, and curative services are to be considered as a supportive framework of such services and not the core of the health programme.

Health is a product of simple things—adequate nourishment, safe water, hygiene and protection from infection. But these should happen to the maximum of people and not to a privileged few. Economic and social investment in many developing countries has hitherto followed the historical trend of producing goods and services best suited to the needs of a limited proportion of people. By its very definition, absolute poverty means no access to productive assets nor to food, water, health and education. It is these nutritional and environmental deficiencies, and the formidable clustering of disadvantage that accompanies them, against which health programmes have to provide a shield, and not merely give out pills against poverty.

What the above proposals envisage is not the setting up of an alternative system of care for the poor, but a restructuring of community health services and ensuring adequate coverage to the rural and the urban poor with such restructured services. The existing hospitals will need to strengthen their supportive and training roles for primary health care in order to become true staging posts for the above programmes.

The several programmes listed above are further discussed below in the context of the model presented in figure 5.1.

Regular health supervision of vulnerable groups

The impact of preventive and promotive services is best seen when they are at the level of the individual or the family group. Thus, in England and Wales infant and child mortality rates remained high until the beginning of this century when child welfare services were established, and within a short time there was a dramatic improvement (see figure 5.3). The discovery of antibiotics and other pharmacologic agents, improvements in living stan-

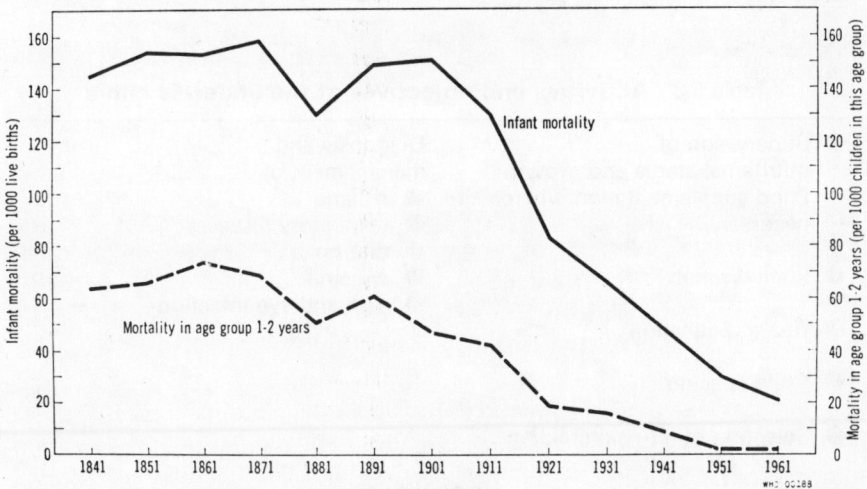

Figure 5.3   Mortality rates and mortality ratios in age group 1–2 years in England and Wales.

dards, the establishment of a National Health Service, etc. have all made a welcome contribution to improvement in health and yet their impact has never been as strong as that of the maternal and child welfare services. Such a programme brings to bear on the individual child all the available health and social resources in the community and contributes to the maintenance of health.

The principles of child welfare work combined with a simple out-patient curative service were applied in the *under-5s clinic* in West Africa and within a year the impact on mortality and moridity was noticed (see table 5.2).

Table 5.2 **Effect of child welfare work and simple out-patient curative service, Imesi, West Africa**

	Stillbirth	Neonatal deaths	Infant Mortality	Deaths 1–4 years
Before 1957	41	78	295	69
1962–65	36.4	21.9	72	28.1

Inherent in the concept of the under-5s clinic is the principle of comprehensive care and the application of both curative and preventive care in the individual child. As it evolved, the under-5s clinic is a daily-run out-patient clinic for children with the added functions of the traditional child welfare clinic. Thus the activities and objectives of the under-5s clinic can be summarised in table 5.3

Table 5.3 **Activities and objectives of the under-5s clinic**

● Supervision of nutritional status and growth. Food supplementation where necessary.

● Immunisation

● Health Education

● Child spacing

● Selection of 'at-risk' children

Diagnosis and management of
  ● malaria
  ● respiratory diseases
  ● diarrhoea
  ● anaemia
  ● skin and eye infection

Home Visiting
of problem cases and defaulters

The under-5s clinic is a basic service for children and not a 'speciality' clinic. It has the advantage of flexibility so that, depending upon the personnel available, it can vary from being a very basic service utilising minimally-trained auxiliaries and community health volunteers to a complex and well-coordinated activity. In general, the under-5s clinic does not require highly trained personnel nor expensive equipment and buildings (see figures 5.4 and 5.5), and is cost-effective. An evaluation of the under-5s clinic at Imesi mentioned above showed that 10 years later the clinic was continuing to have its impact on the health of the children in the village. Coverage was in the region of 96 per cent with immunisation rates being 80–90 per cent; undernutrition was being prevented for a significant number of children and mortality in children under the age of 5 was 35 per cent of that in a nearby comparison village. One useful feature of the under-5s clinic is its adaptability. For example, measurement of the weights of children is one of the important tasks performed in the clinic. But weighing scales may not be available, or parents may not know the exact ages of their children. In such a case measurement of the arm circumference, which changes very little between the ages of 1 and 5, may be substituted for weight in identifying malnourished children. The measuring tape may be made from an old X-ray film which is cheap and does not stretch (see figure 5.6). The tape may be coloured to indicate the danger zones and to make interpretation easy, thus obviating the need for the health worker to be literate. Any child whose arm circumference is below 12.5 cm—that is, the red zone—is considered to be malnourished;

Figure 5.4   Under-5s clinic in Tanzania.

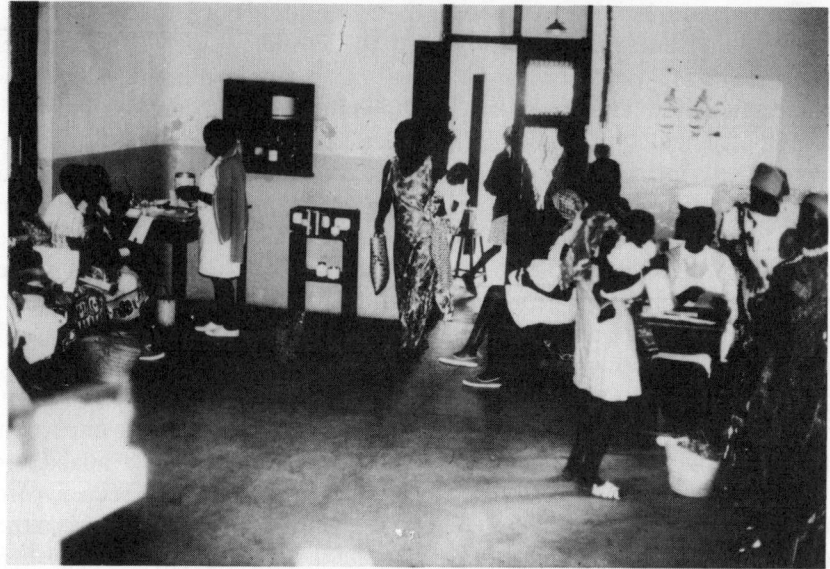

Figure 5.5   Under-5s clinic in Tanzania.

12.5–13.5 cm is borderline, and above 13.5 cm the child is adequately nourished.

Further experience with the under-5s clinic has shown that its effectiveness depends upon the following considerations:

(1) The frequency with which it is run. A daily clinic will be more beneficial than a weekly one. The ideal will be to have a daily clinic in each village, but this is not always possible, and a compromise can be made by organising a rotating clinic for each cluster of villages, such that no home is a distance of more than 2 km away from the clinic on any given day.
(2) At least 80 per cent of the children in the area should be regular attenders.
(3) An individual child should attend at least once a month for health surveillance, and within a day of the onset of any illness.
(4) There should be home visiting and follow-up care of problem cases or of non-attenders.
(5) A parent-retained weight chart should be available (see figure 5.7). The parent-retained weight chart is essential because parents will be reassured that information concerning their children is not being made public. If details about parental attitudes concerning family planning and the contraceptive methods practised by them are also being entered on the weight chart, then its retention at home by the parents is all the more necessary.
(6) Established criteria should exist for the identification of the child who is 'at risk' of disease.

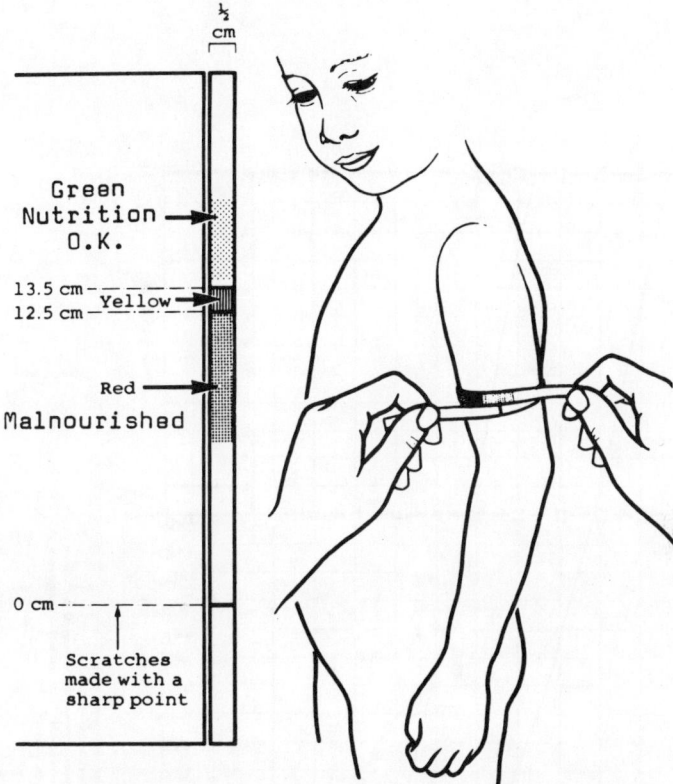

½ cm

Green
Nutrition →
O.K.

13.5 cm ———————
            Yellow →
12.5 cm ———————

Red →
Malnourished

0 cm ———————

Scratches
made with a
sharp point

Figure 5.6   Measuring the arm circumference for assessment of nutritional status.

(7) Community health volunteers who are residents of the villages should participate in the running of the clinic, and continue with the day-to-day work of counselling and treatment during the intervening period.

The concept of the under-5s clinic has spread since it was first described in 1963, and it is now part of the general child health services in many countries. Unfortunately, in common with other health programmes the coverage is inadequate (<20 per cent), especially amongst the disadvantaged groups. Secondly, all the above-mentioned conditions necessary for its success are not being ensured during the planning and running of the service, with the result that this very useful service remains virtually unexploited. Some of the principles of the under-5s clinic have been adapted for the Integrated Child Development Scheme (ICDS) launched by the government of India in 1975. The ICDS provides a 'package' of services to children up to 6 years old, pregnant women and lactating mothers. Services include immunisation, nutritional supplementation, nutritional rehabilitation of malnourished chil-

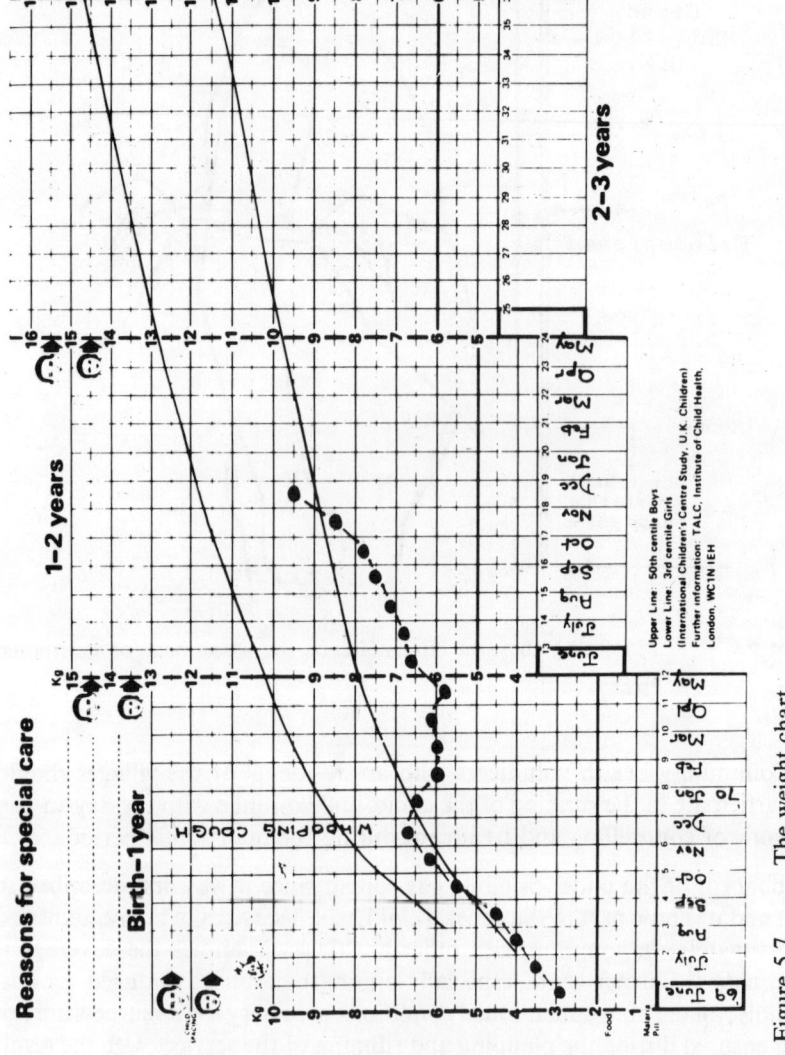

Figure 5.7   The weight chart.

dren, health surveillance of children and pregnant women, treatment of minor illnesses, pre-school education and health as well as nutrition education. The programme is specifically aimed at families living below the poverty line in the more remote rural and tribal areas of the country as well as in the urban slums. Several evaluations testify to the benefits of the programme.

The antenatal clinic

The antenatal clinic is another activity comparable with the under-5s clinic in providing regular supervision of a vulnerable group and can produce a similar impact on perinatal health. For example, the British Perinatal Mortality Survey (1958) showed that perinatal risks become five times the average when there has been an absence of antenatal care. The improvement in perinatal mortality reported from most industrialised societies is due to a reduction of late fetal deaths rather than any marked improvement in neonatal deaths (see figure 5.8 and table 5.4), and yet the one service that can make an immediate impact on perinatal health at minimum cost — antenatal care — is the least developed of all services. Most developing countries quote rates of 25–30 per cent for pregnant women receiving antenatal care, and most of these figures are made up from urban areas. Antenatal registration around 1977 was 27 per cent of all births in Senegal, 24 per cent in Nigeria, 37 per cent in Egypt, 40

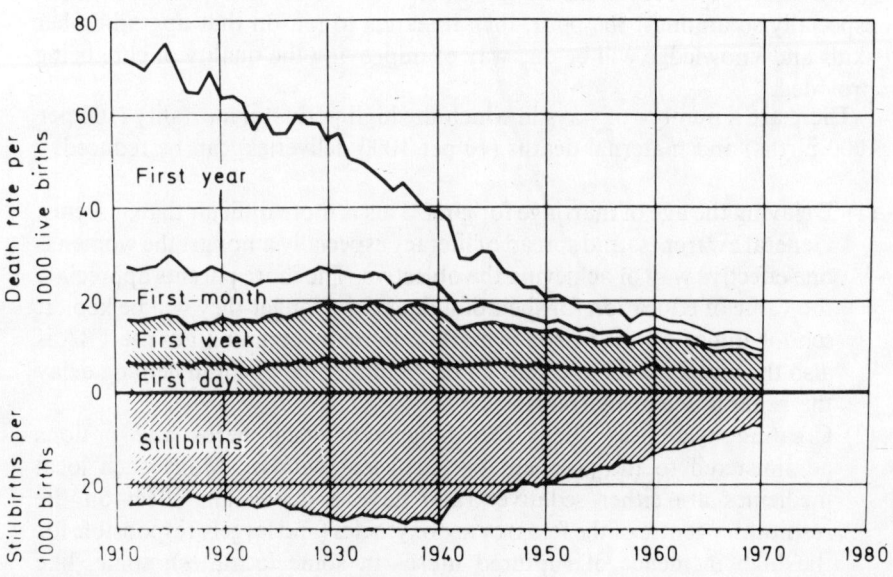

Figure 5.8   Perinatal mortality in Sweden.

Table 5.4   **Reduction of perinatal mortality in West European countries**

Country	Perinatal deaths 1956	1966	Late fetal deaths 1956	1966	Death in first week 1956	1966
England & Wales	37.6	26.7	23.4	15.6	14.1	11.1
Sweden	28.8	19.0	17.0	10.0	11.7	8.8
Italy	45.4	36.2	26.2	19.7	18.8	17.1

per cent in Costa Rica, 19 per cent in India and 31 per cent in the Republic of Korea. In Zaria, Nigeria, antenatal care has been the single most effective means of saving the lives of the mothers and their infants. Maternal mortality was less by 17-fold, perinatal mortality by sixfold and the prevalence of low birth weight was less by nearly threefold in mothers who received antenatal care compared with those who did not. In all traditional societies, pregnancy and childbirth require the performance of rites and rituals which are part of the 'rites of passage' described by anthropologists. Hence there is a reluctance to accept maternity care from the health services and the traditional methods are preferred instead. In this respect, the traditional midwife has a crucial role to play and many countries have instituted programmes of training for the traditional midwives in order to improve their skills and to integrate them into the overall system of health care. If more than 80 per cent of all deliveries in the Third World are conducted by the traditional birth attendant (TBA), and especially so amongst the poor, then it stands to reason that upgrading her skills and knowledge will be one way of improving the quality of care being provided.

There are a number of ways in which the high perinatal mortality (100 per 1000 births) and maternal deaths (10 per 1000 deliveries) can be reduced:

(1) Delaying the age of marriage for girls. This is more difficult than it seems. General awareness and spread of literacy especially amongst the women is one effective way of achieving the objective. The more parents appreciate the value of education for their daughters, the longer they will be kept at school and so off the marriage market! In many communities the TBA is also the matchmaker and she can be an influential agent in helping delay the general age of marriage.

(2) Creating awareness about the dangers of local herbs and potions administered to the pregnant or parturient woman. Many such local medicines are either sedatives (and have a depressant effect on the respiratory centre of the fetus) or are oxytocics (and largely responsible for the high incidence of ruptured uterus in some localities); some, like 'kanywa' in northern Nigeria, cause an excessive electrolyte load and precipitate post-partum cardiac failure.

(3) Creating awareness of the nutritional needs of the pregnant woman to counter the general attitude of eating less so as to have easy labour. In the Gambia, an increase in daily intake of energy by as little as 430 kcal (1.8 MJ) reduced the incidence of low birth weight (<2500 g) from a typical developing world level of 28.2 per cent to a desirable affluent world level of 4.7 per cent. This amounts to cooking daily a handful of rice or half that quantity of groundnuts *extra* for the pregnant woman. The very poor may need food supplementation, and especially during the stressful wet season in the rural areas. The TBA can be trained to identify women for food supplementation by monitoring fetal growth and well-being through serial measurements of fundal height and abdominal girth. She can also act as the source for issuing iron, folic acid as well as antimalarials to pregnant women.

(4) Training the TBA in clean cord-handling techniques and encouraging the mothers to be immunised with the tetanus toxoid. In the Khanna study in North Pubjab it was found that neonatal tetanus was an important cause of perinatal mortality, being responsible for 20.3 deaths per thousand live births, which is more than the total perinatal mortality rates of many countries in western Europe. By training the indigenous midwife in clean cord-handling techniques and immunising the mothers against tetanus during the last trimester of pregnancy, it was possible to reduce deaths from tetanus by two-thirds within a period of 6 months. In 1981, death rates from neonatal tetanus varied from 3 to 67 deaths per 1000 live births in a number of special surveys sponsored by the World Health Organization in several developing countries.

(5) Training the TBA in selecting the high-risk pregnancies for referral to health facilities where more advanced skills and equipment are available. Similarly, training her to monitor labour using simple techniques like the partogram and thereby anticipate problems during labour (see figure 5.9).

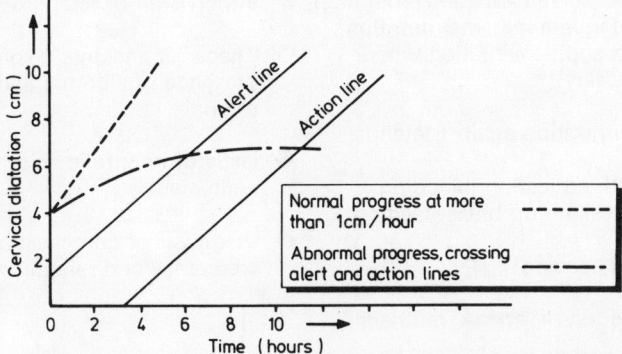

Figure 5.9   The partogram. The normal rate of cervical dilatation is about 1 cm/h (the slope of the alert and action lines). The examples shown are for women found to be 4 cm dilated on admission in labour.

(6) Creating awareness and training the TBA in helping mothers to space their pregnancies. There is now evidence from many developing countries that when pregnancies are closely spaced, the risks of fetal wastage and child mortality are increased several-fold. It is generally held that a period of at least 24 months on an adequate diet is needed for the mother to recoup her body stores of nutrients after a pregnancy. With subsistance level of nutrition, recovery is likely to take longer and hence the need for counselling about child-spacing.

In short improvement in the general health and nutrition of the mother through adequate coverage with prenatal care, ensuring fetal growth and the selection of the high-risk mothers for more skilled attention, is the most logical approach for decreasing the mortality risks for the baby and the mother in disadvantaged groups. For all the above-mentioned activities the TBA is an important intermediary since she is already providing obstetric care. Upgrading her skills will be an effective way of improving maternity care in disadvantaged communities. Experience with such training programmes indicates that the TBAs are more effective when trained to deal with specific problems like reducing the prevalence of neonatal tetanus, and when they are closely supported and linked with highly professional and sympathetic systems of maternal care.

As in the case of the under-5s clinic, the objectives and activities of the antenatal clinic may be summarised as in table 5.5. In order to make a measurable impact, the antenatal care programme should fulfil the following requirements:

Table 5.5   **Objectives and activities of the antenatal clinic**

● Health surveillance and promotion of adequate maternal nutrition. Food supplementation where necessary.	● Supervision of fetal growth
	● Check for anaemia, hypertension, presence of albumin and sugar in urine.
● Immunisation against tetanus	
	● Issue of iron, folic acid, antimalarials
● Health education including counselling on breast feeding.	
	● Diagnosis of complications of pregnancy and referral
● Child spacing	
● Selection of 'at-risk' mothers	

Home visiting of problem cases and defaulters

(1) At least 80 per cent of the mothers, especially amongst the poor, should be reached by the service on a regular basis.
(2) The earlier in pregnancy the prenatal checks commence, the better. An average mother should make a minimum of five visits, of which at least three should be in the last trimester.
(3) A system of record-keeping should exist to maintain adequate records on all women in the reproductive phase of life.
(4) There should be facilities for follow-up of defaulters and non-attenders.
(5) Early diagnosis and treatment of common illnesses should be included in the work of the clinic.
(6) Criteria should be established to identify the mother who is 'at risk'.

The 'at risk' concept

Inherent in the concept of regular health surveillance of the vulnerable groups is the principle of identifying those 'at risk' and early action to prevent disease. An individual may be 'at risk' because of bio-medical, social or environmental reasons, which may vary from one place to another and even from one village or urban neighbourhood to another. In each geographical area, specific criteria for the identification of those 'at risk' need to be defined and should be well known to the primary health workers. Some of the well-known criteria are mentioned in table 5.6.

Services of health surveillance like the under-5s and antenatal clinics are more in the nature of social services than strictly medical. Diagnosis of 'interesting' pathology is of secondary importance. Through continuing contact with a large number of families they help to build rapport besides being a valuable source of information about the community, and act as a vital interface between the community and the health service. If good coverage of the disadvantaged groups is achieved, the influence of the services can be made to be felt in every rural home.

In the case of the individual 'at risk', the remedial action usually consists of providing help through the available medical and social services in the community. This may be in the form of regular home visiting and health education, issue of food supplements, admission to the nutrition rehabilitation centre, family planning, referral to agricultural extension or other social services in the area, or referral to the health centre and/or district hospital. In every MCH clinic, at every level of health organisation, one day a week should be assigned to discussions on those 'at risk' among the attenders, the remedial action taken and their follow-up. Such meetings should take place under the chairmanship of the visiting senior personnel from the district hospital or the health centre (see table 5.7) so that a database of mothers and children 'at risk' in the locality is built up within the health system.

Table 5.6 **Selection of 'at-risk' mothers and children**

'At-risk' mother	*'At-risk' child*
● Age below 15 and over 40 ● Height below 150 cm ● First and after the fifth pregnancy ● Pre-pregnancy weight of less than 40 kg or weight gain of less than 7 kg in pregnancy ● Previous history of stillbirth, neonatal death, difficult labour or low birth weight ● Anaemia in pregnancy ● Social problems like alcoholism or unemployment in the family ● Abandoned mothers ● Socially deprived ethnic groups ● Short birth interval (<24 months)	● Low birth weight ● Multiple pregnancy—twins, triplets etc. ● Birth order of 5 and above ● Pregnancy in the mother before the child is 18 months old ● Recent measles, whooping cough, diarrhoea or any other major illness ● History of malnutrition or death in a sibling ● Lack of weight gain in the last 2 months ● Social problems: (a) Illegitimate child, one-parent family, abandoned child (b) Unemployment, chronic illness or alcoholism in parent (c) Socially deprived ethnic groups

The above-mentioned activities—health surveillance of children and women of child-bearing age as well as lactating mothers, treatment of the common illnesses, nutritional care and counselling, family spacing, immunisation, and the training of health workers to carry out the tasks involved—will form the core of a community health programme. The appalling hardships faced by the poor affect most severely women of child-bearing age and children. Hence a total coverage of the disadvantaged group is essential. The selection of those 'at risk' is at its most effective only when coverage with services is adequate.

The above core programme should be responsive to seasonal needs. Thus measures against seasonal infections like malaria and diarrhoea, programmes for health and nutrition education according to season, increasing the energy intake of women and children at critical times of the year, seasonal stocking of drugs and vaccines as well as increased intensity of travel and supervision should be built into the programme.

Table 5.7 Health institutions, their staff, local activities and mutual responsibilities in the total system of health care

Institution	Local health functions	Responsibility to other health institutions

District Hospital
Existing Staff:
Doctors 4
Sisters 4
Med. Asst. 4
Trained Nurses 4
Nurse Aides 15
Public Health Nurse 1
Health Inspector 1
Health Educator/Nutrition Instructor 1
 	
Visiting Staff:
Once a month from regional hospital
(i) Consultations
(ii) Evaluation of MCH activities
(iii) Evaluation of public health activities
	(i) In-patient and out-patient work
	(ii) MCH work—'at risk' meetings
	(iii) Nutrition Rehabilitation Centre
	(iv) Health and Nutrition Education
	(v) Organization of community programme
	(vi) Under-five play groups
	(vii) Communicable disease control
	(viii) Public Health activities
	    (a) Sanitation
	    (b) Water supply
	(ix) Acceptance of emergencies and referrals
		Rural Health Centre
		Supervision and assistance with activities (i) to (viii) at the Rural Health Centre.
		
		Visits as follows:
		One doctor fortnightly—consultation, participation in 'at risk' meetings, supervision of nutrition rehabilitation centre and in-patients, supervision of MCH activities and communicable disease control.
		
		One public health nurse fortnightly, alternating with doctor, to participate in 'at risk' meetings and assist with MCH clinics.
		
		Health Inspector
		Nutrition Instructor } weekly, together with visiting doctor or public health nurse for:
		Health Educator
		
		Supervision of communicable disease control
		Supervision of nutrition rehabilitation centre
		Nutrition demonstration
		Health education
		Participation in 'at risk' meetings

Table 5.7 Health institutions, their staff, local activities and mutual responsibilities in the total system of health care

Institution	Local health functions	Responsibility to other health institutions
Rural Health Centre Medical Assistant 2 Rural Medical Aide 3 Nurse/Midwife 1 Community Nurse 1 Nurse Aides 4 Assistant Health Inspector 1 Visiting Staff: Once a week from district hospital (i) Consultations (ii) Evaluation of MCH activities (iii) Evaluation of public health work	(i) Out-patient work and some in-patients (ii) (iii) (iv) (vi) (vii) and (viii) as above	*Dispensary (sub-centre)* Supervision and assistance with functions (ii), (iv), (v), (vi) and (viii). Visits as follows: One doctor Health Inspector Nutrition Instructor Health Educator } once a month *Dispensaries* Supervision and assistance with (i) (ii) (iv) (v) (vi) and (vii) Visits as follows: One medical assistant One public health nurse One assistant health inspector } once a month Participate in 'at risk' meeting, health education, communicable disease control

Dispensary (sub-centre)
Existing Staff:
Rural Medical Aide   1
Nursing Aides   3

MCH Aides   3

Visiting Staff:
Once a week from
health centre

Village Level Health Workers

(i)   Out-patient work
(ii) MCH work
(iii) Nutrition supplementation and
      rehabilitation

(vi) (v) (vi) (vii) and (viii) as above

(i)   Out-patient work
(ii)   MCH work
(iii) Nutrition education
(iv)   (v) (vi) (vii) and (viii) under
       guidance of Rural Medical Aide
       from the Sub-centre

Village level health worker
Visits and assistance with (i) (ii) (iv) (v) (vi) and
(vii)

Visits as follows:
One Rural Medical Aid visits the villages in
rotation
One Nursing Aid visits the villages in rotation.
(The Rural Medical Aid's visits coincide with
major under-five clinic. The Nursing Aid's
visits coincide with antenatal clinics.)

Visits the dispensary or sub-centre on day of
visits by the Health Centre personnel

Communicable disease control

The control of communicable diseases amongst the rural and urban poor can be considered under four headings: preventable infectious illnesses, strategies for dealing with respiratory infections and diarrhoea, the control of chronic infectious diseases, and the control of illnesses caused by parasites.

Preventable infectious diseases (see figure 5.10)

The control of common infectious diseases preventable by immunisations, many of which can be carried out in the under-5s clinics, can be effectively mounted through the use of such clinics. The aim is to create adequate group immunity amongst the susceptibles to break the chain of transmission of an infective illness. In a given community resistance of a group to the spread of infectious illness is a product of the number susceptible 'n' and the probability 'p' of the susceptibles coming into contact with an infected person. Computer simulation models show that the phenomenon of 'herd immunity' depends not on the number immune but on the number of susceptibles and their distribution in the community. If there is adequate 'herd immunity' in a group, not all susceptible individuals will be infected in an epidemic. Susceptibles are not distributed homogeneously but tend to cluster in sub-groups defined by ethnicity, social class and age. It is necessary therefore to build up a high level of immunity amongst the poor in order to prevent regular epidemics. In the USA, for example, a high level of coverage with measles immunisation has been achieved but measles continues to occur in sub-groups with low social status and education level. Thus maximal effort to reduce the concentration of susceptibles throughout the community is necessary rather than achieving any specific target of immunised individuals in the overall population.

Even though a well-organised under-5s clinic programme can provide immunisation for a large number of children in the community, it is found that to reach the *minimum* target of 80–90 per cent, regular mass immunisation campaigns are necessary. Experience in several countries has shown that the actual target groups reached may be less than the proportions estimated by clinic records, and amongst those unreached, the majority are geographically clustered. Mass campaigns are thus a mopping-up operation aimed at avoiding a build-up of susceptibles. They should logically begin with the most disadvantaged localities and then spread out to the rest of the community.

The mere availability of vaccines is not enough and does not make a programme. There should be channels for regular supply, facilities for adequate storage and transport of vaccines carefully watched over by a supervisor. There should also exist an efficient system of surveillance to ensure that sufficiently large numbers of children are being immunised, and to maintain records of notified illness in order to identify new pockets of

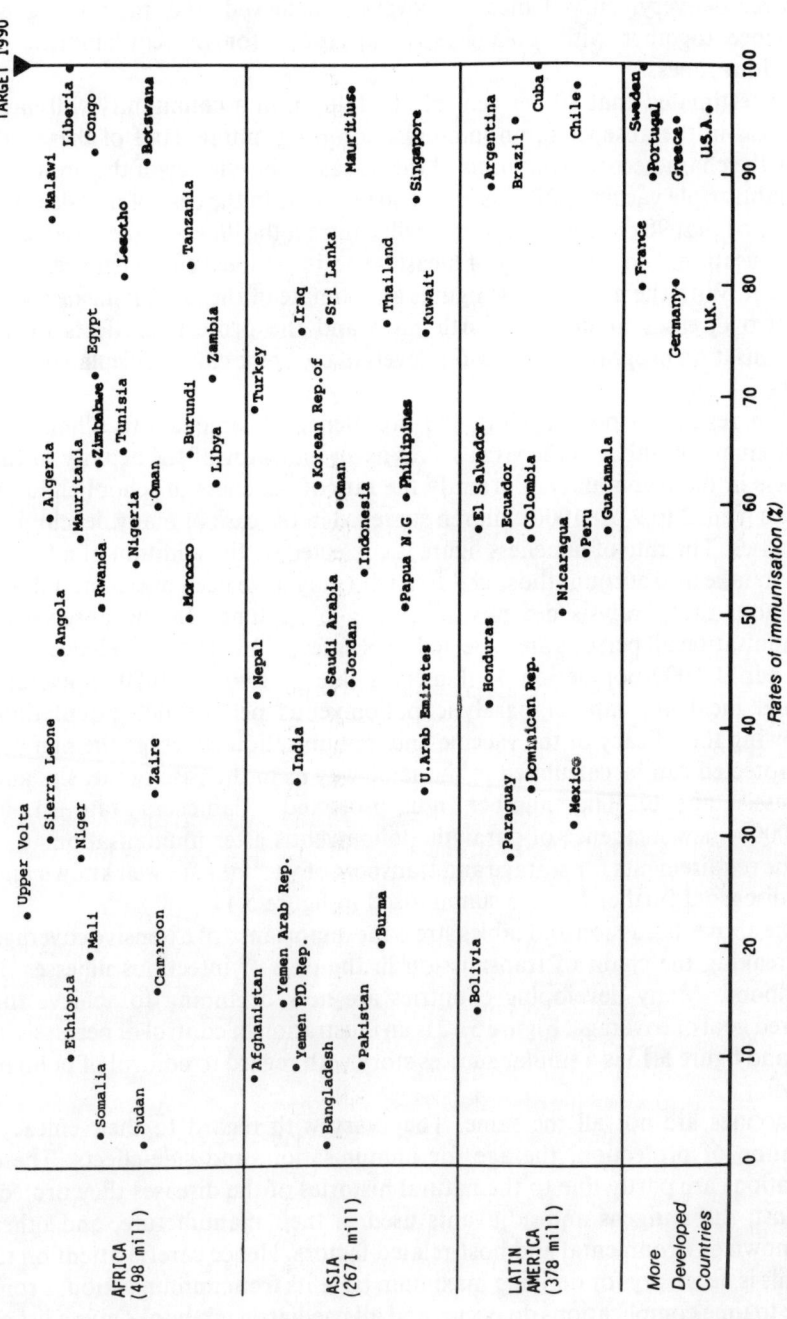

Figure 5.10   Rates of immunisation.

infections. The best vaccines are worthless without an adequate system of storage, delivery, surveillance of coverage achieved and monitoring of incidence together with an aggressive approach for the containment of infectious illness.

It is estimated that 80 per cent of all children in a community will have pertussis in the absence of an immunisation programme. Half of these will show the characteristic symptoms of the disease. The efficacy of the presently available triple vaccine (DPT) is about 80 per cent. In the case of measles, it is estimated that 90 per cent of children will contract the illness in the absence of immunisation, and the efficacy of measles vaccine in ideal circumstances is 95 per cent. With the help of these figures an estimate of the annual incidence of the two diseases at different birth rates and the protective effects of an immunisation programme at various levels of coverage can be calculated as in tables 5.8 and 5.9.

With regard to poliomyelitis, the prevalence of lameness in school-age children attributable to the virus serves as an indicator of the activity of the disease in the community. Currently the rate of lameness in school children ranges from 2 to 9 per 1000 children surveyed in the case of many developing countries. The rate of lameness figure is corrected by the addition of a factor 1.66 to take into account those children who may have been missed and those in whom the paralysis did not affect the lower limb. In the absence of immunisation all persons are expected to be infected by the virus. Hence birth rate per 100 000 population × (lameness rate + 1.66) ÷ 1000 = average annual incidence rate of paralytic poliomyelitis per 100 000 population. Knowing the efficacy of the vaccine and immunisation coverage the number of protected can be calculated in the same way as in the case of measles and pertussis above. The number not protected × (lameness rate + 1.66) ÷ 1000 = new incidence of paralytic poliomyelitis after immunisation.

The requirements for storage and transport of vaccines are well known and not discussed further but are summarised in figure 5.11.

The above discussion and tables stress the importance of extensive coverage in breaking the chain of transmission in the case of infectious illnesses of childhood. Many developing countries are now beginning to achieve the desired goal of coverage. Figure 5.12 is an illustration of control of pertussis in Fiji and figure 5.13 is a similar success story with regard to control of polio in Brazil.

Vaccines are not all the same. They vary with regard to their efficacy, duration of protection, the age for immunisation, and side-effects. These variations are partly due to the natural histories of the diseases they protect against, the antigens and adjuvants used in their manufacture, and other unknown environmental and host-related factors. Hence careful attention to details is necessary for deriving maximum benefits from immunisation. From time to time complications do occur, and all paediatric textbooks give a list of contraindications when immunisation is best withheld. Table 5.10 gives the

Table 5.8 Estimates of protection by immunisation with measles vaccine

Birth rate (births/ 100 000 population)	Measles incidence rate with no immunisation	Measles vaccine efficacy (%)	Immunisation coverage (%)	No. of children protected by imm.	Measles incidence rate expected with immunisation programme	Percentage reduction in incidence from immunisation
4000	3600	95	90	3420	522	86
			80	3040	864	76
			20	760	2916	19
3500	3150	95	90	2993	456	86
			80	2660	756	76
			20	665	2552	19
3000	2700	95	90	2565	392	86
			80	2280	648	76
			20	570	2187	19
2500	2250	95	90	2138	326	86
			80	1900	540	76
			20	475	1823	19

Table 5.9 **Estimates of protection by immunisation against whooping cough**

Birth rate (births/100 000 population)	Pertussis incidence rate with no immunisation	Efficacy of vaccine (%)	Immunisation coverage (%)	No. of children protected by imm.	Pertussis incidence rate with immunisation	Percentage reduction in pertussis
4000	3200	80	80	2560	512	64
			50	1600	1280	40
			20	640	2048	16
3500	2800	80	80	2240	448	64
			50	1400	1120	40
			20	560	1792	16
3000	2400	80	80	1920	384	64
			50	1200	960	40
			20	480	1536	16
2500	2000	80	80	1600	320	64
			50	1000	800	40
			20	400	1280	16

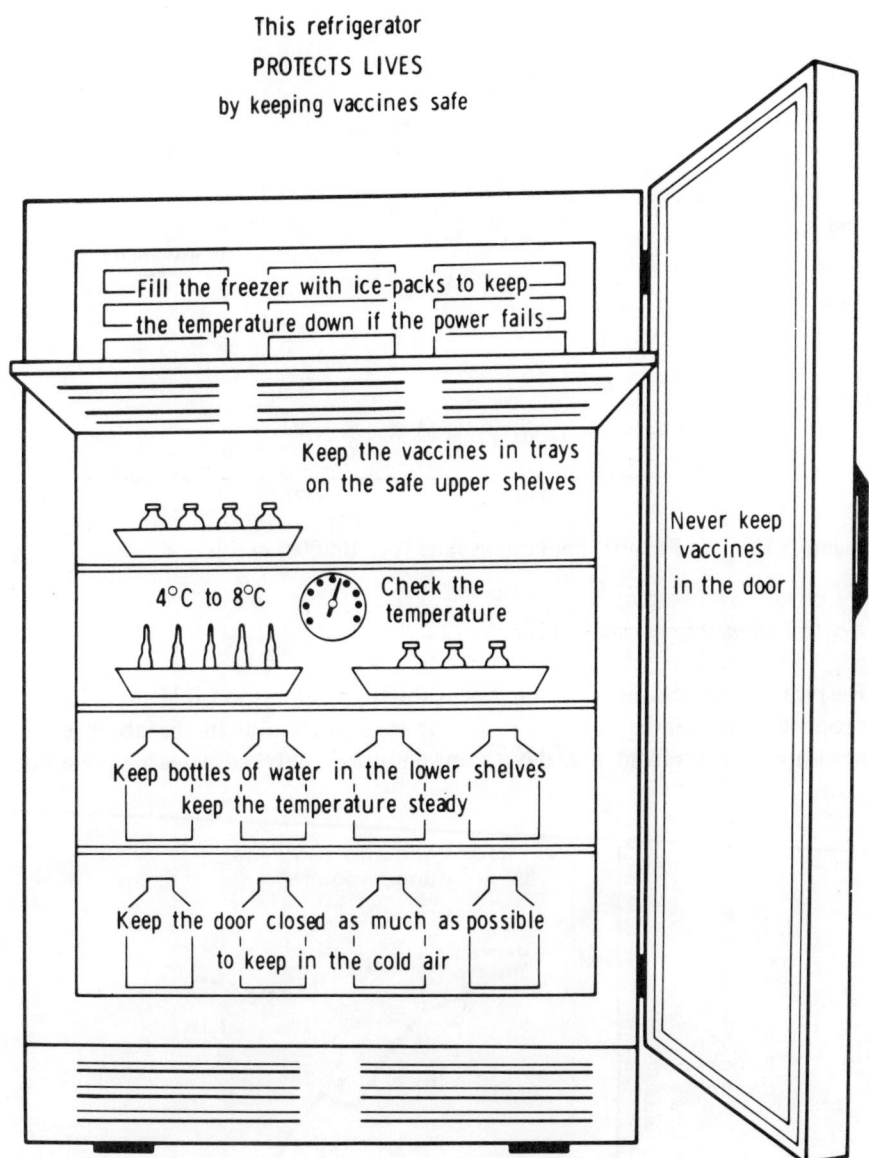

This refrigerator
PROTECTS LIVES
by keeping vaccines safe

Fill the freezer with ice-packs to keep the temperature down if the power fails

Keep the vaccines in trays on the safe upper shelves

4°C to 8°C   Check the temperature

Never keep vaccines in the door

Keep bottles of water in the lower shelves keep the temperature steady

Keep the door closed as much as possible to keep in the cold air

The refrigerator is a vital member of the health team

Figure 5.11   Storage of vaccines.

estimated rates of adverse reactions with different vaccines, and compares them with rates of complications during a natural infection.

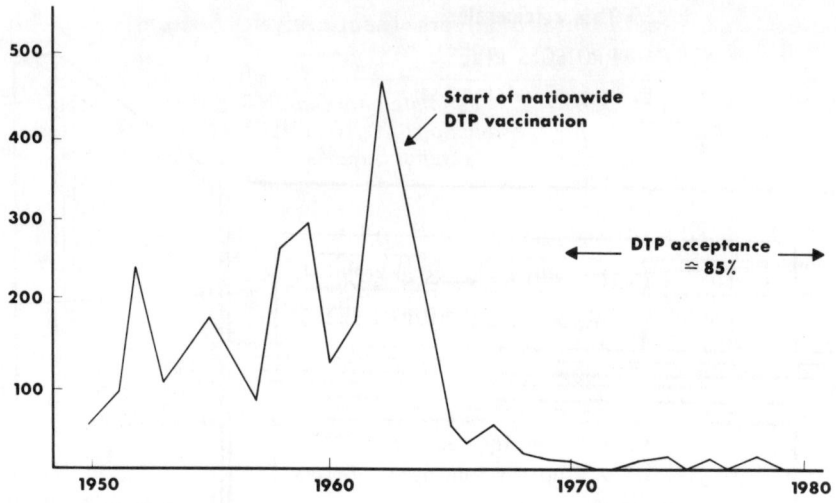

Figure 5.12   Pertussis notification rates (per 100 000) in Fiji.

Control of pneumonia and diarrhoea

Respiratory infections and diarrhoea are together responsible for a large proportion of deaths in children less than 3 years old. In the absence of accurate statistics from most developing countries, only estimates are possible

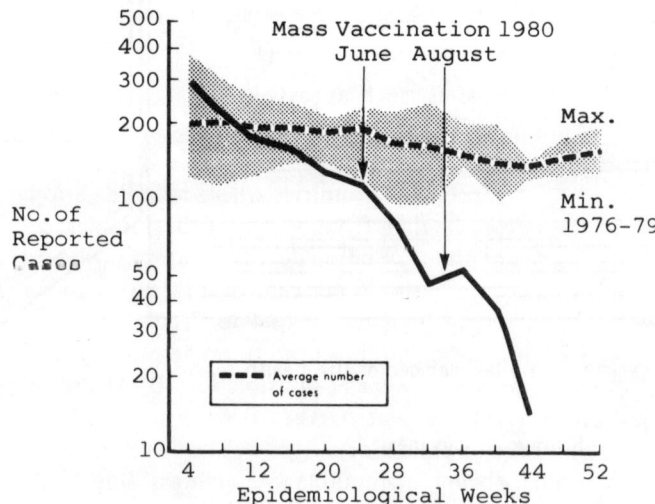

Figure 5.13   Poliomyelitis in Brazil, 1980.
Source: EPI Newsletter. Feb. 1981.

Table 5.10 **Estimated rates of adverse reactions with presently available vaccines**

Vaccine	Estimated adverse reactions per 100 000 immunisations	Rates of complications per 100 000 cases of the disease
BCG:		
Disseminated BCG infection	<0.1	—
Osteitis/osteomyelitis	<0.1–30	—
Suppurative adenitis	100–4300 (0.1–4.3%)	—
Triple vaccine (DPT):		
Permanent brain damage	0.2–0.6	600–2000 (0.6–2.0%)
Deaths	0.2	100–4000 (0.1–4.0%)
Encephalopathy	0.1–3.0	90–4000 (0.09–4.0%)
Convulsions	0.3–90	600–8000 (0.6–8.0%)
Shock	0.5–30	—
Measles:		
Encephalitis encephalopathy	0.1	50–400 (0.05–0.4%)
Subacute sclerosing panencephalitis	0.05–0.1	0.5–2.0
Pneumonia	—	3800–7300 (3.8–7.3%)
Convulsions	0.02–190	500–1000 (0.5–1.0%)
Death	0.02–0.03	10–10 000 (0.01–10%)
Oral polio vaccine:		
Paralytic illness	0.1	>28

by piecing together evidence from countries where reliable national records are maintained. Based on the data from 88 out of the 156 member states of WHO, it is estimated that about 2 million deaths occur each year due to acute respiratory infections representing 6 per cent of all deaths. In Bangladesh, respiratory infections were responsible for 10.4 deaths per 1000 in infants and 1.6 deaths per 1000 in older children. In the Inter-American Study of Child Mortality, respiratory diseases were responsible for 40–44 deaths per 1000 children aged under 1 year in some parts of Bolivia and Brazil.

The effect of diarrhoea on child mortality is well known, with an estimated 5 million deaths annually being attributable to diarrhoea. Both diarrhoea and respiratory illness also contribute to deterioration in the nutritional status of the child and, together with measles and pertussis, are significant aetiological factors in the events that lead to malnutrition.

Prompt intervention in the case of both pneumonia and diarrhoea is effective in lowering mortality. In a health programme in 13 villages in the Punjab, a 50 per cent reduction in death rates for diarrhoea and 45 per cent reduction in the case of respiratory illness was noticeable within a short time of the commencement of a programme. The basic principles of the programme were twofold: (1) awareness amongst the health workers and the community of pneumonia and diarrhoea as serious illnesses by singling them out as important causes of deaths in children; (2) transfer of technology for treatment and decision-making from the health centre to the village level.

Since effective interventions for the management of respiratory infections and diarrhoea are now available, they should be the priority targets, especially with regard to the poor amongst whom these illnesses are more frequent. Continuous availability of penicillin or co-trimoxazole in the poor neighbourhoods, together with the ingredients for oral rehydration fluids, *and* training of community health volunteers in the use of them, together with appropriate back-up are the main features of such a programme. The principles of oral rehydration are well known and not further discussed, but summarised in figure 5.14. Appropriate technology for measuring the requisite amounts of the ingredients like the double-ended spoon and bottle-tops used as a measuring device is illustrated in figures 5.15 and 5.16. In Jamkhed minimally trained village health workers carry out oral rehydration using the hand as a measure for sugar and a two-finger pinch for measuring salt with the juice of freshly cut lemon for palatability and some potassium. For more than 5 years now there has not been a single death from diarrhoea in the 40 or so villages served by the comprehensive health programme in Jamkhed. Such community health workers help to provide a continuum of oral rehydration between home-based local mixtures, the distribution of packets with correctly measured ingredients, and intravenous therapy at the health centres.

In the case of several chronic infectious diseases like tuberculosis, leprosy, trachoma and venereal diseases, there is social stigma, so that patients do not readily come for treatment, and because of superstitious beliefs or tradition tend to prefer indigenous remedies. Thus in the case of pulmonary tuberculosis, it has been estimated that in the average district of India there is a point prevalence rate of 5000 cases, but only 900 are being diagnosed every year by the health institutions (see figure 5.17).

As in all infectious diseases, each individual with the disease constitutes a portion of the reservoir of the diseases in the community and this reservoir in turn determines new infections and prevalence rates for the community. Thus in the case of *tuberculosis*, one adult patient infects two or three persons per year, and without medical treatment is expected to live an average of 3–4 years. On the basis of such data, a model for the community prevalence of tuberculosis in the average district of India can be formulated as follows.

At present 900 cases are being diagnosed per year; of these only 300 complete the full 9 months of treatment and may be considered 'cured'.

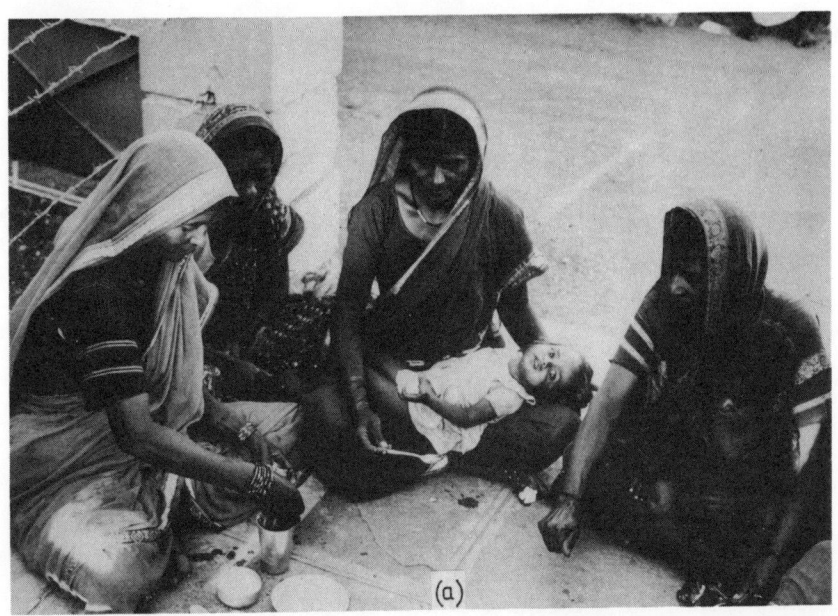

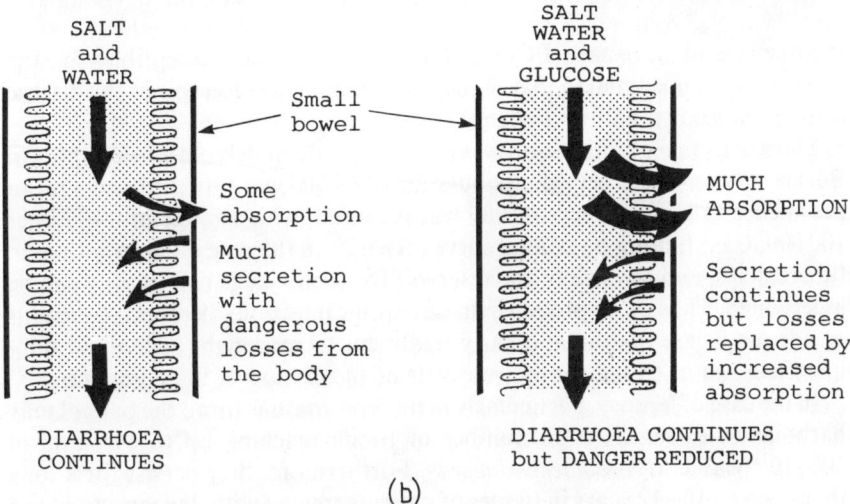

Figure 5.14   Oral rehydration. (a) By village health workers in Jamkhed. (b) Principles.

Another 300 complete 2–3 months of treatment and then give up. Some are rendered sputum negative and non-infectious, though not 'cured'.

The estimated diagnostic *potential of the health centre* is 2000 cases per year. If this potential can be fully realised, then with improved case finding and

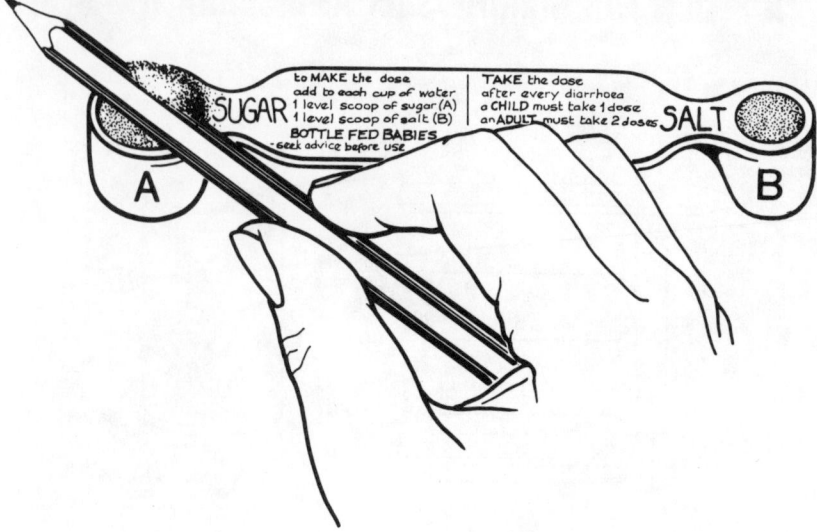

To MAKE the dose
add to each cup of water
1 level scoop of sugar (A)
1 level scoop of salt (B)
BOTTLE FED BABIES
seek advice before use

TAKE the dose
after every diarrhoea
a CHILD must take 1 dose
an ADULT must take 2 doses

SUGAR   SALT

A   B

Figure 5.15   Two-ended spoon for oral rehydration.

treatment and adequate BCG immunisation of the susceptibles in the community, it is estimated that in the above model the reservoir of the disease can be reduced to half its size in 25 years.

The situation regarding *leprosy* is known less adequately. In a field survey in Burma, over a 4-year period a population of 69 000 was surveyed and a mean prevalence rate of 316 per 100 000 was recorded, with a range of 0–797 per 100 000. Case finding by annual survey is easier in the case of leprosy than in tuberculosis, and the size of the reservoir for each village community can be ascertained. Thus the approach in these chronic infectious diseases is by means of adequate case finding and early treatment to render the individual non-infectious, so as to reduce the reservoir of the disease in the community.

In the case of leprosy, particularly in the lepromatous form, the patient may harbour an extremely high number of bacilli reaching up to the level of 10^9–10^{11} viable *Mycobacterium leprae*. Furthermore, they persist for a long time—up to 10–12 years in tissues of patients treated with dapsone and for 5 years when treated with rifampicin as monotherapy. This explains the clustering of infectioin in familial and household close contacts of the patient. Both tuberculosis and leprosy are not only associated with poverty, but also, on account of the associated social stigma and debility, they are generators of poverty. Hence an aggressive programme for their containment and control is an essential part of any anti-poverty programme in the developing world. Case-finding does not always require sophisticated diagnostic methods. In the case of leprosy, regular surveys in the community and schools with contact

A SPOON FOR MAKING SALT AND SUGAR WATER

FOR TREATING DIARRHOEA

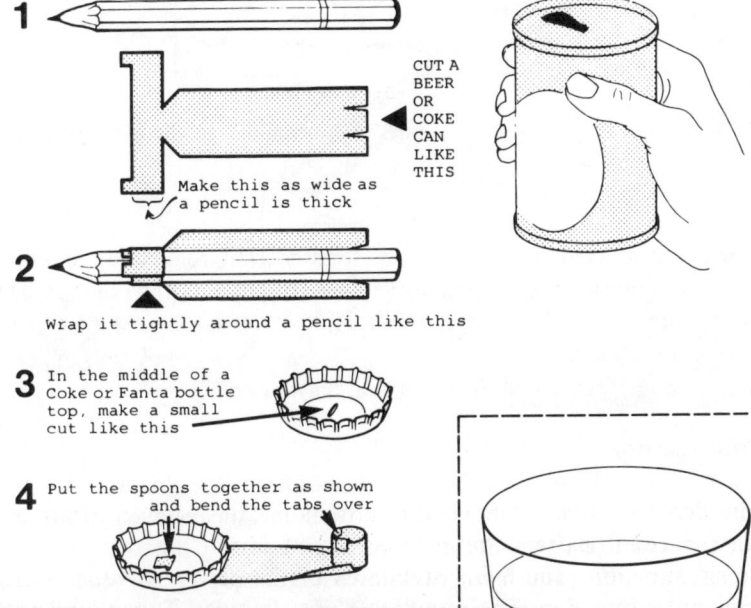

There are many things you can use to make spoons
to measure the right amount of SUGAR and of SALT

Here is one idea
BE SURE TO MAKE THE SPOONS THE RIGHT SIZE

1

CUT A
BEER
OR
COKE
CAN
LIKE
THIS

Make this as wide as
a pencil is thick

2

Wrap it tightly around a pencil like this

3 In the middle of a
Coke or Fanta bottle
top, make a small
cut like this

4 Put the spoons together as shown
and bend the tabs over

TO MAKE THE DRINK FOR A DEHYDRATED CHILD

5 Heap the bottle   Fill the little
    cap with   spoon with
    SUGAR   **SALT**

And mix it in a medium-sized glass of WATER
(or a Coke can or a standard beer can full
of water)

Before
using

taste the
water and
be sure
it has no
more salt
in it than
tears

Figure 5.16   Bottle-tops for oral rehydration.

tracing is usually enough. In the case of tuberculosis, the microscope for
examination of sputa is more useful than the X-ray machine, since the danger
to the community is greater from 'open' cases excreting the bacilli in their
sputa.

The treatment regimens have been described in standard textbooks and are

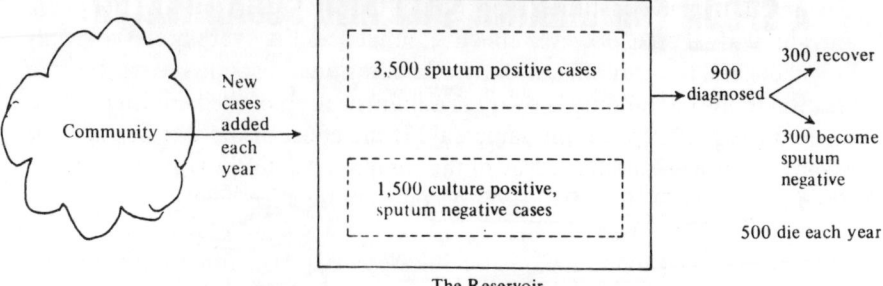

Figure 5.17   Epidemiological model of tuberculosis in the average district in India.

not further discussed. It is, however, stressed that regular availability of chemotherapeutic agents, regular surveillance of patients and contacts as well as maintenance of adequate epidemiologic records are essential for an effective programme.

Parasitic diseases

The incidence of several parasitic infections is decreasing in a number of developing countries who have succeeded in improving their social and economic situation. The living standards of the people serve as a crucial determinant of infections. In Costa Rica, Cuba, Trinidad-Tobago and Taiwan there has been a continuing and persistent decline in the incidence of malaria, hookworm and other helminthic infections, indicating that poverty, lack of education and overcrowding are important determinants of parasitic illnesses. These factors determine to a large extent the choice of habitat, the way of life, adequacy or otherwise of personal hygiene, and above all the available home technology. This technology is related to the handling and storage of water, the preparation, handling and storage of food; the care of children in health and illness; the disposal of excreta and waste and the inclination for improving housing and sanitation. Thus, one major step in dealing with parasitic diseases is improving parental competence by the transfer of technologies for the improvement of the environment to an organised community, especially of the poor.

The advent of effective and non-toxic pharmaceutical preparations has made the treatment of the individual case relatively easy, so that most individuals can be treated on an out-patient basis. At the same time, the use of an epidemiologic model, similar to the one described above with relation to tuberculosis, helps to create the possibility of mass therapy. Thus each individual with an intestinal parasite is part of the total pool of the disease in the community and constitutes a portion of the total reservoir. The treatment of the individual case, however effective, influences the overall reservoir only marginally and the only effective way of making an impact on the reservoir of infection in the community is by mass administration of the vermifuge to the susceptible age-groups on the same day. If the effect of the weather and the seasons on the eggs and the larvae of the common helminths is also taken into consideration, mass administration becomes more effective if carried out at specific times in the year.

For most of the common parasitic illnesses a sequence of options becomes available as follows:

(1) Reduction and prevention of mortality. This is the traditional curative approach hitherto employed with the benefits largely accruing to the privileged classes in most countries.
(2) Prevention of morbidity in the most vulnerable groups.
(3) Overall reduction of prevalence by attacking the 'reservoir' of the disease.
(4) Eradication, which requires the implementation of several interrelated measures, aimed at reducing the reservoir together with improving the living standards, like, for example, environmental sanitation and protection of the water supply.

On the basis of the above discussion, the following strategy of attacking the reservoir of the disease is suggested, taking into account options (1)–(3). When this strategy is considered together with the section on 'water supply and sanitation' as well as 'community organisation' discussed in Chapter 6, option (4) also becomes feasible.

Ascariasis—Mass treatment, with a single administration of piperazine or levamisole, of a large number of persons in the community has been shown to interrupt transmission. In many places transmission is continuous and occurs all the year round. In such cases mass treatment may be required every 3 months or so. On the other hand, in some places there are marked seasonal variations in transmission. In such places mass treatment should commence about 4–6 weeks after the transmission season begins and should be continued at 3-month intervals while it lasts. The seasons, environmental temperatures and the soil determine the differences in transmission. It has been shown experimentally that eggs placed in soil became infective only when the soil temperature reached 20°C in the summer months, and at temperatures of 40°C or higher, all eggs were killed. Similarly, eggs placed 1 cm deep in the soil were killed when soil humidity fell below 4 per cent, but with higher humidity 53–98 per cent of the eggs became infective. Knowledge of this nature may help to time the mass campaign in a way that will produce maximum benefit.

Ankylostomiasis—Bephenium, like piperazine, is relatively non-toxic and is the vermifuge of choice for the individual case. Tetramisole (a racemic form of levamisole) is a broad-spectrum anthelmintic and gives cure rates of 90 per cent with roundworm and 80 per cent with hookworm infections. Meben-dazole is also a broad-spectrum anthelmintic effective against *Ascaris*, hookworm and *Trichuris* infections. Unlike ascariasis, the transmission of ankylostomiasis is more dependent on the rainy season, the maximum transmission occurring about 2 months after the end of the rainy season. Owing to this seasonal dependence of transmission it should be possible to mount two 'rounds' of mass therapy in order to break the cycle of transmission in the community.

Schistosomiasis used to be one of the most difficult of the parasitic infections to eradicate. Recent success in China where eradication was achieved by burying the breeding grounds of the parasite-bearing snail along the banks of irrigation canals has demonstrated the effectiveness of community action, and of mass campaigns for dealing with the reservoir of infection. The advent of more effective and nontoxic chemotherapeutic agents like Praziquantel which can be administered orally in a single dose has made mass campaigns possible. The most heavily infected segment of the population are school-age children who are the logical target group. In a number of studies mass chemotherapy has been shown to result in reduced transmission of infection. Targeted mass chemotherapy by itself is not enough for long-term reduction of prevalence. It needs to be combined with programmes for sanitation and disposal of human waste as well as reduction of frequency of contact with water sources. Observations in St. Lucia showed that most of the infection is acquired at the water course, usually during the washing of clothes or the drawing of water. Whilst women were involved in these tasks, the accompanying children played in water and got infected. Communal laundry facilities and protected wells can help to reduce these risks.

Malaria—During the past 25 years the attempts to control and eradicate malaria have provided a number of interesting lessons and results. Malaria has been largely eradicated from temperate and subtropical zones. The countries concerned possessed the resources and expertise to exploit the use of residual insecticides and antimalarial drugs. Besides, they had well-structured health services which could easily take on the challenge of sustaining the malaria eradication programme, not counting the fact that for climatic reasons the disease had a precarious foothold in those countries. By contrast, malaria is firmly entrenched in the tropics and the vectors have feeding and resting habits which do not allow a successful use of residual insecticides. The social, educational and economic levels of development necessary for the successful control of endemic malaria are absent in many of the affected countries. It is presently estimated that of the approximately 200 million people exposed to the dangers of malaria, 80 per cent live on the African continent. It is in tropical Africa where a fresh approach to the control of malaria is needed. Malaria is a social disease largely affecting the poorer segments of the population. Because of its debilitating effect it reduces the productivity of the working members of the family during the stressful wet season, and makes poverty worse. A combination of measures like dealing with the breeding grounds of the vector, draining stagnant water, encouraging the use of personal protective measures against the mosquito in addition to chemoprophylaxis of selected groups may help to reduce the transmission rate as suggested in the model in figure 5.18.

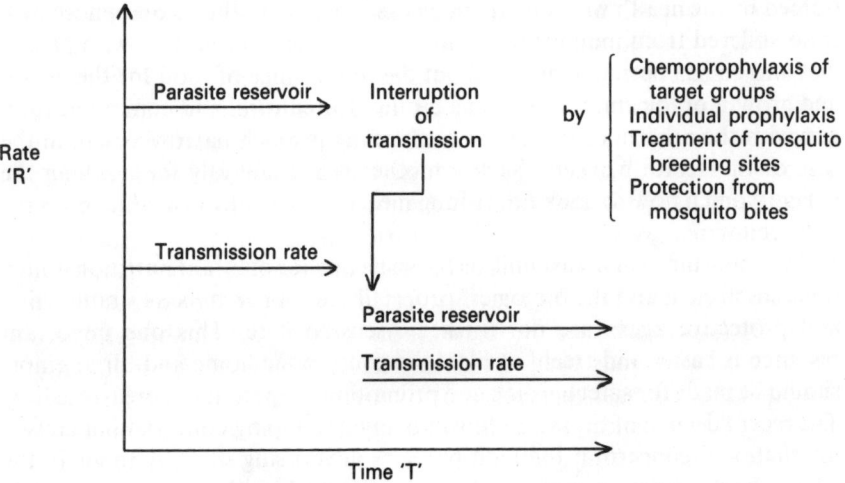

Figure 5.18   A model to show the effects of combined intervention on the transmission of malaria in the community.

Some of the important principles in malaria control are:

(1) Chemoprophylaxis should be offered only to vulnerable groups like small children and pregnant women, in order not to interfere with the acquisition of immunity.
(2) Health education should be provided together with chemoprophylaxis, so that adequate measures are taken by individual families for protection against mosquito bites.
(3) Community participation and organisation are vital for the successful control of malaria transmission.

Nutrition programmes

The under-5s clinic and the antenatal clinic provide a good working base for all programmes of nutrition promotion in the community. With a little imagination these clinics can serve as the means of integrating health and nutrition activities. Moreover, the outreach clinics and home visiting further extend the scope of the health services into remote communities and homes. The mothers and families are interested in the nutrition of the child and of the pregnant woman, and there are opportunities for them to learn by participation in nutrition demonstrations and health education. Experience has shown that for the rural and urban poor the best educator is a mother who has been trained by the health workers. In many cases such a mother is one whose own child suffered from malnutrition and who has seen him recover with proper diet and so has been convinced about the importance of food for the health and growth of the child. For such a mother the cultural and communication gap with the other mothers of the community is much narrower than in the case of the health workers. Such a mother is a useful ally for teaching the village women how to cook nourishing meals from locally available foods for their children.

The importance of breast milk as the sheet anchor of infant nutrition is now well established, and the biological properties of human milk as a nourishing and protective agent are not further discussed here. This one important resource is easily and freely available in every poor home and all attempts should be made for safeguarding and promoting the practice of breast feeding. The recent decline of breast feeding in many developing countries has caused international concern at the high-pressure advertising of baby foods in the Third World. Consequently, in 1981 the World Health Assembly voted in favour of an international code of ethics for member states to adopt for the control of advertising. Unfortunately, under the prompting of the baby food industry, several countries have passed national codes which are no better than a cosmetic exercise. At the same time, much of the promotion has become subtle and is shifted to the more remote rural areas and urban squatter communities. Programmes for primary health care in these communities are likely to encounter the promotion of bottle feeding in various forms and must develop strategies to counteract it.

Besides being generally supportive of breast feeding in all health activities, there is also a need to eliminate some of the medical rituals and practices known to have adverse effects on breast feeding and to modify the training of health workers accordingly. These are listed in table 5.11.

The remarkable ability of breast milk to support the very rapid growth of early infancy despite a relatively low amount of protein (1.2 g/100 ml) indicates that its property as a nutrient is largely due to its energy content, and to its energy/protein ratio. In fact, at 6 kcal/g of solid matter (24 kJ/g) breast milk has six times the energy density of many traditionally used gruels in developing countries, and three times that of commercially available weaning foods. Studies of food intakes in healthy children in Uganda have shown that in the second year of life those who were weaned had 25 per cent less energy intake compared with those who were still breast feeding, even though the former were being offered 60 per cent more solids. Thus even in the second

Table 5.11 **Practices interfering with successful lactation**

Practices	Effect on lactation	Modifications
Delaying first breast feed	Inadequate stimulation of let-down reflex	Putting infant to the breast immediately after birth
Excess maternal analgesia resulting in heavily sedated newborn	Weak, unco-ordinated suckling	Avoidance of excessive sedation of the mother
Giving prelacteal glucose feeds to the infant	Weakening of the suckling stimulus	Avoidance
Rigid 4-hourly routine of feeding with no night feeds	Anxious mother and a hungry, fretful baby	Frequent on-demand feeding during the day as well as the night
Separation of the infant from the mother	Suppression of lactation	Rooming-in
Uninformed, unsupported mother	Interference with the let-down reflex	Preparation of the mother for lactation during pregnancy and counselling from lactation advisers with emotional support in puerperium
Excessive use of instrumental delivery (pain + anaesthesia)	Suppression of lactation	Avoidance
Unsympathetic, inexperienced staff	Anxiety and frustration in the mother	Adequately trained staff skilled in the management of breast feeding
Provision of 'gift packs', visits by 'milk nurses' and use of posters and brochures advertising baby foods	Suppression of let-down reflex and the drying-up of milk e.g. by deciding to try the gift pack	Hospital policies prohibiting all such practices

year of life, breast milk is a valuable source of energy besides providing protein of high biological value.

A number of simple manuals are now available giving information on the preparation of weaning diets out of multi-mixes from local foods. Such multi-mixes ensure adequate and balanced consumption of amino acids. But the major deficiency in traditional weaning foods is that of energy and not protein. Hence the use of edible oils and fats as well as the use of energy-containing foods like ground nuts, soya, coconut, sesame, palm oil and so on needs to be popularised. Besides providing energy and improving palatability,

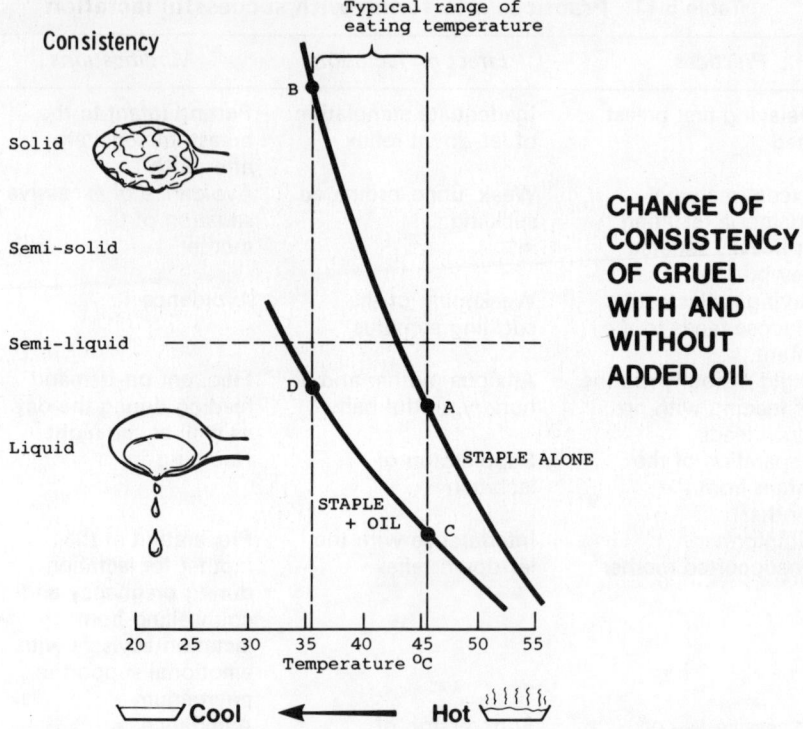

Figure 5.19   Adding oil to gruel improves the energy density and reduces the viscosity.

the use of oil helps to keep the traditional gruel more fluid and facilitates its handling by the infant's mouth (see figure 5.19).

Presently in the average rural community at any point in time about a quarter of the children enjoy adequate nutrition and growth, approximately 60–65 per cent show slow growth and in about 10 per cent growth is minimal or has ceased. Some children in this last group may show clinical signs of malnutrition. Many of the parents of children showing a flat growth curve can be helped by advice, nutrition demonstrations and home visiting, but in those cases where growth is minimal or has ceased, food supplements are necessary. Locally available foods may be used to prepare these supplements. This has been demonstrated by the National Institute of Nutrition in Hyderabad, India. The food supplement provided consists of a mixture of wheat 35 g, Bengal gram 17.5 g, ground nuts 6.0 g and jaggery 11.5 g. The ingredients are cooked by roasting on an open fire and then milled together into a powder, which is sealed in a small polythene packet. Each packet provides one day's food supplement for a child. The foods are bought from the local farmers and

Figure 5.20   Members of the women's club preparing 'Hyderabad Mix'.

prepared and packed by the local women's clubs (see figure 5.20). It has been found that the use of the locally available foods in preparing food supplements creates a local demand and the farmers thus find an incentive to grow more of such foods, and often use them in their own dietary.

Improving the food chain

In a given district the nutrition activities and programmes are part of the food chain which is the channel through which nutrients pass from suppliers (local growers and imports) through distributors and the processing media to the consumer. The effectiveness of the food chain in reaching families and communities at the social periphery will determine their state of nutrition. A number of interventions are necessary to ensure the supply of nutrients for the poor. The health system provides many opportunities for such interventions like, for example, health surveillance of vulnerable groups, nutrition education, provision of supplements, rehabilitation of the malnourished and so on. The impact of such direct interventions is strengthened by indirect preventive action to increase the production and availability of food like backyard gardening, to improving the distribution system, increasing the purchasing power through community development activities and improving the environ-

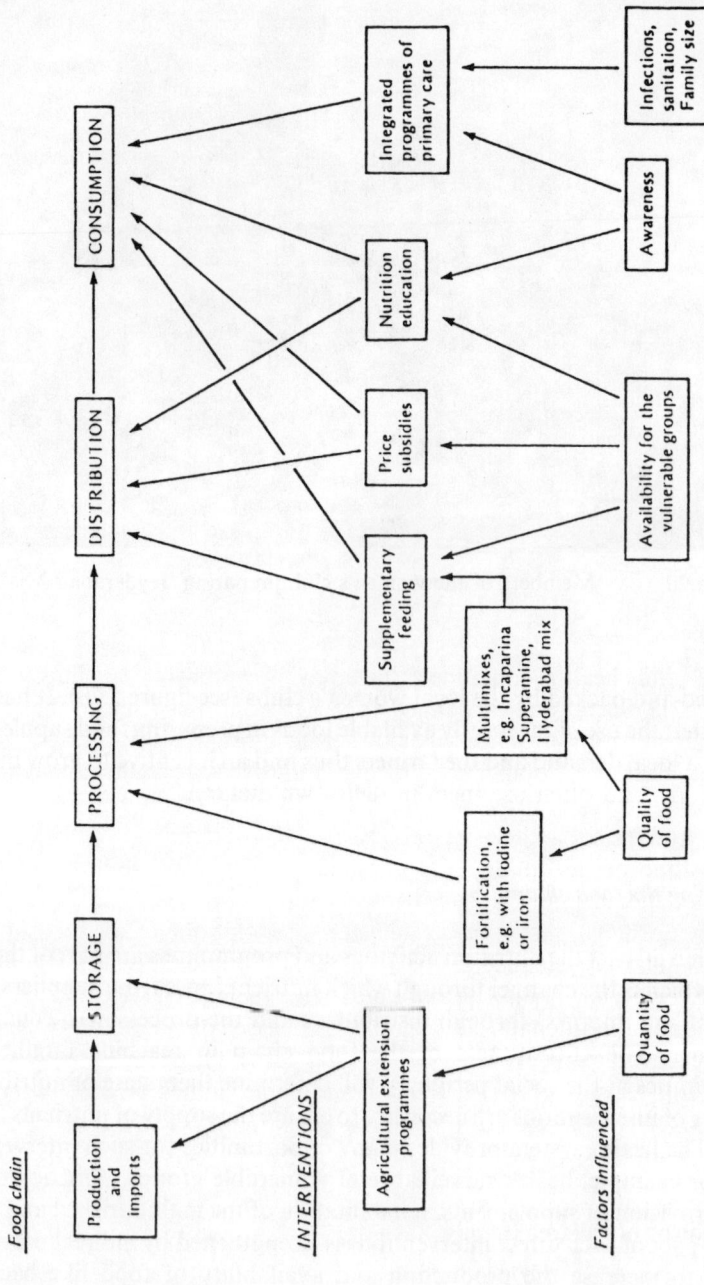

Figure 5.21   The food chain.

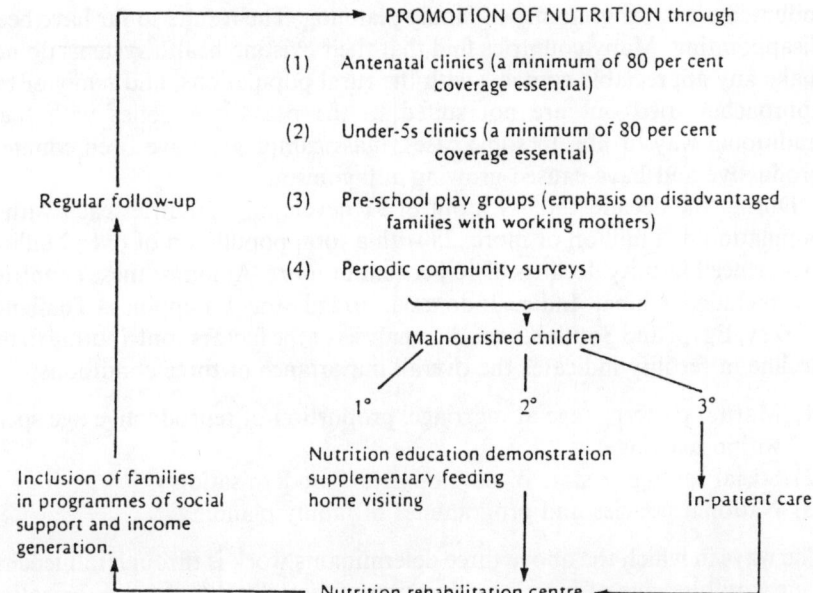

Figure 5.22   Integration of nutrition intervention and surveillance services.

mental and health conditions including the control of infection (see figure 5.21). Such a multi-pronged approach addresses itself to the observation that nutrition problems are not solved through hand-outs of food but require basic development tools like improved agricultural techniques; facilities for preservation, storage and transport; credit facilities; national wages and prices policies; and education programmes. Nutrition is the cornerstone of health. In all community health programmes, nutritional activities should have the major role.

An important aspect of the strategy for the promotion of adequate nutrition is the regular surveillance of the vulnerable groups, especially amongst the poorer neighbourhoods. The usefulness of surveillance services like the under-5s clinic and the antenatal clinic has been discussed on pages 103–13, and they must reach out to all, even in a rudimentary form. The integration of nutrition interventions and surveillance services into the unified scheme is shown in figure 5.22.

The spacing of children (family planning)

The urgent need to restrict the growth of their populations has been felt by many countries, and several nations, especially in South-East Asia, have mounted crash programmes of family planning. The results so far have been disappointing. Many countries find that their existing health systems do not make any appreciable contacts with the rural populations, and many of the approaches tried out are not suited to the peasant societies with their traditional way of life. In some cases, mass campaigns have been counter-productive and have caused growing antagonism.

During the decade 1965–75, out of 91 developing countries each with a population of 1 million or more, 28 with a total population of over 2 billion experienced fertility declines of 10 per cent or more. Amongst these countries are included China, India, Indonesia, Brazil, the Philippines, Thailand, Turkey, Egypt and South Korea. An analysis of the factors contributing to the decline in fertility indicates the overall importance of three conditions:

(1) Marital patterns (age at marriage, proportion of reproductive age spent within marriage).
(2) Social setting or state of development ('modernisation').
(3) National policies and programmes of family planning.

The ways in which the above three determinants work is through influencing four variables: age of marriage, duration of lactation, the family formation behaviour including methods used to avoid conception, and fetal loss. These four variables largely explain the differences in fertility rates between populations.

Recent estimates by the World Health Organization are that only 17 per cent of couples in developing countries are using modern forms of contraception. The remaining 83 per cent are dependent on natural and traditional methods to check their fertility. The decline in fertility during the decade 1965–75 is largely due to later marriages. In societies that advocate early marriage—such as India, Pakistan, Nepal, Bangladesh and Indonesia—the median age at marriage (the age at which half of all women are married) is rising on account of greater awareness and the spread of education. The median age at marriage is generally low for the poor compared with the upper socio-economic classes. The use of the TBA, a continuing dialogue for creating awareness about the dangers of child marriage, and spread of education amongst the poor will help to avoid early marriages.

The spacing of children is a highly personal matter and requires a personal approach built upon a long-standing relationship. The child health worker is more intimately in contact with parents and families than any other member of the health team and the under-5s clinic holds the potential for a sound approach to family health through child spacing. The rationale of the method is as follows. If the average birth interval in a community is studied, it is possible to calculate the earliest period when the 5th percentile of women are likely to become pregnant again after bearing a child. The period of risk for conception to occur in a mother is then marked on the child's weight chart and the health worker then knows when a dialogue with the mother should begin, so as to motivate her to use contraceptives. Thus if an investigation of birth interval in a given community shows that the birth interval is 17 months, the average mother is at maximum risk of conception when her infant is 8 months old. This period is marked on the weight card of the infant, and the dialogue for motivation begins with the mother a few months before this period.

The traditional approach to family planning has been through women's clubs by education, through antenatal and postnatal clinics, and in maternity wards. In the last three situations the mother is least interested, because she knows that there is no immediate danger of pregnancy. The approach through under-5s clinics is directed towards mothers who know that they are vulnerable to another pregnancy, are interested in delaying it because of their concern for the well-being of the small infants and are prepared to act upon the advice given because it comes from the health worker who regularly supervises the health of their children and with whom a bond of trust and friendship exists. The approach to child-spacing through the under-5s clinic adds yet one more dimension to the family planning programme—a dimension that may well turn out to be a strong feature of the programme, since child-spacing is closely related to the health and survival of the other children in the family (see figure 5.23).

The contraceptive effect of breast feeding is now better understood. The observed incidence of conception during lactational amenorrhoea is 2–8 per cent. On the basis of such information as well as controlled observations in defined populations, it is estimated that about 5 per cent of women who are fully breast feeding (including night-time feeding) are likely to become pregnant before the first menstruation. The value of such data for the poor communities is obvious. In Bangladesh, where only 9 per cent of women use contraceptives and the duration of lactational amenorrhoea is $18\frac{1}{2}$ months, the use of contraceptives would have to rise to 43 per cent merely to hold fertility at its present level, if lactational amenorrhoea were to decline to 6 months.

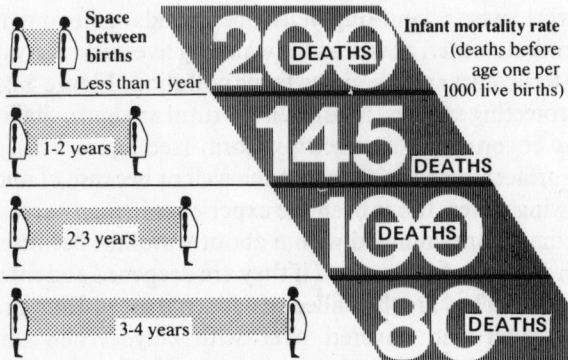

Figure 5.23   Spacing births reduces deaths.
Source: WHO survey of 6000 women in South India.

In certain cases a medical or social reason may exist for the parents to avoid another pregnancy so as to be able to devote time and attention to the child 'at risk'. These are cases of chronic illness such as nephrosis or sickle cell anaemia, a handicapping illness in one of the parents, or a social problem in the family. The use of IUD, the pill, or Depo-Provera may be indicated in such cases.

Water and sanitation

Availability of water which is safe for drinking is an important target in any programme of community health. For the family, and particularly the mother, nearby safe water in adequate quantity will save labour and effort in water haulage. The nearest source of water supply may be a mile or two away and the water has to be transported in buckets or gourds carried by the womenfolk or older children in the family. In a study of a typical East African village it was found that the source of water supply was a stream 1.5 km distant and 1000 m below the village. The women carried water in 4-gallon (18 l) kegs or cans, walking down to the river and trudging back, 3–5 times each day, each round trip requiring about an hour.

Greater health benefits seem to result from adequate assured supplies of safe water than from limited supplies of pure water. This is because health benefits derive from the hygienic use of water not only for direct consumption but also for the washing of food and for cooking as well as hand washing and bathing. Water provided in adequate amounts in the home cuts down on the likelihood of contamination.

Much of the surface water easily becomes polluted. Thus in a survey in Sannaa, Yemen, it was found that as many as 80 per cent of the water sources used for domestic purposes were contaminated owing to lack of well covers and unwashed water buckets. This is usually the case in much of the developing world where hand-dug wells, open ponds or streams are used as the sources of drinking water, as well as for watering livestock and washing. Much can be done to protect these sources from pollution. Figure 5.24 illustrates a method of protecting springs. Most wells in rural areas are shallow, and carry no protective covering, or a raised platform (see figure 5.25). The water is polluted by surface water draining into the well or because of unclean buckets used for drawing water. It has been the experience in many areas that a newly dug well becomes contaminated within about 9 months because of the above factors. Such wells can be improved if they are deepened and fitted with a tube and a hand pump. They are then filled in with coarse sand and gravel up to the level of the water and covered over with clay. When this filling has consolidated, a platform with drainage can be built on it. The cost of the operation has been estimated at US $500–700 and the water obtained from such wells is of reasonable purity.

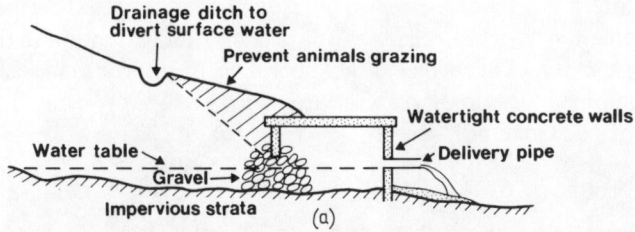

Figure 5.24   Protecting the spring. (a) Principles. (b) In practice.

The technology for digging wells is sufficiently advanced so that in most situations it is possible to provide reasonably safe water by simple and economical means. Water obtained from a deep tube well is usually safe for drinking. High-speed drilling rigs can bore through 50 m of hard rock in 2 days—a feat which used to take as many months in the past. Plastic pipe is coming into use for lining tube wells. Using high-speed drilling in a rocky country, the capital cost of drilling and casing a well serving 200 people is of the order of US $60/m (1980 prices) i.e. $3000 for a 50 m well). In easier geological conditions, the cost of sinking wells is proportionately less.

Several countries have embarked on programmes of providing water for their rural populations through shallow wells. This method has the added

Figure 5.25   Traditional water source.

Figure 5.26   A well constructed from pre-cast concrete rings.

Figure 5.27   Casting concrete rings.

advantage of utilising simple technology to sink pre-cast concrete rings into the soil as shown in figures 5.26–5.28.

A simultaneous campaign of health education should actively dissuade

Figure 5.28   Shallow wells.

people from using surface water like tanks, canals, springs and rivers. The use of clean water will be more popular and the campaign of health education more successful if the digging of new wells and improvement of existing ones, as described above, is carried out through self-help schemes. The village community is invited to contribute labour and sometimes material so as to develop a sense of pride and ownership. Whenever water supply has been left solely to an outside agency or a government, the local community assumes no responsibility, so that there is lack of maintenance of equipment. It is also possible that villagers who have co-operated in installing a water system may be prepared to go on to the next step of wider health-oriented activities like sanitation, home improvements, and give local support to other health and social services, etc.

In communities with marked social disparities, many of the water resources are monopolised by the upper classes. Use of wells and springs may be denied to the poor as is the case with the caste system in India, or to the poor ethnic minorities as in some countries of tropical Africa. In such a situation it is important to ensure development of water resources for the poor whose needs are greater on account of their overcrowded living conditions and unhygienic or dirty occupations.

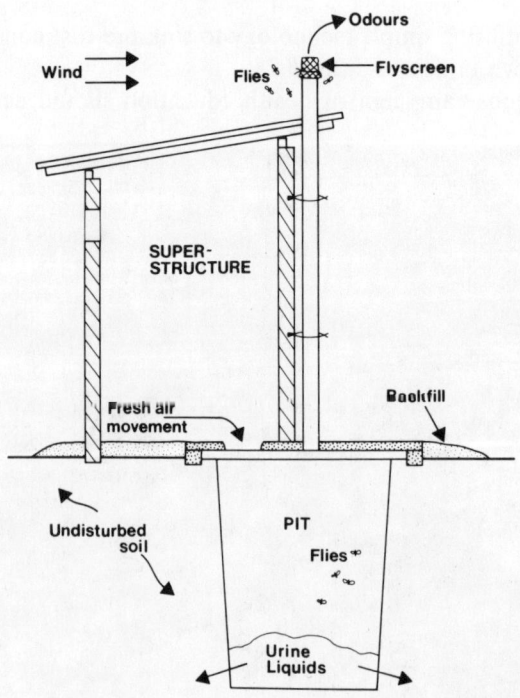

Figure 5.29   The ventilated improved pit latrine.

During epidemics of water-borne diseases and in the rainy season when surface water is likely to be contaminated, all shallow wells in the area should be regularly chlorinated, using the same epidemiologic principles as mentioned in relation to the control of communicable disease, so that all shallow wells in the district are chlorinated on the same day, the process being repeated every 3 weeks until the risk of water pollution subsides.

The programme for developing water resources must go hand in hand with one for improving sanitation. Hitherto, the only technology for the disposal of human waste which was practical within the means of the poor has been the pit latrine. But the pit latrine has several defects. The odour discourages its use; flies and mosquitoes breed in the pit and are a health hazard, and cockroaches can be a nuisance. A number of improvements have been introduced in the original design to overcome the above disadvantages. The Ventilated Improved Pit (VIP) latrine first developed in Zimbabwe to provide sanitation

Figure 5.30   A ventilated improved pit latrine in Zimbabwe.

independent of removal by water has become popular (see figures 5.29 and 5.30). By 1981, 30 000 units had been built. In the VIP a slab with two openings covers a pit which is well sealed. A ventilation pipe is fitted on one of the openings. The other opening is the squatting hole. Fresh air is drawn through the squatting hole and up the pipe setting up an air current, and the latrine remains odourless. The top of the ventilation pipe is fitted with a corrosion-resistant flyscreen. The flies from the outside cannot get in and those in the pit are attracted by the light from the top of the vent pipe but remain trapped and cannot get out.

Further experience has shown that wind speed and direction are the two factors primarily responsible for ventilation. Thermally induced updraught in the vent pipe is only of minor importance. Black paint on the vent pipe to absorb solar heat helps a little. A large diameter, 200 mm or so, is more effective than pipes of smaller diameter.

Modification of the design (see figure 5.31) to make two pits serving the single superstructure has been developed in Botswana. This design may be more useful in high-density areas especially if municipal facilities are available for emptying the pits at intervals, usually of 1 year or more.

In the Far East human waste is used as manure, and the practice in many rural areas is to apply it to the soil untreated. In Vietnam, however, the double-vault composting latrine (see figure 5.32) has become popular because of the dual advantage of getting rid of waste and turning it into useful compost. The vaults to receive waste are built above ground level to facilitate emptying. The vaults are built adjacent and are served by the same superstructure. When one vault is about three-quarters full it is filled with earth and sealed and the other

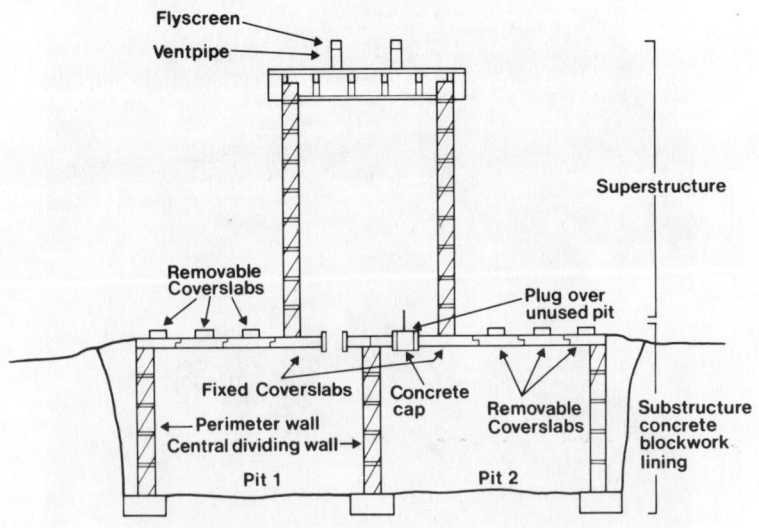

Figure 5.31   A ventilated double pit latrine in Botswana.

Figure 5.32   Double vault latrine.

vault is then used. Ash and farm or kitchen refuse are added from time to time to the vault to absorb moisture and odours, and also before sealing it. This helps to provide a suitable carbon/nitrogen ratio for efficient composting. In

Figure 5.33   Fish pond latrine.

the Vietnamese toilet urine is excluded by means of a shallow gutter running in front of the squatting hole. It drains off into a soakway or is collected to be used as a liquid nitrogenous fertiliser. The exclusion of urine also helps to control the moisture in the vault. These toilets need a great deal of conscientious care by the user, and also an understanding of the value of compost for agriculture.

A number of other simple technologies have been developed e.g. fish pond latrine (see figure 5.33) and are described in special texts. Among these the biogas and aqua privy are best suited for communal use because of costs. These are described in special texts to which the interested reader is referred.

Community organisation for participation in health programmes

This important topic is further considered in Chapter 6. Health workers in most developing countries have singularly failed in establishing an ongoing dialogue and rapport with the communities they serve. Countries like China and Cuba which have achieved a breakthrough in health in a remarkably short time ascribe their successes largely to popular awareness and participation in health activities and not to advanced technologies operating from within hospitals. It should be emphasised that the success of a community-based health programme is to be judged not so much by the improvements in vital statistics as by the increased knowledge and skills of the people to manage and solve their health problems. A tangible evidence of such an approach will be the extent to which local resources and initiatives have been mobilised for sustained efforts over time.

Most ministries of health do not have the ability to undertake the dual task of delivering health services and mobilising communities for more than routine activities over short periods of time. Self-help schemes to build clinics, improving water resources or building access roads have been some of the few examples of activities undertaken. The enthusiasm soon wanes after the task is completed, and without continuing support or encouragement interest is not sustained. A number of factors inhibiting community participation can be identified as follows:

(1) There may be a lack of perceived usefulness of the proposed activities.
(2) Communities may not be accustomed to collective problem-solving. In traditional societies most joint activities take place within the framework of family, caste, tribal or religious linkages.
(3) There is the historic mistrust and cynicism of governments and bureaucracies.
(4) Governments are often cool to the idea of popular participation because it creates demands, raises expectations and generates political unrest.

(5) The local élite feel threatened when the poor organise themselves into action groups.

Grass-root organisations greatly enhance the opportunities for the poor to improve their own lives. Thus in Jamkhed it was found that in project villages with farmers' clubs and women's groups (*Mahila Mandals*) the awareness amongst the people of agricultural and health matters was far greater compared with nearby non-project villages, even though both the groups of villages were equally served by governmental health and agricultural services. In the case of the non-project villages the big farmers and the upper-class élite were the main beneficiaries of governmental services.

Creating community groups and social structures for participation in health programmes may be a key factor in bridging the gap between knowledge and its application, but is not easy. It raises questions which may be difficult to handle. These are the questions of who is doing the choosing, how the choices are enforced and whether the style of health development treats participation mainly as the means for achieving defined objectives or as the *true* aim of the programme. The process of true participation is a long, painstaking one. There is first the phase of developing the *psychological base*, through dialogue and discussions. Next is the phase of creating the *social infrastructure* wherein the community forms several care-taker groups on whom the health programme must come to rest. Then is the phase of creating the *physical infrastructure* where the necessary activities like improving local clinics or schools through self-help schemes, improving the water supply, building access roads and so on are carried out. Simultaneously with all these activities there is the slow process of building the *technological infrastructure* in which the local knowledge and technical know-how are being upgraded.

When fully functional the activities of the community groups are complementary to the objectives of the health development programme. They provide volunteers and sometimes essential support besides being the 'enablers' through mobilising the community to take full benefit of the services. By attracting the more forward-looking individuals in the community, such groups also become the training grounds for leadership. A conceptual framework for the interrelationship between health development programmes and community groups is given in figure 5.34.

The poor usually have a very good idea of what is required to meet their needs, and to solve their problems. But this does not necessarily mean that they know all the obstacles which are likely to crop up, and are not knowledgeable about alternatives. They are also disorganised and rarely united. The organisations that emerge are initially fragile and need a considerable amount of support and encouragement. Long delays, bureaucratic red tape, and demands for written reports work adversely and stifle them. And yet there are no other ways for the poor to resist the forces of impoverishment except by organising themselves and pooling their resources.

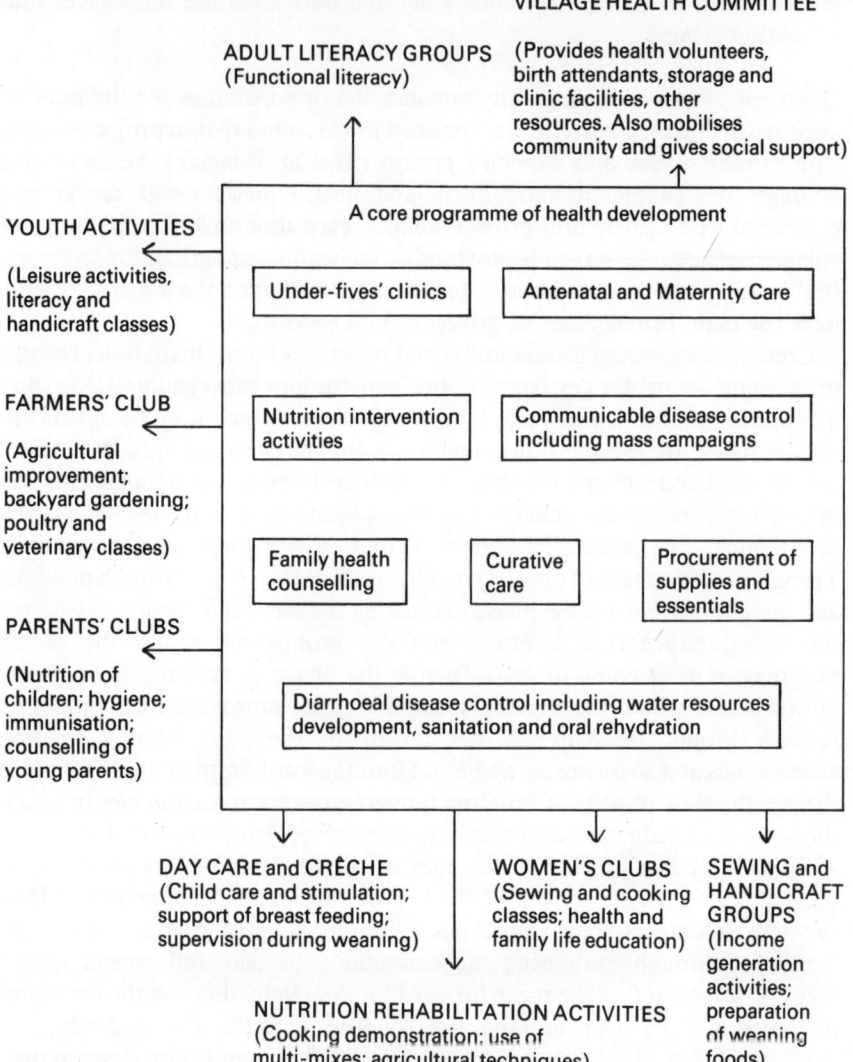

Figure 5.34   A conceptual framework for the interrelationship between health programmes and community groups.

All of the four known modes of impoverishment respond to the power of a united and organised response. These modes are as follows:

(1) Geographical where natural or ecological factors are predominant.
(2) Social where pauperisation is part of the process of exploitation along the ground rules of that society.

(3) Economic where market forces are responsible for loss of livelihood.
(4) Political where poverty is imposed by the power of the state.

These activities and programmes provide a framework of 'minimum goals' in health to be aimed at. Once these 'core' activities are established and community trust and support generated, the programme can grow in a number of other directions. Child-to-child activities and promotion of mental · health are other priorities, not discussed here, which could be added to the package of activities. They form the core of the package of health services in the basic needs approach for the removal of poverty. Together with other services like education, food production, development of water resources, housing, and so on, they constitute the basic tools of human development.

It may be argued that in most developing countries the beginnings of these programmes have already been made and that in the district hospital/health centre/sub-centre complex the seeds of comprehensive health services exist. It is only a matter of time before services can grow and reach out to all. Such an argument has been pursued by health planners everywhere, but it has two major weaknesses. First, primary health care is more than the mere extension of basic health services. It has social and developmental dimensions which are far more important. Social goals like the improvement of the quality of life and maximum health benefits for the greatest number should determine the direction of health services and not high-technology care for the chosen few. Social goals are usually attained through social means. Acceptance of greater responsibility by communities and individuals for their own health and their active participation in attaining it will open the way for achieving these social goals. Secondly, a preferential allocation of resources to the social periphery in order to overcome years of neglect and to satisfy their essential needs is now urgent in most countries. True national development revolves round this crucial issue. Just as economic development helps to achieve social goals, so also is social development necessary for economic progress.

In the next chapter the weak links in the existing health programmes of countries are discussed and ways and means of strengthening them are considered.

Further reading

Ebrahim, G. J. (1981). *Pediatric Practice in Developing Countries*. Macmillan Press, Basingstoke and London.
Ebrahim, G. J. (1979). *Care of the Newborn in Developing Countries*. Macmillan Press, Basingstoke and London.
Ebrahim, G. J. (1978). *Practical Mother and Child Health in Developing Countries*. Macmillan Press, Basingstoke and London.

Ebrahim, G. J. (1983). *Nutrition in Mother and Child Health*. Macmillan Press, Basingstoke and London.

Gwatkin, D. R., Wilcox, J. R. and Wray, J. D. (1980). *Can Health and Nutrition Interventions Made a Difference?* Overseas Development Council, Washington. Monograph No. 13.

Morley, D. C. (1973). *Pediatric Priorities in Developing Countries*. Butterworths, London.

Morley, D. and Woodland, M. (1979). *See How They Grow: Monitoring Child Growth for Appropriate Care in Developing Countries*. Macmillan Press, London and Basingstoke.

Pacey, A. (ed.) (1978). *Sanitation in Developing Countries*. John Wiley & Sons, Chichester.

Walt, G. and Vaughan, P. (1981). *An Introduction to the Primary Health Care Approach in Developing Countries*. Ross Institute, London. Publication No. 13.

6 Crucial Issues in Reaching the Poor with Health Services

During the last two decades all developing countries have invested large sums of money in building the health infrastructures and in training programmes, and yet the impact on the overall health situation has been marginal. Some of the reasons for this failure have been considered on pages 49–50. Coverage with health services continues to remain low in most countries of the Third World. The gap between existing medical knowledge and the health needs of the poor remains difficult to bridge, because of the weakness or even absence of several vital links in the existing systems of delivery of health care. The deficiencies in the formulation of health policies and the resulting disparities in health activities are described on page 15. There are similar defects in training programmes, and the following statement of the revolutionary committee of the Shanghai First Medical College reporting on medical education prior to 1966 has a ring of truth for many medical schools in the developing world:

'Under its decayed system . . . were trained so-called "first-rate" doctors who were divorced from proletarian politics; divorced from the workers, peasants and soldiers; and divorced from practice—bourgeois intellec-tual aristocrats who rode over the working people and thought of nothing else than personal fame, wealth and position. It ignored the 500 million peasants and served only the cities. The curriculum required students to study as long as 6 or even 8 years but after graduation they were unable to treat even the most frequently encountered diseases. . . . Students concentrated all their energies on the treatment of rare diseases and difficult cases, and were oblivious of the commonly seen diseases that most affect the working people.'

A major tenet of the primary health care approach is that the existing inequalities in health are unacceptable, and that health services need to be reorganised to serve all people. In achieving that objective, communities have a crucial role to play. Besides being involved in designing, implementing and evaluating health activities, it is also desirable that health care at the level of the community should be provided by persons from within the community. But moving beyond the rhetoric into practicalities is difficult for a number of reasons. First, hospital services aggravate the logistical and financial problems of primary health care services by siphoning off the drugs and supplies available, as well as the best staff. Since in-patients usually have more acute and serious illnesses, the needs of the hospital services are considered paramount. Secondly, the training of the medical personnel may not prepare them for understanding the true problems of the poor: that geographical distance means also being peripheral to available services; that being on the social fringe also means denial of basic needs and services; and that poverty is made worse by the appropriation of developmental tools and resources by the local power groups, rarely enters into the training of the district medical officer. There is little scientific awareness of the fact that in the statistics of mortality and morbidity being so painstakingly collected, it is the poor and their families who largely show up. Thirdly, setting up a primary health care structure means establishing numerous service points at the periphery, all requiring continuous support in terms of essential drugs, regular training, organisation of community groups and so on. The start-up is always easy but service delivery flounders from lack of support on account of dependence on vehicles and fuel, poor road conditions, and geographic terrain. Besides, in most developing countries the management capabilities within the health services are weak to begin with. Hence the building up of support capabilities must precede service delivery programmes. To take the analogy of the industrial sector (as first developed on page 25), in many developing countries large industrial complexes have been imposed from above by political leaders impatient for results and copying the surface appearance of Western economies but ignoring the process by which they were arrived at. Similarly, large tertiary-care hospitals have been built on the pattern of the affluent societies but ignoring the fact that much of the health development in the West stems from adequate nutrition, hygiene, water and sanitation, education and availability of primary care services.

Some of the more important deficiencies in the organisation of health care in developing countries, and the weak or missing links in the existing health system, are further considered below.

Faulty assumptions in health planning

Much of the organisation and planning of health care systems in the past has been based on the following assumptions:

(1) More and more curative services will assure improved health. This fallacy has now been sufficiently exposed.
(2) Only highly trained manpower can deliver good care.
(3) Medical activity is independent of such activities as community organisa-

tion and participation, agriculture improvement, development and protection of water resources, child care centres, school health, women's clubs, and other similar activities. Such an integrated approach is yet to become common.

(4) A hospital-centred system focusing on disease can solve the problem of community health.

In many cases the *inherent fallacies* of the above approach have become apparent, but change has been found to be difficult. The reasons are that programmes based on such assumptions have been put into effect, institutions have been built and administrative channels developed and above all a tradition has been implanted, so that a reversal of the process can be achieved only with great difficulty. New approaches and ideas arising out of the evaluation of present programmes of community health care will have to be grafted on the health system, and a re-thinking is necessary at all levels of medical administration. The training institutions are thus faced with the challenge of creating programmes of training relevant to the nation's problems and needs in the face of entrenched traditions.

Lack of resident staff at village level

The greatest weakness of all existing patterns is the lack of health personnel resident in each village or community group, and who are part of the entire system. A dispensary looking after a population of 10 000 people is in effect looking after five or six villages with an average distance of 1–8 km (0.5–5 miles) from one another. This means a large area to be covered—approximately 60–75 km² (23–30 miles²)—on foot or bicycle. This is not always possible. It stands to reason that in each village there should be a person resident in the community who can act as a health scout and promoter. He will be able to provide relief or treatment for most common illnesses on the spot, and at the same time will be the community's agent for liaising with the health service personnel. It is important that this person be a part of the village community—selected by them and recompensed by the community for the services he renders. It is unlikely that such a person will be able to earn his livelihood entirely from the health work that he does in the village. Hence such work is done on a part-time basis and the rest of the time he or she carries on with the usual work as a full participant in the social and economic life of the village.

This concept has been developed in an effective manner in the Chinese system of delivery of health care in the form of the '*barefoot doctor*'. Several experiments in other countries have shown that such a concept is feasible. Thus in Guatemala various persons selected by rural communities have been trained as health promoters and are able to make a contribution to the health of the community after a short period of training lasting 4–6 months. In a village health programme near Bombay, it has been shown that 'part-time social workers' can be trained to do extension work in the MCH programme of the area. Sudan and Indonesia have been training indigenous midwives in aseptic techniques and recognition of complications for several years. Recently Tanzania has commenced a programme for training village MCH aides who will be resident in '*Ujamaa*' villages and provide on-the-spot health care as well as participating in various health programmes as they apply to the village community. There are several variations on the same theme, but all point to the feasibility of the concept and its usefulness in making a health impact on the community.

Besides providing emergency care for the episodes of illness in the community, the resident health workers should organise and run the antenatal and under-5s clinics in the village in co-operation with visiting staff from the local dispensary; participate in campaigns of immunisation, of mass treatments, and of chlorination of water; notify communicable diseases; issue a supply of drugs in cases of tuberculosis and leprosy every month under guidance from the dispensary; gather health information; act as a health scout in the community; and mobilise the community for participation in health activities. Such a person will be the driving force for health activities related to promotion and monitoring of growth, oral rehydration, breast feeding and immunisation (GOBI) at the level of the village or neighbourhood.

Since a large proportion of morbidity in rural areas is caused by a small number of diseases, the diagnostic and therapeutic knowledge required of the health worker is not very extensive. It is suggested that the village health worker should be knowledgeable in the use of the following drugs:

(1) Aspirin.
(2) Sulfa drugs.
(3) Iron and vitamins.
(4) Antimalarials.
(5) Vermifuges (chiefly piperazine and bephenium).
(6) Anti-tuberculosis and anti-leprosy drugs (to be issued only under instructions from the local dispensary).
(7) Antibiotic eye ointment and local antiseptic preparations.

The village or community health worker (VHW) is the visible outcome of primary health care activity. As countries have launched national plans for primary health care, a number of schemes for training VHWs have come into existence. With more experience, the initial enthusiasm is being tempered with caution concerning the tasks the VHWs can undertake, their selection, methods of remuneration and training. After visiting nearly 40 rural health projects in nine Latin American countries, David Werner, the author of *Where There is No Doctor* expressed his misgivings in a thought-provoking paper

entitled *The Village Health Worker: Lackey or Liberator?* In his experience
external factors rather than intrinsic elements of training or recruitment
largely influenced the performance of the VHWs. Programmes which were
committed to making communities self-reliant and genuinely encouraged
responsibility, initiative and decision-making were able to bring out the best
among the VHWs compared with programmes which were paternalistic in
outlook and authoritarian. Sadly, in his experience most of the government-
sponsored programmes fell into the latter 'community oppressive' category
(see figure 6.1).

Political factors will unquestionably constitute a decisive element in
whether the VHW becomes part of a community supportive programme. This
is as much true for local level community politics as for national politics.
Medical politics are also part of the overall scepticism surrounding the
question whether the 'barefoot doctor' concept is exportable. Long-term
experience with community-based health programmes has shown that like the
medical auxiliary, the VHWs are necessary in their own right, and not as a
matter of expediency.

The VHW is part of the local network of extension workers for bringing
scientific knowledge and appropriate technology to the local community.
Ideally she has regular contacts with the upper echelons of the health service to
whom she refers patients beyond her competence to manage and from whom
she receives patients below their competence for looking after. She has a
horizontal relationship with the local birth attendant and the traditional
healer. She is one of them, except for her special training to deal with specific
problems. She has an angular relationship with agricultural extension

Figure 6.1   The village health worker: lackey or liberator?
            Source: Werner, D. *Where There is No Doctor*. Macmillan, London and
            Basingstoke. 1985.

workers, school teachers, and auxiliary sanitarians. Such a network of local relationships is the essence of community-based health development.

The VHW has essentially a dual role. That concerning the health of the families is mainly curative with some promotion and motivation. Her curative work is related to the treatment of common illnesses and thereby she reduces the danger of ignorant selection of medicines which her neighbour is going to buy anyhow. The role with regard to the community is mainly preventive/promotive like monitoring the growth of children, oral rehydration, promotion of breast feeding, motivating families to make use of immunisation campaigns, hygiene and sanitation within the home, and the care of water resources. Her 'core' training should have the following elements:

(1) *Communication*—The art of motivating people.
(2) *Food*—What to grow, what local foods are best value, and recognition of undernutrition.
(3) *Water*—Care of water resources, storage of water in the home, oral rehydration.
(4) *Cleanliness*—Food care, personal cleanliness, waste disposal.
(5) *Family health*—Care during pregnancy and labour. Child spacing, tetanus prevention, support of breast feeding, good weaning.
(6) *Control and treatment of common illnesses*—Malaria, diarrhoea, worms, immunisation, tuberculosis/leprosy.

For such grass-root workers, continuous training and support are as important as initial training. With the above definition of the role of the village (or community) health worker and her training, it is now possible to consider the place of the VHW and the TBA *vis-à-vis* the professional in caring for the poor. This is set out under different headings in table 6.1.

Inadequate use of the health auxiliary

Many countries have yet to develop a system of auxiliary health personnel. Thus in India, the Philippines, Indonesia, the Middle East and almost all of South America there is no cadre equivalent to the Medical Assistant and the Rural Medical Aide found in some of the African countries. In all the countries mentioned, medical education has been concentrated on the training of professionals, and it has been assumed that the laws of supply and demand will tend gradually to push the professionals into rural areas. This has not occurred and the trained professional prefers to live on a meagre income in urban cities or even emigrate rather than go to work in the villages.

Obviously, many of the community health problems of rural areas do not require diagnostic and therapeutic skills as much as those of management, administration and communication. With adequate training and proper supervision the auxiliary is able to implement health programmes effectively.

Table 6.1 **The role of the professional and the village health worker in caring for the poor**

The professional	*The community health worker*
Class background	
Usually from the upper social class	From amongst the poor
Residence	
Usually in a city. Visits the village (or community) at intervals by vehicular transport. Rarely spends the night in the locality	Long-term resident of the area
How chosen	
By the training institution on the basis of academic grade	By the community on the basis of compassion and willingness to help others
Training	
Mainly institutional, concentrating on technology. Highly qualified to diagnose and treat individual cases; interested in rare illnesses. Less interested in the everyday common ailments. Poorly qualified in communication with the poor and the illiterate	Intimate knowledge of the community, the language and the customs. Training mainly experimental. Good at communicating with the people. Not qualifieid to deal with uncommon problems
Primary interest	
Largely professional—the challenging cases. Often bored by common ailments	Helping people resolve their health problems because they are neighbours and friends
Attitude towards the sick	
Paternalistic; creates dependency	Treats patients as equals, because selected by the community
Attitude of the sick towards him	
Hold him in awe. Know he charges heavily	See him as friend and feel free to question him
How he uses his knowledge	
Hoards it; keeps patient dependent	Shares it; generates self-reliance
Accessibility	
Not easily accessible to the poor	Very accessible. Lives in their midst
Relative permanence	
Is always looking for promotion	Permanent member of the community
Cost-effectiveness	
Too expensive for the meagre resources of the poor. Requires expensive facilities and equipment. Drains resources of the community	Low cost. Operate from own home. Helps the community to use its resources more effectively

Source: Adapted from Werner, D. *Wld. Hlth. Forum* (1981) **2**: 52–4

Proper identification of the roles of the various health institutions like the dispensary, the sub-centre, the health centre and the district hospital in the overall system of delivery of health care is necessary in order to define the roles of the health personnel who work in these institutions. A job description of this nature is necessary for evolving relevant training programmes for the auxiliary and the professional. In the absence of such an approach, the training of the auxiliary becomes a watered-down replica of the curriculum of the professional, which itself is inappropriate in many cases.

The above statement on proper identification of the role of the health institutions and job description of the health personnel presupposes good administration and management of the service. But in practice there are several administrative flaws, so that health centres without doctors, or dispensaries without drugs, are common occurrences. The service provided by such institutions becomes irregular and the public loses confidence in the capability of the institutions.

The existing social imbalance in many of the developing countries

As we have seen, many of the developing countries have two levels of society—the *urban élite* with all the available facilities and benefits of modern civilisation and the *rural masses* who do not have even the basic requirements like food and clean water. The former group produces the professionals, the technicians, and key personnel who implement the programmes of the country. Very often the administrator does not have any knowledge of the workings of the rural society of his country. Under such an imbalance a larger proportion of the resources of the country are consumed by the urban population. Furthermore, there exists a tendency for any new inputs to be divided disproportionately, unless a special effort is made to effect a more equitable distribution.

One can carry the same reasoning down to smaller social groups like villages. If there exists any stratification in the society and the existing tradition and culture supports such stratification (e.g. the caste system), then it is likely that new inputs in any discipline would be distributed in a disproportionate manner so that the underprivileged groups get very little benefit from it. The cycle of deprivation is perpetuated from one generation to another and the deprived groups may receive virtually no benefits from new programmes, unless special care is exercised to divert the effort towards them. The 19 villages study in India (mentioned on page 86) found that irrespective of the range and activities in rural development all programmes were mostly mediated and controlled by the privileged classes. By controlling the public distribution system for commodities such as food grains, sugar, kerosene, cement, fertiliser, high-yielding variety of seeds and credit facilities, the upper class derived considerable profit and political leverage. Relief work in the form of construction of roads or housing got them remunerative contracts, and governmental expenditure for strengthening the irrigation system was usually manipulated to improve agricultural production and marketing by the upper-class landowners. Such a powerful grip of the affluent classes over almost all the facets of the lives of a substantial section of the population is the most outstanding feature of all social interaction in most of Latin America, several countries of tropical Africa and in south-east Asia. The rural élites command votes from the poor which in turn are used to strike bargains with the politicians for the issue of licences and monopolies.

The health service is part of the other services in the society and is subjected to the same social forces that control the benefits accruing to different social groups. Even in a country like Britain, where a National Health Service has been in operation for more than 30 years and the sick have a right to free access to health care, irrespective of class and income, it has been found that the 'social class gradient increases with successive censuses, so that in 1959–63 the standardised mortality ratio for social class I is half that of social class V' (Registrar-General, 1961, 1971). More recently it was shown that for 49 out of 85 separate causes of death applying to men, and for 54 out of 87 applying to women, standardised mortality ratios for social classes IV and V were higher than those for I and II. If the mortality experience of social class I had applied to social class V during the period 1959–63, only just over half of the reported deaths would have occurred and 40 000 lives would have been spared during that 5-year period.

There is a need for most service programmes including those of health development to be made accountable to the people rather than to distant supervisors and administrators.

Within such a framework of imbalance, primary health care activities aim to focus on the needy and to ensure that their basic health needs are provided. Caring for the poor requires not only increased health awakening in the disadvantaged but also an awareness amongst the planners and the providers of care that all services are largely monopolised by the élite. A shift in emphasis is needed to get the objective right before committing any further resources. Without such a reappraisal of objectives, all new inputs will only end up with benefiting the rich. The direction of the transformation needed at the various levels of health planning can be determined by asking certain fundamental questions, as indicated in table 6.2 below.

Lack of community involvement

It is not unusual to find that the village community considers health services as part of the government administrative system and as something imposed on them by an 'outside' authority. The lack of communication between health

Table 6.2 **Essential changes needed in health planning**

	Present	Shift of emphasis	To this
Who are served?	The urban élite and the upper social classes → in the rural areas	Increasing coverage of the rural and urban poor →	Equal accessibility of care for all with emphasis on the needy
Who are the grass-roots of the services?	Professionals and → specialists	Increasing localisation →	Village health workers, trained birth attendants and auxiliaries
Where is the main emphasis in health programmes?	Intensive and → sophisticated care in centres of excellence	Alleviating the → effects of malnutrition and infection	Improving nutrition, environmental sanitation, immunisation, oral rehydration, care of vulnerable groups
How is health care provided?	Through hospitals →	Health centres and smaller units →	Inside the home in villages and shanty towns
What are the main health interventions?	Curative →	Preventive/ promotive →	Comprehensive care ensuring that basic health needs are met
Where is training carried out?	In urban teaching hospitals →	Teaching/learning in the community →	Amongst the disadvantaged with emphasis on diseases of poverty
What is the coverage in health?	<20 per cent	→	>80 per cent

personnel and the villagers, together with the social, cultural and educational gaps between them, often leads to alienation of the people. Traditional methods based on superstition and indigenous practitioners are preferred, even though they may be more expensive.

In order to overcome mistrust and alienation and to create a sense of pride and belonging, active involvement of the community is necessary. Community leaders, elected and traditional, should be invited to participate in the formulation, implementation and evaluation of programmes. Such involvement may also help in mobilising community resources which may supplement the efforts of the health workers. Thus, village improvement schemes, digging of wells or the improvement of existing ones, nutrition rehabilitation programmes, day-care centres, school vegetable gardens, mass campaigns etc. can all benefit from a spirit of self-help in the community. When the village community has helped to build institutions and to create facilities, they are more likely to make use of them on a regular basis, and to register dissatisfaction if these do not meet their expectations.

Several issues concerning community participation have been discussed in Chapter 5 on page 150. It was pointed out that these issues address themselves to the important questions of who is doing the choosing, how the choices are enforced, and whether the health programme considers participation mainly as the means for achieving health objectives or as the end i.e. a true end-result to be achieved. Successful community organisations are usually the ones where people have a voice in their running, and which can ensure equitable distribution of benefits. Many such community structures are understandably fragile to begin with and can only grow in strength by gaining experience. Organisation patterns created for one project will provide the basis and the stimulus for other projects when the first one succeeds.

It is now being increasingly realised that all community programmes should involve the total care of the community and not be restricted to only health or any one single aspect. Health programmes provide many entry points into the community and afford opportunities for establishing rapport with the rural folk and for gaining their confidence. They form the basis for the introduction of other programmes, like improved agriculture and food production, education, home improvements, and the general upliftment of rural life.

A common mistake has been to seek the involvement of the community only at the stage of implementation, so that the people feel that they are being asked to carry out schemes imposed by an outside agency which has no insight into their real problems and thus lose the feeling of pulling together. The tendency that the professional knows best has been the cause of failure in many a programme. In the words of Julius Nyerere of Tanzania, 'to plan is to choose [from alternatives]'; the main contribution of the professional is in the technical implementation of programmes selected by the people themselves.

Community participation is usually through their elected leaders. All rural communities have established methods of selecting their leaders or 'elders'. Even where democratic processes of selection exist, e.g. selection of the Gram Panchayat in India, there may also exist a parallel system of traditional leaders, e.g. the Jati or Caste Panchayat. Thus the socio-political life of the community may show a dichotomy between the two systems: the traditional and the secular – modern. The leaders in the two systems of organisation are not necessarily the same. Traditional leaders may not always be successful in elections. None the less, their influence on the decision-making process is important. In all such community councils, it is important to see that the socially underprivileged groups are well represented. Such persons are immigrants into the area who may be employed as landless agricultural labourers or as serfs (as among the Burundi immigrants in Baganda), persons of a social status traditionally considered low (e.g. the Harijans in India), or women, who by tradition are often not allowed an active part in the political life of the community.

The village council may not be able to administer all the various aspects of a programme and should be encouraged to evolve a social and administrative framework for the supervision of various activities. Thus women's clubs, youth clubs, parent–teacher associations and farmers' clubs are useful devices for the sharing of responsibilities.

Felt needs and real needs

In any discussion with village communities the gap between felt and real needs soon becomes apparent. The professional is more concerned with the health of the people, but this may hold a low priority for the community. Their abiding interest is the day-to-day toil on the land to earn a livelihood. Agriculture, water for the crops, the welfare of the cattle, etc. may be foremost in the minds of the people. This is understandable. In places where each mouthful of food has to be wrested from the land, it is only natural that the growing of food crops is most important to the people. Many programmes of community health have felt the need for including various extension activities as well, depending upon the needs of the community, so that the objective becomes the overall improvement of rural life. This, of course, meets the additional difficulty of resistance to change, because not only attitudes to health but the entire life style of rural communities is bound in tradition.

In introducing changes in rural societies, the following principles should be observed:

(1) All innovations should be simple and within the technical competence and economic resources of the community.
(2) All local initiative should be supported and encouraged.
(3) The aim should be to utilise existing structure, whether administrative or buildings, and strengthen this structure with a view to inducing growth in the system.
(4) Training of personnel and the education of the people is as important as the delivery of service.
(5) There should be regular evaluation by the community and a regular feedback of the information so obtained in order to bring about necessary changes in the programme.

Assigning priorities in health

In assigning priorities to the community's health problems, account is taken of the true and felt needs, the community's concern about a particular problem, the vulnerability of the disease to available measures, and the cost. Various methods are described of assigning scores to each of these criteria and of calculating the final score. On the basis of the total score the problem may then be given a high or low priority rating. The Ministry of Health in Tanzania has prepared a list of the main health problems of the country by using such a method of scoring, which is shown in table 6.3.

Table 6.3 **Disease priorities in the health programme of Tanzania**

Problem	Vulnera-bility	Magni-tude	Impor-tance	Cost	Total score	Rank
Pneumonia	3	3	2	2	36	2
Malaria	2	3	3	1	18	4
Diarrhoea	3	3	3	3	81	1
Tuberculosis	3	3	2	2	36	2
Defective nutrition	3	3	3	3	81	1
Measles	3	3	3	1	27	3
Diseases of the heart	1	2	1	1	2	8
Maternal deaths	3	2	2	3	36	2
Accidents	3	2	2	2	24	3
Venereal diseases	1	2	2	2	8	6
Schistosomiasis	1	2	2	1	4	7
Leprosy	2	2	2	2	16	5
Hookworm	3	3	3	3	81	1
Onchocerciasis	2	2	1	1	4	7
Tetanus	3	2	2	3	36	2

Methods of community involvement

Self-help schemes—Many countries have now had long experience with self-help schemes in rural areas. It is agreed that when communities have helped to build institutions and to create facilities they are more likely to use them on a regular basis. Self-help projects have hitherto been directed towards construction—the building of health centres and sub-centres, schools, roads, and occasionally irrigation projects. Recently, this principle has been used in agricultural extension programmes where new varieties of grain are grown on land belonging to the village, by voluntary labour, making use of fertilisers or new agricultural techniques.

Payment of fees—There is a general tendency not to appreciate what comes free. Hence in many instances small registration fees are charged for a child to be registered at the under-5s clinic, or a mother to be registered at the antenatal clinic. In some cases such fees are used as payment for record cards with the result that such cards are lost less frequently. In some clinics a portion of the fee is refunded at subsequent visits, with a resultant improvement in repeat attendances for immunisations, etc. In some cases the fees are paid into a village improvement fund under the administration of the village government.

Partnership in projects—The village community makes a part contribution to a project and as such becomes committed to its success.

Commitment of individuals on account of credit facilities made available to them through the interventions of the health projects.

Lack of fundamental concepts in the operational framework of the health institutions

The various health institutions in the district health service act as autonomous institutions carrying out a limited amount of curative and preventive functions. The concepts depicted in the model of district health services (see page 97) are non-existent, with the result that most health centres have become extensions of hospital out-patient departments, and the health personnel spend a large proportion of their time on curative medicine on a basis of episodic care.

The important epidemiologic concepts regarding reservoirs of a disease in the community are also missing, so that whereas the affected individual may receive treatment, the reservoir in the community remains unchanged. Mass campaigns in immunisation and chemotherapy are not undertaken, and no active effort is made at case finding in the community for diseases like tuberculosis and leprosy.

Regular health supervision of vulnerable groups with a view to identifying those 'at risk' is virtually non-existent. It is taken for granted that the creation of such surveillance services as antenatal clinics and the under-5s clinic will lead to a maximum number of people making use of them, and that the very act of operating such services will in itself make a health impact. The minimum requirement for such clinics to make a measurable improvement in health indices is not taken into consideration.

Absence of 'at risk' consultations

An important reason for regular health surveillance of vulnerable groups is to identify those at risk of illness and for whom routine care is not adequate.

Social, health and other community resources need to be mobilised for the well-being of such individuals. In many cases intensive health education or home visiting may be necessary for such families. In a rural child care programme at Palghar, near Bombay, it was found that two-thirds of deaths in children under the age of 5 years occurred among those in the 'at risk' category. Similarly, in Britain, the 2nd National Study on Morbidity Statistics from General Practice, 1970–71, found that among those consulting their general practitioners, two-thirds were from among those who can be defined as 'at risk'. Clearly there is a need for all health institutions to maintain a register of those 'at risk' in the communities they serve, and the 'at risk' meetings are necessary not only at the level of each individual institution but also at the level of the entire district. They not only help in identifying problem families but can also provide a clue to the kind of social services required.

Lack of a system for gathering and utilising health statistics

In most developing countries there is no system for regular measurement of the impact of the health services on the community. Even though it is customary for dispensaries and health centres to send regular returns to the district health office, the collection of such information is never supervised, so that even ministries of health consider all their vital statistics as estimates rather than a reflection of the true state of affairs. There may even be a paradox in that the health information from an area is forwarded to the provincial and national headquarters and gets compiled into statistics, but the district health team remains totally unaware of the true health status of the communities they are serving.

The trend has been to concentrate largely on data that would enable the calculation of mortality and morbidity in different age groups. The complexity of data processing has been found discouraging by the majority of health workers in national health services. A great deal of useful information can be obtained by concentrating on selected indicators instead of hard statistical data. In this respect indicators are to be looked upon as indirect or partial measures of a complex situation. When they are measured sequentially over a period of time they indicate the direction and speed of change. For example, the proportion of infants born with a low birth weight is a useful indicator of the health and nutritional status of pregnant women, and the trend over a period of time will provide a measure of the effectiveness of prenatal care services.

In all programmes aimed at improving the situation of the poor it is essential that one should be continually measuring the degree of equity in health status and services. Indicators like the proportion without basic health care, lack of adequate water and sanitation, literacy and school enrolment, proportion of infants born with a low birth weight and prevalence of malnutrition in young children or anaemia amongst women, help in assessing the degree to which inequity has been corrected. Similarly, an assessment of the effectiveness of the mechanisms created for the poor to express their needs, and the level of their involvement in decision-making, can provide the measure of the participation of the poor in decision-making.

A fundamental issue in health care is that of accessibility of health services to the poor—geographically, economically and socially. Hence it is necessary to be vigilant about monitoring the availability of essential drugs (see page 158) and primary health care services within the community at all times. Secondly, to assess whether services for antenatal care, under-5s care and for immunisation are available regularly and whether facilities exist for delivery care all the time. Thirdly, first-level referral services should be available within 1 hour's travel time for all. It is not unusual to find that creating equity in health care is not merely a matter of extending coverage by involving communities or training village and community health workers, but that a more fundamental structural change is needed in the existing services.

In a community-based health programme the workers at the grass-roots level should also be trained to gather information which will enable them to interpret health events in the context of the physical and socio-cultural environment in which they occur. A good knowledge of the current situation of the people and their environment coupled with what goes on—the health events—is usually adequate for such 'barefoot epidemiology'. As mentioned earlier, these grass-root workers are to be looked upon more as agents of change than as 'mini-doctors'. If they can relate health events to the situation, work patterns and life styles of their communities they will be able to appreciate the significance of the various determinants of health in their communities. They should be trained and encouraged to gather information on:

(1) The situation of the community, e.g. the total number; the demographic pattern; the occupations of various family groups; the different social groups; the common practices and life styles.
(2) The environment—e.g. the natural environment of geography, seasons and climate as well as their effects on health patterns and work; the soil, crops and animals; housing, water and disposal of waste; the common vectors and animal hosts of disease; the social environment, like local political, economic and social activities.
(3) The vital events like births, deaths, illnesses, accidents and changes in social and economic status.
(4) What people do, e.g. marriages, divorces, family crises and so on.

In their regular meetings with the community and village health workers the supervisors should be concerned not only with updating knowledge but also must focus the discussion on questions such as:

(1) What can be done to reduce a given problem and its consequence?
(2) How can it be prevented in the future?
(3) What actions should be taken by the community? By the health service? By other sectors? Which groups are at greatest risk and for whom these activities should be carried out?
(4) What resources are needed? How are the activities to be organised?
(5) What should be the role of the community health worker?
(6) What difficulties may be anticipated and how might they be overcome?

Health needs are not always solely met by the health system. A great deal of intervention at the grass-root level requires an intersectoral approach. The framework for an integrated approach is best laid by considering questions like the above in group discussions and in meetings with the community.

Much of the present discrepancy and waste of effort in national health systems can be corrected by devising a simple *system of data collection* along the following lines:

(1) A tally system at all under-5s and antenatal clinics in the district to show the number of new attenders and repeat attenders according to the number of visits made in the year. Such a system is currently in use in Tanzania.
(2) A tally system to indicate the various immunisations given in each clinic and the infectious illnesses diagnosed at the clinic (see figure 6.2).
(3) The data from the above tallies should be analysed at regular intervals, monthly or quarterly, and discussed by the health team with a view to bringing about modifications and improvement in the health activities.
(4) Similarly, a data sheet of vital events can be provided to all community health workers (see figure 6.3).
(5) Maintenance of 'at risk' lists at each sub-centre or health-post (indicating the particulars of the 'at risk' individuals in the villages served), at the health centres (indicating the 'at risk' individuals at each health-post area served by the health centre and also particulars of the 'at risk' individuals in the population regularly attending the health centre), and at the district hospital.
(6) Regular surveys in the community for evaluating the acceptance of health care. Such surveys need not be elaborate statistical exercises but simple enquiries which can often be carried out by a team of secondary school children with a few health workers. In these enquiries, randomly selected homes in a village are visited and the number of pre-school children, pregnant women and sick persons in the household are noted. In the case of pregnant women and children, a further enquiry is made into whether a clinic card is available, and if so the number of visits made to the clinic and the immunisations given are noted. In the case of the sick person, whether the services of the dispensary or health centre have been utilised is noted. In this way one part of the community—the schools—help in the

ILLNESSES DIAGNOSED

CHILDREN	MALNUTRITION	00000 00000 00000 00000 00000	00000 00000 00000 00000 00000	00000 00000 00000 00000 00000	00000 00000 00000 00000 00000	00000 00000 00000 00000 00000	00000 00000 00000 00000 00000	00000 00000 00000 00000 00000	Total
	DIARRHOEA	00000 00000	00000 00000	00000 00000	00000 00000	00000 00000	00000 00000	00000 00000	
	MEASLES	00000	00000	00000	00000	00000	00000	00000	
	'AT RISK'	00000 00000	00000 00000	00000 00000	00000 00000	00000 00000	00000 00000	00000 00000	
MOTHERS	RAISED BLOOD PRESSURE	00000	00000	00000	00000	00000	00000	00000	
	ANAEMIA	00000	00000	00000	00000	00000	00000	00000	
	FIRST ATTENDANCE IN THIRD TRIMESTER	00000	00000	00000	00000	00000	00000	00000	
	'AT RISK'	00000	00000	00000	00000	00000	00000	00000	

IMMUNIZATION

CHILDREN	BCG	00000 00000	00000 00000	00000 00000	00000 00000	00000 00000	00000 00000	00000 00000	00000 00000	Total
	SMALLPOX	00000 00000	00000 00000	00000 00000	00000 00000	00000 00000	00000 00000	00000 00000	00000 00000	
		1st Injection			2nd Injection			3rd Injection		
	DPT	00000 00000 00000 00000 00000	00000 00000 00000 00000 00000	Total	00000 00000 00000 00000 00000	00000 00000 00000 00000 00000	Total	00000 00000 00000 00000 00000	00000 00000 00000 00000 00000	Total
		1st Dose			2nd Dose			3rd Dose		
	POLIO	00000 00000 00000 00000 00000	00000 00000 00000 00000 00000	Total	00000 00000 00000 00000 00000	00000 00000 00000 00000 00000	Total	00000 00000 00000 00000 00000	00000 00000 00000 00000 00000	Total
	MEASLES	00000	00000	00000	00000	00000	00000	00000	00000	
MOTHERS		1st Injection			2nd Injection			3rd Injection		
	TETANUS	00000 00000 00000 00000 00000	00000 00000 00000 00000 00000	Total	00000 00000 00000 00000 00000	00000 00000 00000 00000 00000	Total	00000 00000 00000 00000 00000	00000 00000 00000 00000 00000	Total

Figure 6.2 The tally system as used in Tanzania.

assessment of acceptance of health care by the community, and the findings can be discussed in joint meetings between the health workers and the community leaders.

What you have seen	Cases	Total	What you have seen	Cases
Kwashiorkor	○○○○○ ○○○○○ / ○○○○○ ○○○○○		Off breast before walking	○○○○○ ○○○○○ / ○○○○○ ○○○○○
Marasmus	○○○○○ ○○○○○ / ○○○○○ ○○○○○			
Measles	○○○○○ ○○○○○ / ○○○○○ ○○○○○		Second ANC visit	○○○○○ ○○○○○ / ○○○○○ ○○○○○
Whooping Cough	○○○○○ ○○○○○ / ○○○○○ ○○○○○		Deliveries assisted	○○○○○ ○○○○○ / ○○○○○ ○○○○○
Eye Infection	○○○○○ ○○○○○ / ○○○○○ ○○○○○		Births	○○○○○ ○○○○○ / ○○○○○ ○○○○○
Skin Problems	○○○○○ ○○○○○ / ○○○○○ ○○○○○		Deaths under one year	○○○○○ ○○○○○ / ○○○○○ ○○○○○
Diarrhoea	○○○○○ ○○○○○ / ○○○○○ ○○○○○		New Latrines	○○○○○ ○○○○○ / ○○○○○ ○○○○○

Figure 6.3   Data sheet for the village health workers.

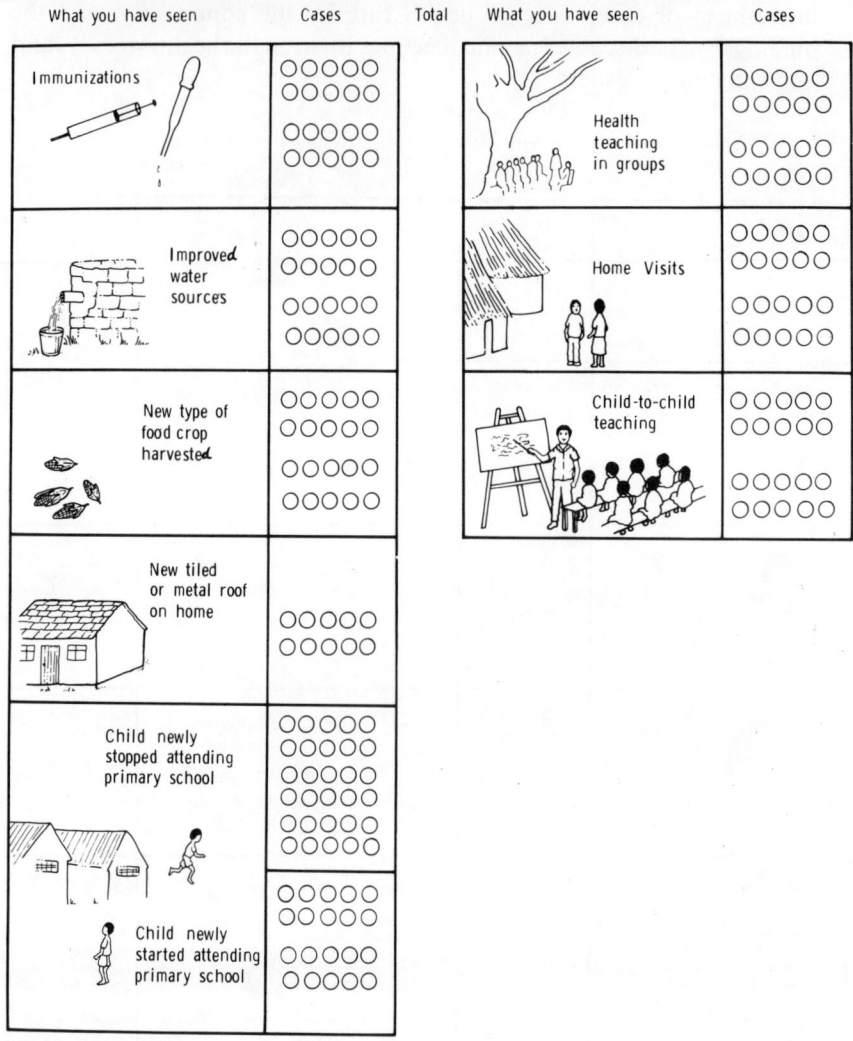

Figure 6.3 (continued)

For continous monitoring of health programmes and assessing their effectiveness, basic epidemiologic tools should be available at all health facilities. These are:

(1) Maps to indicate where health events commonly occur, and where those at special risk may be found.
(2) Population data—including demographic and social profile and the major community and social structures like health committees, youth

clubs, women's groups, etc. together with the names of those taking leading roles in the activities.

(3) Diaries of health events.
(4) Time charts and graphs where possible.
(5) Results of community surveys carried out in previous years.
(6) List of 'at risk' families and data compiled from tally sheets described above.

'Medical audit' of community health programmes

It is agreed that in the present state of medical knowledge and technology, it should be possible to prevent almost all the major illnesses afflicting the disadvantaged communities of the developing world. The means to apply this knowledge and technology to benefit the masses are developing into health programmes reaching out to communities through a health infrastructure. However, several crucial goals still remain to be achieved. The success of each health programme revolves round these goals and is in direct proportion to the extent to which they have been met. These are:

(1) A strong and effective management component in the health organisation of the district, so that all the different units operate as one integral whole rather than as autonomous institutions. Any efficient management system requires regular problem analysis, evaluation of programmes and techniques, analysis of resources and measurement of results. In the organisation of health services, collection of health information and its analysis in relation to health problems is vital to good management and planning.
(2) Unreserved acceptance of health programmes by the community. It is obvious that utilisation of health services by the community on a regular basis is important for producing any measurable impact on the health situation and yet in programme evaluation this factor is rarely taken into account. Most systems for collection of health data are preoccupied with collection of information on morbidity and mortality patterns and virtually no information is collected about utilisation of services. Lack of such information make the management of health programmes ineffective.

It is suggested that in addition to collection of the usual health data, there should be a regular 'audit' of all health programmes to assess the utilisation of services by the community.

From the management point of view, such an 'audit' will be of greater use than the conventional methods of assessing benefits. For example, if the impact of a nutrition programme is to be assessed, the conventional method will be to carry out a cross-sectional anthropometric survey before and after the institution of the programme and to subject the data to statistical analysis—a major undertaking beyond the means of the ordinary district health service. On the other hand, one knows that the impact of applied nutrition programmes depends upon the type of nutrition education provided and the techniques used, the proportion of target population reached and, in the final analysis, on the improvement in the food intake of the average individual. This can be expressed as a formula:

Effectiveness of the programme = applied nutrition activity × per cent target population reached × improved nutrition intake

From the medical audit point of view, the smaller the percentage of the target population covered, the less is the impact. On the other hand, even with a good programme and full coverage of the target population, if there is no change in the daily nutritional intake of the average child, the programme is unsuccessful. A similar argument is used to produce the following formulae as further examples of measuring the effectiveness of health programmes:

Provision of clean water

Effectiveness = technology used × number of wells protected × percentage population ingesting clean water

With available technology it is possible to provide 90 per cent protection of the well-water, but if only a few wells are so treated, or if the people do not use the water from 'safe' wells, the programme will be ineffective. On the other hand, even if all wells in the area were made safe but the water became contaminated during storage, the effectiveness of the programme would be undermined.

Tuberculosis control

Effectiveness = technology × (susceptibles protected + reservoir of infection treated) × co-operation

As regards the technology, both BCG and anti-tuberculosis drugs can provide protection rates of 80 per cent and more. It is possible to protect 75–80 per cent of pre-school children in a district with mass campaigns, but the most difficult factor is adequate coverage of the reservoir of infection in the community. It is estimated that less than half the sputum-positive cases in an area are being diagnosed; furthermore there is poor patient co-operation with chemotherapy, so that of those diagnosed and put on to treatment, only 30 per cent complete the full course of treatment. At the present rate, the effectiveness as regards the treatment of the reservoir of infection is $0.8 \times 0.5 \times 0.3 = 0.12$, or only 10–12 per cent.

Health needs and the utilisation of health services

The health needs of the community and the use of health services will vary from one place to another, depending upon the environmental and living conditions, the occupation, and the cultural attitudes towards health. Very few studies of health needs in quantitative terms have been made on disadvantaged communities, and most of the time the plight of the poor remains excluded from the consciousness of those in government bureaucracies with the power to act. However, it is now generally recognised that a large proportion of the statistics on mortality and morbidity come from amongst the disadvantaged.

Table 6.4   **Causes and symptoms, from Indian health centre villages**

Cause and prominent symptoms	1966 (%)	1967 (%)	1968 (%)	1969 (%)
Violence or injury	3.7	4.1	4.3	3.5
Diarrhoea	11.1	9.7	9.4	9.2
Childbirth and complicated pregnancy	1.5	1.4	1.3	1.3
Coughs	26.5	23.8	24.6	24.5
Swellings	7.4	7.2	8.0	8.0
Fevers	21.4	22.0	19.4	20.6
Other infant deaths	9.6	11.1	11.0	11.1
Other clear symptoms	4.8	5.0	5.2	5.0
Miscellaneous, including extreme old age	14.0	15.7	16.8	16.8

The Registrar-General's office in India has been carrying out sample surveys of causes of death in rural areas by using enumerators who record all health events in health centre villages. Data recorded from 786 health centre villages with a total population of 2.3 million show very little change in the health picture from 1966 to 1969 (see table 6.4). These causes arranged in descending order of importance and according to the age of the individual show the following distribution (see table 6.5).

These data provide an indication of the service needs in the rural community and the curative workload of the most peripheral unit. They also help to determine the range of therapeutic agents which should be made available to the rural health institutions for providing relief of symptoms and cure, as well as the knowledge and skill attributes of the persons working in the rural community.

Table 6.5   **Causes of mortality in various age groups (in years) in rural India (1967)**

Cause	Total (%)	0–1	1–4	5–14	15–34	35–54	Over 55
Coughs	5145 (24.5)	833	928	266	371	798	1949
Fevers	4315 (20.6)	534	1280	577	446	739	939
Other infant deaths	2326 (11.1)	2326	—	—	—	—	—
Diarrhoea	1929 (9.2)	320	605	235	154	191	424
Swellings	1666 (8.0)	45	176	86	176	390	793
Other clear symptoms	1058 (5.0)	299	88	54	79	142	383
Violence or injury	736 (3.5)	18	56	140	252	160	110
Childbirth and complicated pregnancy	276 (1.3)	—	—	—	205	71	—
Miscellaneous, including extreme old age	3513 (16.8)	85	394	88	159	187	2600

Mother and child health workload

The workload for maternal and child care is easier to estimate than demands for curative services. In many countries a sub-centre is expected to cater for the needs of 10 000 people, and the following estimates are based on that number.

In a population group of 10 000, the following vital events can be expected:

Births at the rate of 40/1000 population	400
Stillbirths at the rate of 25/1000 live births	12
Neonatal mortality at the rate of 40/1000 live births	16
Total pregnancies approximately	428

At the infant mortality rate of 120/1000, 30 infant deaths can be expected every year. The morbidity may be 3–4 times the mortality figures, hence 90–120 serious infant illnesses may be expected. The under 1 year population forms 2.5 per cent of the total population. Therefore 250 infants would require regular health supervision. The 1–5 years age group comprises 12 per cent of the population. Therefore 1250 children in the age range 1–5 years require regular health supervision. The 1–5 years' mortality has been estimated at 62/1000 live births. Hence 30–40 illnesses of children in the age group 1–5 resulting in death can be expected, and the morbidity in this age group may be estimated at 3–4 times the above numbers.

Thus the MCH workload on the smallest unit, the sub-centre, is relatively high. If to this were added other functions like control of communicable diseases and provision of clean water over a geographical area covering 7–10 villages, it is likely that the resources would be stretched considerably. Hence the need for the implementation of priority interventions in growth monitoring, oral rehydration, breast feeding and immunisation (GOBI) in all communities, and for enabling the people to become the prime movers in the development of their own health.

In conclusion, this chapter identifies a number of crucial issues in the development of health services for the poor. Just having a variety of interventions as outlined in the preceding chapter is not enough. There is a need for integration between the different aspects of the health services, a need for integration between different sectors like agriculture, water development, education and social services with health programmes and a linking up of the primary health care activities with the higher echelons of the health services for adequate back-up. The extent to which such an objective is achieved will depend upon the quality of management, and on the epidemiological approach in health planning. Accessibility of services and adequate coverage together with full mobilisation of the people to receive the services and mould them in accordance with their needs will largely determine the effectiveness of the health programme.

Further reading

Mandl, P. E. (ed.) (1983). A child survival and development revolution. *Assign. Child.* **61/62**: 11–281.

World Health Organization (1981). *Development of Indicators for Monitoring Progress Towards Health for all by the Year 2000*. WHO, Geneva.

World Health Organization (1981). *Health Programme Evaluation*. WHO, Geneva.

World Health Organization (1974). *New Approaches in Health Statistics. Technical Report Series No. 559*. WHO, Geneva.

World Health Organization (1982). *The Place of Epidemiology in Local Health Work. Offset Publication No. 70*. WHO, Geneva.

7 Health Care for the Urban Poor

Growth of large urban conurbations is a relatively recent phenomenon. Before 1850 no nation was fully urbanised and at the beginning of this century there was only one, namely Britain. Today most industrial nations of Western Europe and North America as well as Japan are in effect urbanised societies and there is remarkable urban growth occurring in many less developed countries. On present trends it is estimated that by the year 2000 over half the people of the world will be residing in cities with populations of 100 000 or more (see figure 7.1).

Because of the rapidity of urbanisation, sociological studies of the urban community are relatively few. Several fundamental questions need answers. How will a species that has evolved during hundreds of millenia in small communities and rural settlements adapt to existence in huge dense agglomerations? The background to man's religious and cultural heritage is

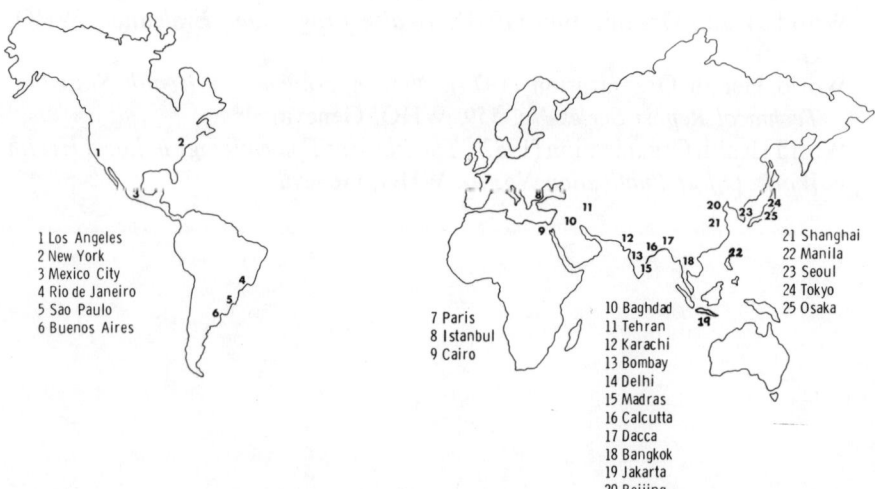

1 Los Angeles		21 Shanghai
2 New York		22 Manila
3 Mexico City		23 Seoul
4 Rio de Janeiro		24 Tokyo
5 Sao Paulo	7 Paris	10 Baghdad	25 Osaka
6 Buenos Aires	8 Istanbul	11 Tehran
	9 Cairo	12 Karachi
		13 Bombay
		14 Delhi
		15 Madras
		16 Calcutta
		17 Dacca
		18 Bangkok
		19 Jakarta
		20 Beijing

Figure 7.1   Cities with projected populations of over 10 million in the year 2000.

overwhelmingly rural. Besides cultural adaptation there are also problems of physical conditioning. The change has been too rapid for the process of natural selection to occur, and the adaptive process between man and cities consists mainly of physical alterations in the cities. The more complex the technology for adapting to city life, the larger have the cities grown, and the more elaborate have become the techniques needed to adjust them to man.

During the growth of many of the cities in the Western industrial world there was a phase of high morbidity and mortality amongst their populations compared with the countryside. The townsfolk were more exposed to disease because of living in close proximity, because of unhygienic surroundings, because of trade and travel (e.g. cholera in London), and because the cities provided the opportunity for multiplication of pests and vectors (e.g. the black death), and on account of pollution of food and drink. It is only since the beginning of the present century, and in some cases the post-war period, that death rates in Western industrial cities have dropped to their present levels.

Urbanisation in the developing world

In the developing world rapid population growth has created a process of hyperurbanisation. Since 1950, in the case of 171 developing countries the population living in cities of 100 000 and above has grown by 67 per cent per decade, doubling over 13 or so years! During the same period the population in rural areas has grown by 16 per cent per decade, outstripping the capacity of the cities to absorb immigrants from the countryside. Therefore, when the new migrants come, they live a peripheral existence unable to participate in the economic, political and social life of the cities. This phenomenon has resulted in the sprawling shanty towns, the *barriadas* and *favellas* of the cities. Compared with the so-called modern urban sector with its orderly life of municipal authorities, the police and other civic services, in the shanty towns there is a life of exploitation, violence and crime with street gangs, bullies and

Table 7.1 **Proportion of urban population and projected increase in 109 developing countries, 1980 to the year 2000**

Proportion urban population (%)	1980 No. (%) countries	2000 No. (%) countries
0–25	*41 (37)*	*19 (17)*
26–50	*38 (35)*	*32 (29)*
51–75	*22 (20)*	*42 (38)*
Over 75	*8 (7)*	*16 (15)*

extortionists holding sway. In many cities of the Third World slum dwellers and squatters already represent between 40 and 60 per cent of the population. It is estimated that in Delhi, Calcutta and Madras, up to 40 per cent of the city population consists of squatters, and for India as a whole, 20–30 per cent of the total urban population consists of squatters. This is equally true for several developing countries. A study of 109 such countries in 1980 showed that for 22 of them (20 per cent) more than half the population was already urban. This number is expected to increase to 42 (39 per cent) by the year 2000 at present rates of population growth and the number of countries with over half of their population in urban areas will have doubled (see table 7.1).

Unprecedented urban growth has come to be the dominant demographic feature, particularly in Latin America (see table 7.2).

Table 7.2   **Growth of cities in the developing world**

Population	No. of cities		Projected increase
(million)	1980	2000	(%)
>1	118	284	140
>5	16	45	181

Most of the urban growth in the developing world (an estimated 1.2 billion people in the last quarter of this century) is likely to be in the form of the urban poor or 'the marginals' thereby creating another unprecedented social phenomenon—marked growth in the number of the urban poor (see table 7.3).

Measuring health and welfare

The above data indicate that the cities of the developing world will be called upon to absorb around 70 per cent of the projected population increase of Asia, Africa and Latin America, and the welfare of the urban poor will be of particular concern to health planners. The health status of the populations of many developing countries today is no better than that of nineteenth-century Europe, and the quality of life in some rural and urban groups is even worse. It has been recently suggested that vital statistics, however useful, do not project a full measure of the quality of life and welfare enjoyed by a population and instead the Physical Quality of Life Index (PQLI) has been suggested as a more adequate measure as described on page 33.

There are very few studies carried out amongst the urban poor but the

Table 7.3 **Proportion of squatters and slum dwellers in selected cities**

Region and city	Year	Population (thousands)	Squatters and slum dwellers (thousands)	Percentage squatters and slum dwellers
		Africa		
Addis Ababa	1981	1200	948	79
Casablanca	1971	1506	1054	70
Kinshasa	1969	1288	733	60
Nairobi	1970	535	177	33
Dakar	1969	500	150	30
		Latin America		
Bogota	1969	2294	1376	60
Buenos Aires	1970	2972	1486	50
Mexico City	1966	3287	1500	46
Caracas	1974	2369	1000	42
Lima	1970	2877	1148	40
Rio de Janeiro	1970	4855	1456	30
Santiago	1964	2184	546	25
		South Asia		
Calcutta	1971	8000	5328	67
Bombay	1971	6000	2475	41
Delhi	1970	3877	1400	36
Dacca	1973	1700	300	35
Karachi	1971	3428	800	23
		East Asia		
Manila	1972	4400	1540	35
Pusan	1969	1675	527	31
Seoul	1969	4600	1320	29
Jakarta	1972	4576	1190	26
Bangkok	1970	3041	600	20
Hong Kong	1969	3617	600	17

indications are that the PQLI in the squatter settlements is likely to be very low. Several studies indicate that even though immigration into the cities is largely in search of jobs, the modern urban sector does not employ more than 5 per cent of its regular labour force from amongst the squatter areas. The urban poor generate their own sources of livelihood engaging in small-scale retail trade (street vendors, pavement stores, food and drink stands), transport (taxis, rickshaws, porters, handcarts), personal services (house servants, laundry, shoe-shine), refuse collection (dustmen, night-soil collection, sweepers), security services (car park or bicycle stand attendants, night watchmen), casual labour or dealing in contraband. Many of the major cities of the developing world report infant mortality rates of between 75 and 90 per thousand births, but amongst the urban poor these rates are far higher. In the *bustees* of New Delhi the overall child mortality rate (0–5 years) is 221 per

1000 children, but reaches twice that number amongst certain castes. In the city of Manila, the infant mortality rate is three times higher in the slums compared with the rest of the city. In the same study the rates for tuberculosis per 100 000 population were nine times higher and diarrhoea twice as common as in the rest of the city. Twice as many people were found to be anaemic and three times as many were suffering from malnutrition as compared with the rest of the city.

Urban poverty largely caused by the overflow of rural poverty into cities

The unrelieved poverty in most developing countries is in some degree due to the pattern of economic growth. During the period 1960 to 1980 Third World average life expectancy went up by 10 years; birth rates fell by 20 per cent; literacy rose by 30–50 per cent. Per capita food production has been roughly stable in the past 30 years and the population increase of some 1500 million during the period has been matched by increases in agricultural productivity and by new land brought under production. But the progress has not been uniform and there are differences between regions, between countries within the same region and between population groups within individual countries. There are still 50 developing countries where 15 per cent or more of the population are officially designated as malnourished. In 14 African countries agricultural production has lagged behind the growth of population. The pattern of industrial growth in the developing world has been such that it has been largely capital intensive and has not significantly increased employment. However, the most pervasive influence has been of the way that national resources and power are distributed. According to a UN survey of 83 countries, approximately 3 per cent of all landlords have come to control almost 80 per cent of the land. Another measure of inequality is the access to credit. In many countries only 5–20 per cent of all producers have access to institutional credit. The rest must turn to landlords and money-lenders. Whenever governments have pursued strategies that have ignored the issue of control of production they have set in motion a chain of events which worsens the plight of the poor. The introduction of new agricultural technology has largely favoured the big farmer. In India, the percentage of work force that is landless has doubled since the Green Revolution. In north-west Mexico, the birthplace of the Green Revolution, the average farm size has jumped from 200 to 2000 acres with over three-quarters of the rural labour force now deprived of any land at all. In Brazil large estates control over 43 per cent of the farmland.

Developments and conditions as described above have resulted in dispossessed families moving to the cities in search of livelihoods. By now several generations have been born and have grown up in circumstances of urban poverty. A recent UN study has shown that natural increase is responsible for an average of 61 per cent of urban population growth in developing countries compared with only 39 per cent from rural migration. In spite of living in the city for a considerable number of years the urban poor lack the necessary knowledge and skills to perform effectively in a modern city. Moreover, the existing social and commercial systems often operate against them, leading to their exclusion from service and welfare programmes. A vast majority live a precarious existence. In Lima's Cono Sur shanty town, 53.6 per cent of the population have to depend on their own initiatives to earn their living. The wage-earners who constitute 37.4 per cent have an average monthly income of US $50 and a third earn less than US $30. Naturally, the nutritional status is poor and virtually 60 per cent of the community are malnourished, on account of their inability to meet even 80 per cent of their caloric requirements. More than three-quarters are living below the bread line. Only 7 per cent of families have running water in their homes, 72 per cent obtain water from standpipes or public fountains and another 21 per cent rely on private water trucks. Another measure of precarious livelihood in Cono Sur is the quality of the environment. In the absence of services, 195 tons of solid waste have to be disposed of daily, commonly by tipping at the periphery of the inhabited area, thus creating vast piles of refuse and litter and a proliferation of insects, rodents and scavenging dogs. The home environment is equally poor with low rates of female literacy and little stimulation or education of children at home. The ground is well set for creating intergenerational transmission of disadvantage. The above description is typical of slums elsewhere and provides a measure of the precariousness of the lives of people who live in them.

Inner city areas of the industrial world

Cities of the affluent industrial world, having been through similar experiences as described above, are facing a different set of problems. The major challenge is provision of services in the inner city areas. Many of the hospitals and other services were originally founded in populous working-class areas where there were sufficient patients to justify the existence of a large expensive hospital. The patients have moved away from the city centres to the peripheral suburbs but the city hospitals have not followed. In fact, up until the mid-1970s many were still undergoing expensive modernisation even though denuded of their clientele. The migration of the young skilled workers from the city centres has left an unbalanced population structure with a high concentration of the poor, the old, and the vulnerable groups like single-parent families, the psychiatrically disturbed, the homeless, those addicted to drugs and alcohol. Amongst this residual population of inner city areas, rates of illegitimacy, stillbirth, perinatal and infant mortality are high. There is also a high prevalence of sexually transmitted diseases and of mental illness.

Common health problems of the urban poor in the developing world

The presence of a large number of susceptible human hosts living in overcrowded circumstances in the septic fringes of the cities creates an ideal situation for epidemics of infective illness and for reservoirs of infective illness to build up. In the slums of industrial London in the nineteenth century a common illness and cause of prolonged debility leading to pauperism was the pyrexia of typhus. Such outbreaks have not yet been described largely on account of the very few and episodic contacts between the urban poor and the formal health services. But the stage is set because of severe overcrowding, poor personal hygiene due to lack of washing facilities, and susceptibility of the host. On the other hand, epidemics of dengue haemorrhagic fever and increased transmission of filariasis have occurred. These vector-borne diseases have been associated with the need of each individual household to store water in iron drums or large earthenware containers leading to the breeding of *A. egypti*. At the same time the accumulation of waste water in pools and puddles around the settlements favours the breeding of *C. fatigans* which is the vector that transmits filariasis. Old scourges like tuberculosis and leprosy continue to be a problem together with nutritional disorders and sexually transmitted diseases. New dangers are likely to arise. In the overcrowded settlements where several thousand live cheek by jowl there is the ever-present danger of meningococcal meningitis. In many of the squatter areas of Latin America the incidence of leishmaniasis has been rising, and several cases of rabies are being reported each year, both of which are due to the presence of a large number of

Figure 7.2   A squatter area in Bangkok.

stray dogs scavenging in the garbage heaps and the ubiquitous litter that surrounds the settlements.

In one study of a large slum in Bombay, half the number of families surveyed reported some major illness during the previous year. The most common complaint was diarrhoea and other gastro-intestinal disorders (19 per cent) and one in ten were reported to be suffering from tuberculosis. The degree of environmental contamination was measured in one study from Jakarta in which cultures were made from specimens of water obtained from a river running through a residential area, from open drains, roadside puddles, riverside wells and ice lollies being sold in the street to schoolchildren. A large number of micro-organisms were found including enteric pathogens, like *Salmonella typhii*, *Shigelle flexner* and *Escherichia coli*. The high bacterial counts, in the range of 3.1×10^4/ml to 3.6×10^7/ml, indicate the degree of environmental contamination. In some specimens the river water contained a density of bacterial population of the same order as in the gut. Such heavy environmental contamination leads to microbial contamination of the gut and oropharyngeal secretions as reported in several studies, and is responsible for a high incidence of diarrhoeal disease. The heavy build-up of a susceptible population with poor hygiene and a contaminated environment (see figure 7.2) has largely been responsible for the recent epidemics of cholera that swept through parts of Asia, Africa and Latin America. As a result, cholera has now become endemic in some countries such as the Philippines, Bangladesh, India and Indonesia. Another recent epidemic illness has been dengue haemorrhagic fever (DHF). Conditions are ideal for outbreaks of a variety of communicable diseases. All that is needed is the introduction of an infective agent, a vector or an intermediate host. Thus there is an urgent need to improve the living conditions and the quality of the physical environment together with facilities for basic health care in order to avoid future epidemics of transmissible illness.

High prevalence rates of preventable infections in children like measles, whooping cough and polio reflect the very low levels of health facilities for the urban poor. Both measles and whooping cough are highly infectious and spread rapidly in communities where overcrowding in the home is such that a family of six shares a small living and sleeping space separated by a flimsy partition made from a mat or plywood from similar families next door. Adequate coverage with immunisation is a priority in such overcrowded communities. Failure to provide such elementary health care is an example of the antipathy with which city health planners view the urban poor.

Malnutrition, the most pervasive symptom of urban poverty

Even though a large proportion of the urban poor left their rural homes because they could not support themselves and their families, the city has changed their lot very little. Between 40 and 60 per cent of the children under the age of 5 in the *bustees* of Delhi show evidence of malnutrition. More than 90 per cent of the squatter families cannot afford a balanced diet in spite of spending more than 80 per cent of their earnings on the purchase of food. When more than two-thirds of an income goes on food, there is little room for being selective. Satisfaction of hunger is the prime need. This leaves little for fuel, rent, clothing and other necessities including education of children, bearing in mind that when individuals or families spend more than half their income on food for obtaining calories, they are customarily defined as poor. Such economic necessity requires all adults to find work including the women. Seventy per cent of the women workers in the *bustees* of Delhi indicated that their earnings go almost entirely towards the purchase of food for the family. When both parents go out to work there are no facilities for the care of children and it is a rare employer who would allow the worker to bring along a child. Forty per cent of the women in the *bustees* of Delhi said they left their children by themselves at home. Infant and child feeding becomes more difficult under such circumstances and the young infant is usually left in the care of an older sibling who offers feeds from a bottle or out of leftovers from the previous day. In a study of families of 100 malnourished children in Jamaica it was found that total family income in the case of 98 per cent was so low that to bottle feed a child adequately would take up half of it, not counting the price of the bottle, the utensils and the fuel for sterilisation.

For most countries it can be said that the poor are seduced into spending a disproportionate amount of their incomes on powdered milk, canned baby foods and similar items at the expense of the more needed and readily available common foods. The presence of large numbers of illiterate and gullible people new to the ways of city life is looked upon as a large untapped market by the baby-food industry. All varieties of seductive persuasion that the imagination of the advertising industry can provide have been let loose on them, resulting in a marked decline in traditional infant-feeding practices. Attempts by governments and civic groups to control the advertising and intensive promotion of baby foods have been thwarted by the manufacturers who point out the sanctity of free trade. The dividing line between free trade and free for all may be narrow and sometimes indistinguishable in societies where democracy has few roots in the cultural and political heritage.

In the meantime, infant feeding practices have changed to an incredible extent amongst the urban poor. Condensed milk, barley water, and aerated soft drinks are used instead of breast milk or even some other form of milk and traditional weaning foods (see figure 7.3). The result has been a rising incidence of blinding malnutrition (xerophthalmia) and marasmus. It is believed that every year some 250 000 children go blind on account of xerophthalmia, chiefly in the countries of south-east Asia. A large proportion of these are the children of the urban poor. In the harsh environment of poverty the blind child has very poor chances of survival. Various studies have shown that between 30 and 40 per cent die within 6 months of discharge from

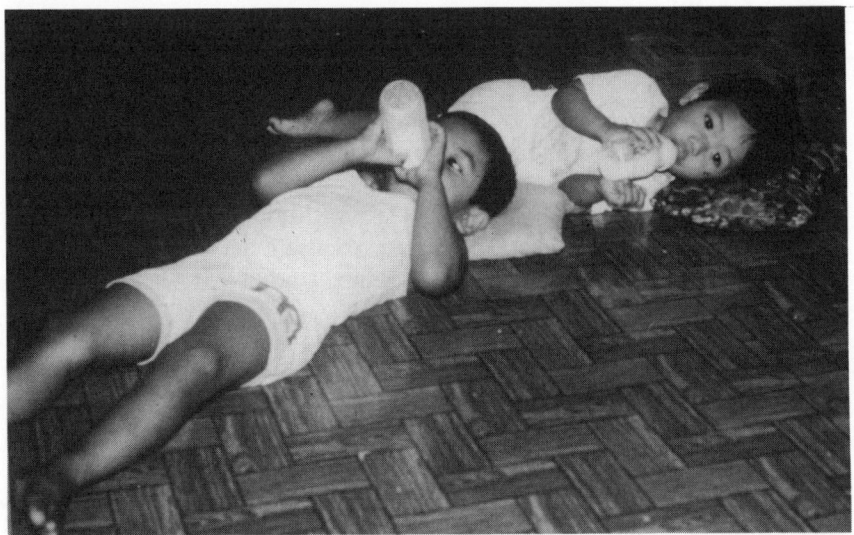

Figure 7.3   Bottle feeding in a squatter area.

hospital. With regard to marasmus, the average age of onset of this severe form of malnutrition has dropped from 18 months to 8 months during the past two decades.

Considering that the brain is the most rapidly growing organ of the body in the first 2 years and that the effect of an environmental insult is most critical on a rapidly growing organ, intellectual stunting is one of the most dreaded sequelae of marasmus. When we take into account the large number of infants being affected by marasmus in the slums and shanty towns there is a danger of creating a permanent under-class of second-rate citizens who will lack the mental capabilities for entering occupations requiring learning and skills.

The rise in commerciogenic malnutrition can be largely ascribed to the fact that the only nutritional or consumer information the urban poor receive is in the form of commercial advertising. In the move to the city the urban poor have lost much of the traditions and customs which encouraged sharing of food resources, however meagre. The complex network of reciprocal obligations between the farmers and the landless helped in the ritual sharing of food after harvest and during festivities. In the crowded city there is also no access to land where vegetables or fruits may be grown. Even though these may not satisfy hunger, they are important sources of nutrients. A handful of amaranth (a form of spinach) leaves, a few carrots, three tomatoes or a slice of pawpaw can provide the daily requirements of vitamin A for a young child. In the chaotic existence of the crowded squatter areas there is no place to call one's own and no possibility of any horticulture. The urban life style imposes an urban economy on the migrants. Everything has to be budgeted for both in terms of time and money, and then purchased in small quantities daily since there is no storage space for food and fuel in the overcrowded shack. The prices paid for such small purchases in the local shops are usually higher than those paid by the more affluent citizens for bulk purchases in the supermarkets. The urban poor tend to rely on ready-made or easy-to-prepare foods. Thus bakery-made bread is preferred to tortillas, and hot-dogs to a traditional meal. Such foods are more expensive and less nutritious. Moreover, in the city there is a wide variety of such unaccustomed foods on sale and it is difficult for the urban poor to choose wisely unless helped to do so.

Water and sanitation, a major need of the urban poor

All the large cities of the developing world are suffering from an acute shortage of water. All the schemes for bringing in more water to the cities suffer from basic in-built inequities so that the more vocal and politically effective élite sector is preferred and the needs of the urban poor get overlooked. Many of the world's largest cities are seaports and underground water is usually not suitable on account of high salinity. Hence water must be pumped over long distances at great costs. In those cases where underground water is suitable, over-pumping over several decades has led to marked and at times disastrous exploitation of the aquifers. Bangkok and Mexico City are both experiencing this problem with many wells running dry and the ground in some areas subsiding.

In many large cities water runs in the mains for a specified number of hours daily. Most dwellings in the modern urban sector are constructed with an underground reservoir which fills when the mains run. The water is then pumped to overhead tanks from which the occupants receive their almost continuous supply. Most residents in the élite sector have rarely experienced shortages and are often unaware of the situation in the squatter areas. Water planning for metropolitan areas makes a distinction between 'primary' and 'secondary' networks. 'Primary' refers to larger pipes carrying water to whole communities and 'secondary' to the network of smaller pipes within the district. In most forms of planning the main brief is for the primary network, and here distribution to squatter areas is rarely specified. Similarly, secondary distribution usually runs along a social gradient and the low-income families tend to be excluded. Thus metropolitan water development projects are mainly responsive to the needs of the modern urban and commercial sectors and millions of families amongst the squatter areas are left to buy water by the tin or pail from water sellers at several times the price paid by the more affluent citizens (see figure 7.4).

Water drainage suffers from the same biases so that squatter settlements

Figure 7.4   The water queue.

tend to have a pervasive smell caused by stagnant water with decomposing household waste. Flooding during heavy rains often carries this highly polluted water into homes in the low-lying parts of the settlements. Part of the sense of exclusion so common amongst squatter families is because of lack of facilities for washing. They know that their dirty clothing and malodorous bodies sets them apart from other social groups. This is especially so for schoolchildren and youths.

The above description is one of a chaotic existence where every day is a struggle for obtaining the basic human needs of shelter, food and water. It is also a description of life on the margin and of exclusion from full participation in the commercial and civic life of the cities. Continuous stress and ostracism breeds alienation, especially where conspicuous consumption lives alongside with destitution. In the slums of Hyderabad, India, 33 per cent of the families studied were without basic services like water, latrines, drainage and bathing facilities. The community was totally disorganised and only 28 per cent could name a local leader. The most common felt needs were for public water taps, street lighting, unblocked sewers and drains and for dustbins to be emptied more frequently. Several families asked for repairs to roads and lanes, provision of public latrines, pest control to counter the large number of rats and cockroaches, mosquito spraying and social amenities or health facilities for women and children.

Appropriate health care for squatter settlements—what do the urban poor need?

Until recently the planners and housers appeared convinced that slums bred the well-known pathologies associated with poverty, and attempted to change the behaviour of the poor by tearing down slums and scattering the inhabitants all over the city. The bulldozing of slums became an obsession with political leaders in several countries. It soon became clear that the so-called urban renewal did nothing but move slum dwellers into other slums. For decades slum dwellers had been saying in country after country that what they needed were more jobs, better wages, more low-cost housing and the basic necessities of life, and not just slum clearance. It was not until they began to oppose urban renewal and then to rebel and riot that the town planners began to take notice of them.

The urban planner largely plans for himself and his peers. He also plans bearing in mind the requirements of the politicians, the business and civic leaders who sit on planning committees. For them and for the planners the ideal city is the one that is good for business and for ownership of property. The urban planner is also planning on the basis of his class culture which is far removed from the culture of poverty.

Planners and bureaucrats often forget that the urban poor suffer not only from economic problems but also from the social and cultural breakdowns that accompany poverty. Alcoholism, family strife, vice and violence are part of life of the urban poor. These pathologies are the by-products of the culture of poverty and are ways of adapting to poverty. City planners are more concerned with downtown residential areas, roads and parks as well as shopping areas which will bring out shoppers in large numbers and attract business. The culture of poverty concerns them only very fleetingly.

So much of medical pathology arises out of social pathology that it would be futile to address the problem of health care without considering the social, economic and physical environments. For example, income-generating activities, adequate and well-enforced minimum wage, job training programmes for the youth, facilities for the care of unmarried mothers, abandoned families, the old and the handicapped are all part of the programme for integrated health care.

This is particularly true for maternal and child health services whose main preoccupation in squatter areas is to devise ways and means of ensuring the health of the family, providing support and counselling during periods of stress and helping to hold the family together at times of family crises. It is the lack of such supportive networks that has resulted in one problem of growing concern in many large cities—the abandonment of women and children. The severing of the extended family and similar social institutions initiated by the move to the city, lack of friends, unemployment, poverty and destitution leading to despair and frustration, are the combined factors that cause family break-up. It is almost always the male head of the household who leaves home first, abandoning the wife to be the sole supporter of her children. With little or no education, and with a full day's housework load already on her hands, and in despair, it is little surprising that the woman is forced to fend for herself. Children drift away or get pushed out and there is a vicious build-up of social pathology. UNICEF estimates that there may be up to 40 million abandoned children in Latin America and the Caribbean. Perhaps abandonment of women and children has not yet become a major problem in the squatter settlements in Africa and Asia because of strong cultural traditions. But as several generations become born in environments of the squatter settlements and grow up knowing nothing better than what the culture of poverty brings, the trend is likely to increase.

Assuming that adequate health care can be organised for the urban poor in all countries, how can a health facility with its roots in a fee-for-service tradition become a force capable of holding together families which are buffeted by strong economic forces in an exploiting city? Surely the traditional nature of health services must change to face this new challenge, and the training of health workers must be modified to promote the required attitudes within the service? Far too many of the world's medical schools prepare doctors not to promote family health but to cure diseases and to do so by the application of increasingly expensive medical technology. Many systems of medical care and the insurance systems that help to support them are oriented towards in-patient hospital care rather than home care and self-care.

Urban health services—experiences in industrial countries

Many of the cities in Europe faced similar challenges during their periods of rapid growth and some of their experiences may be relevant to the problems of the growing cities of the developing world. For example, in Britain almost 92 per cent of the country's population is now urban and major developments in public health in this century took place with a predominantly urban background. The most relevant starting point for an examination of the present day National Health Service (NHS) in Britain is the Royal Commission on the Poor Laws and Relief of Distress which sat in 1909. The existing Poor Law institutions where two-thirds of the sick were being cared for in mixed workhouses were condemned as a public scandal. Poor Law infirmaries were understaffed, had become penal institutions instead of places of care and lacked elementary facilities. Many of the free hospitals in developing countries today cannot be very different from them. The majority and minority reports of the Commission raised between them all the issues which continued to be debated up until 1948 like, for example,

(1) Should a health service be comprehensive providing care for all types of illness and disability as well as prevention, or should some like psychiatric illness be excluded?
(2) Should the services be available to everyone or only to identifiable groups, e.g. those under a certain income limit?
(3) Should it be free when required and financed by some form of insurance and/or taxation, or should it depend on charges for services?
(4) How should the physicians, dentists, nurses and other professionals be paid?
(5) How should the service be administered locally and centrally?
(6) What part, if any, should the professional or academic bodies play in the administrative process?

Statesmen and political visionaries made important contributions to the conceptual processes which sustained the development of the NHS. For example, Lloyd George, one of the most brilliant statesmen in British history, described ill health as a primary cause of poverty and campaigned for National Health Insurance as an attack on poverty by means of cash payments during absence from work on account of sickness in parallel with old-age pensions. The National Health Insurance Bill of 1911 contributed greatly to the relief of poverty among manual workers during sickness and provided minimal care, though not to dependants. This was also the period when the passing of the Midwives Act (1902) had helped to rationalise midwifery care with predictable effects on maternity and neonatal care and on standards of midwifery. Infant Welfare Clinics were started as voluntary services in depressed urban areas. These clinics eventually led to the development and training of professional Health Visitors, and the passing of the Maternal and Child Welfare Act (1918) which made antenatal and young child care as statutory services to be provided by all local authorities. Thus the stage was set for a National Health Service even before the Beveridge Report (1942) which provided the conceptual base for the present-day service. The services as they exist now are centred on a single universal social security scheme which provides insurance against interruption of earning because of sickness, disability, old age, unemployment or injury. There were three basic assumptions made at the inception of the service as follows:

(1) Separate allowances will be paid for the maintenance of dependent children.
(2) Comprehensive health service free to all would be provided.
(3) National policy would be directed towards maintenance of employment and avoidance of mass unemployment.

From the very beginning the NHS has been criticised for not rising to expectations. Environmental services, housing, nutrition, and most preventive health measures have always been outside its scope. Some prevention, however, did come under its concern. Preventive measures for communicable diseases like tuberculosis, polio, sexually transmitted diseases and control through immunisation were applied through the NHS with remarkable success. The most striking characteristics of the emerging service have been:

(1) Its comprehensiveness embodying the existing health and allied services.
(2) Its availability for all. Together with a social insurance system such a health system provided an effective safeguard against destitution.
(3) Its free provision at the time of need.
(4) The growing concern to make the services accessible in all geographical areas and to all social groups.

Principles and concepts arising from the experience of Western Europe in provision of urban health services

Many countries of Western Europe have undergone similar experiences on their way to the development of the Welfare State. In fact, most of the major concepts in public health that have come out of the industrial West during the period 1900–75 are based on the experience of looking after the health of urban populations. The present state of public health in many of the larger cities like London, Paris and Amsterdam is largely a story of the struggle by the town to rid itself of squalor and disease and to provide jobs, homes, schools and medical care. As a result, large concentrations of population are able to live and work together with little detriment to health. Among the main contributions to this progress have been:

(1) Reduction of poverty and the consequent improvement in nutrition and in the provision of other material needs including housing. The central problem of public health at the beginning of this century was poverty. One in 38 of the London population was described as pauper in 1899. More than a quarter were children living in one-parent families. Medicine alone can do little to prevent disease and disability among the poor unless they are first raised out of poverty by social and economic measures. Social security schemes have largely enhanced the effect of health services.
(2) The development of adequate surveillance services appropriate for different vulnerable groups, e.g. Maternal and Child Health Services, School Health Services, Health Visiting and District Nurse Services, the General Practitioner services and so on. The bedrock of better infant care has always been the Health Visitor Service which provided a personal approach to education of the mothers in their homes.
(3) The provision of adequate curative services.
(4) Compulsory primary education which enabled the population to understand health education when it was provided. It had also the sound advantage of taking children out of factories or workshops and into schools.

(5) Absorption of social concepts into medical education so that medical technology came to be the hand-maiden of medical need and not vice versa.

These experiences project health care in a new light. Health services have become part of the process of social engineering to safeguard the weak and to protect them from the strong social and economic currents characteristic of urbanisation.

Concepts into practice—the problems

In parallel with the above development there has also occurred a remarkable growth in medical technology, especially for intensive care of the acutely ill. Large hospitals have been built to house this expensive technology and for the new specialist teaching programmes that have been evolved for the dissemination of this knowledge. Consequently new resources must be found to pay for improving health services for the rural areas and for the urban poor. Assuming that such resources can be mustered, there is every likelihood of competing demands between the hospitals and the peripheral services. The future role of the hospital as being a supportive base of community services, as a staging post for community health activities, and as a monitoring station for measuring changes in disease patterns within the community will need to be carefully worked out. Small, efficient units with flexibility are likely to be more effective than the prestigious ivory towers which sprang up all over the developing world during the last two decades. Thus the debate about the future role of hospitals will centre round two main issues—smaller units as against prestigious large hospitals; and secondly, the training of health workers to fulfil the new roles, e.g. more training in practical epidemiology, managerial techniques, behavioural and social sciences and skills in communication with the semi- or totally illiterate.

In particular, there is a need for developing methods of improving coverage with maternal and child health services, and to shift the emphasis of such services from diagnosis of the rare conditions to surveillance and counselling and to providing support to families during periods of stress and crises.

Concepts into practice—examples of practical application of principles in the urban communities of the developing world

Case Study 1: Hong Kong

The town of Kwun Tong is a new town east of Hong Kong's airport. Close to 700 000 people living in overcrowded industrial and dirty surroundings are responsible for the manufacture of a fifth of Hong Kong's products. A voluntary agency hospital with 580 beds serves the community. The hospital planning team, conscious of the fact that hospitals are not normally designed to influence the health of the surrounding communities, had decided from the outset on helping the community raise its level of health. It was the foremost objective of the planners. A four-pronged programme has been developed as follows:

(1) A system of health centres, each situated in the heart of a housing estate and with several thousand families living within a hundred metres. The health centres provide basic health and dental services and serve as staging posts for community health activities.

(2) Community nursing service to provide home nursing care for early discharge patients from hospital and for long-term illnesses. This service has effectively added 250 convalescent and long-term beds to the hospital bed strength. Besides carrying out home nursing procedures the community nurses have additional training to provide exercise therapy, family health education, social welfare counselling as well as training the volunteer health workers. The community nursing service has increased the outreach of the hospital into housing estates, squatter huts, houseboats anchored in the harbour, and into every conceivable human habitat.

(3) A variety of health maintenance programmes have been commenced, as follows:
(a) Infant health maintenance through monthly weighing and clinical check-up clinics, physical and psychomotor screening, counselling and easy access to curative services if needed;
(b) Schoolchild health maintenance through health screening, curative and dental services and health education;
(c) Adult programme which provides annual screening including laboratory tests and X-rays with special emphasis on reduction of excess weight, smoking, alcoholism, psychological stress and so on;
(d) A geriatric health maintenance programme which provides clubs for old people, medical screening and problems of old age.

Community health workers with a background of training in social work are attached to each of the above programmes. They motivate the people to accept more responsibility for their own health and encourage the formation of neighbourhood health committees, drama clubs, children's organisations, as well as activities like health weeks, and the training of community health volunteers.

(4) The hospital forges links with the community through its training programme. Each student nurse is assigned a family which she visits regularly throughout the 3 years of training. The observations and records of the students provide a useful feedback for the trainers and programme organisers.

Case Study 2: Manila

The Metropolitan Manila region was set up in 1975 by the government of the Philippines. The population of the city was organised into small community units of about 100 families each called *barangays*, and there are about 1800 such *barangays*. The existing community health centres and puericulture centres were integrated as primary health care units (PHCU) and about six *barangays* were allocated to each PHCU. Regular dialogue between the health personnel at the PHCU and the *barangay* residents was initiated to foster community involvement and participation. Four key health programmes were implemented at the PHCU as follows:

(1) Maternal care and family planning.
(2) Child care and nutrition.
(3) Control and treatment of infectious diseases.
(4) Environmental sanitation.

In-service training programmes for workers in the PHCU helped to improve their orientation and abilities to carry out the above activities. At the same time, through health education and information campaigns, people were encouraged to utilise their local health services.

Hospitals were encouraged to form linkages with their catchment area through appropriate service departments and through a reorganised training schedule for the interns.

Such developments are likely to occur in other cities of the Philippines and will create new roles and responsibilities for hospitals. It is recognised that besides the traditional role of providing patient care and of education and training of health personnel, hospitals will have to shift emphasis in research towards epidemiological and social aspects of disease pattern and health care in their catchment areas. Training programmes are being modified as a result of such research, and improved management of health services, especially in the *barangays*, is helping to overcome the phenomenon of by-pass of local facilities.

Case Study 3: Hyderabad, India

In the slums of old Hyderabad city about 60 000 people live in circumstances of near destitution; another 225 000 live in marginal existence and the remainder belong to the low middle class. Seventy per cent of the families have lived in the city since birth. Of these, 42 per cent have been living in the same locality. Sixty-two per cent of the women are illiterate and 71 per cent of the men have some basic education. The families are large and nuclear in character. Up to 44 per cent of the families have more than eight members. Incomes are low (Rs 300). Thirty-three per cent of the families are without basic services like water, latrines, drainage and washing facilities.

The main thrust of the Hyderabad Slum Project is towards social and environmental improvement together with economic development. The objective has been to provide for the immediate needs of the people and work towards long-term changes through people participation. In the past only tax collectors, rent collectors, sanitary inspectors or those canvassing for elections went about visiting homes and asking questions with the result that people did not trust outsiders. Immediate action on pressing problems like blocked drains, street lighting, water connections, helped to build rapport and trust. The main activities generated by the development project are:

(1) Environmental sanitation: provision of water and other physical improvements, e.g. repair of roads, street lighting and so on.
(2) Family health activities, such as (a) immunisation; (b) first aid and family health education; (c) cookery classes for obtaining the best buy in nutrition; (d) health surveillance of mothers and children; (e) eye care; and (f) family planning.
(3) Feeding programmes.
(4) Recreational and cultural activities and youth clubs.
(5) Educational activities, such as (a) play groups and primary schools; (b) night schools; (c) vocational training in the form of sewing classes, typing and shorthand classes, training in photography, radio repairs, car repairs, air conditioner and refrigerator servicing and so on; (d) study tours; (e) cultural activities like community festivals, variety shows, libraries and reading rooms, etc.
(6) Income-generating activities like dressmaking and other co-operatives, facilities for bank loans, etc.
(7) Construction of community halls and improvement of housing.

Many of these activities required active participation by the people as a basic requirement. The community in which previously only 28 per cent could name a local leader is now organised into a number of committees and self-help groups. Matching grants are provided for construction of community halls, community radio sets, charts and toys for play groups, musical instruments for variety shows and so on. Committees are formed to supervise the functioning of the play groups and for women's activities.

The Hyderabad Slum Project has demonstrated the importance of certain basic linkages in the upliftment of squatter communities:

(1) The integration of health with improvement of the physical environment through adequate water supply, drainage, paved lanes, and improved housing.
(2) Linking of slum communities with aid agencies and non-governmental organisations through the formation of local developmental committees, youth clubs, women's organisations and other social groups.
(3) The linking of the income-generating and other business activities in the slums with financial, commercial and industrial institutions in the formal sector of the urban economy.

Case study 4: Mexico City

The new town of Netzahualcoyoti houses between 1.8 and 2 million people. It grew up on the site of an old salt lake and so the land is largely unsuitable for agriculture. Lack of a proper system of garbage collection together with the common practice of open-air defaecation causes large-scale pollution, especially during dust storms which are seasonal. There is a high rate of unemployment; approximately 30 per cent adult men are unemployed. Being a dormitory city, there is very little local employment. For the same reason during the daytime the inhabitants are mainly women and children.

In 1974 the only health facilities in the area consisted of a 259-bedded hospital and one health centre. Since then seven more health centres have been constructed. In the early stages the doctors working in the health centres were mainly residents from specialties and lacked the skills and approaches needed for delivering primary care. Since then a 1-year training programme of work-service has been commenced. The residents and other doctors work in the mornings and attend classes in the afternoons. Each health centre has a geographical catchment area (divisions) with a population of between 100 000 and 400 000. From 1979 onwards smaller catchment areas (micro units) have been defined each consisting of about 3000 people. For each micro unit a community health worker—*Prodiap*—has been trained.

In 1980, the national programme for marginal populations in large cities (PAPMGU) was launched, and in Netzahualcoyoti township 13 sub-centres were constructed under this programme. Each sub-centre is responsible for 10 micro regions (of 30 000 population). The sub-centre has one physician, one nursing assistant and a number of *prodiaps*.

The provision of health care to the marginal population is thus conceptually organised into three levels of care:

(1) First level of health care comprises three basic activities at the micro region level—self-care in the home, health surveillance of mothers and children, first aid and primary care. It is felt that 85 per cent of the health problems can be dealt with at this level of care and 70 per cent of the budget is earmarked for this level. Community leaders, teachers, priests, together with health personnel including the *prodiaps* are the main sources of health care and advice for the population in each micro region.

(2) Second level of care is provided through specialties at the health centre level to deal with referred medical and surgical problems. It is felt that 12 per cent of the health problems require this type of care.

(3) Third level of care is provided in hospitals. Approximately 3 per cent of the health problems need this type of intensive health care in each township.

Concepts into practice—measuring the impact

The above case studies are examples of a variety of approaches being developed in different countries under differing socio-economic circumstances and political climates. Unlike models of integrated health care for rural areas, no well-demarcated approaches have emerged. The trend would appear to be for the development of ways of linking existing hospital services with community health action (e.g. Hong Kong, Manila and Mexico). Only a few cities (e.g. Hyderabad) have been able to evolve an integrated approach wherein environmental improvement, education and income generation are combined with a health component.

These case studies and models, however, indicate a major positive shift in thinking on the part of the urban planners and health officials. Instead of considering the squatters as eyesores calling for demolition and removal, or at best a transitory phenomenon, they are being treated as victims and sufferers from a major social problem facing the cities of the developing world. Their contribution to the economic and commercial activity of the city is being recognised and in some cases the dependence of the formal economic institutions of the city on the informal sector elaborated by the squatters in their quest for livelihood is being appreciated by the decision makers. The welfare of the squatters and their full inclusion into the social and commercial life of the city is beginning to receive attention.

How do the health programmes slowly emerging in squatter areas affect the health of the population? How important are health services to the people's health? These questions are being increasingly asked in all countries, developed and developing alike. Since many of the health activities in the developing world are modelled on the health experiences of the previous world powers in Europe, it will be helpful to consider the trends in mortality in the latter. The British National Health Service (NHS) has been a major academic attraction and a desirable social goal for both commonwealth and non-commonwealth countries. And yet the NHS has failed to reduce mortality and ill amongst the lower social classes to the same extent as in the upper classes (see tables 7.4 and 7.5).

The above data indicate the difficulties of providing health care to working-class groups who largely occupy inner city areas. Several studies in Britain have indicated the poor state of primary care in the inner city areas of London, Glasgow, and other industrial towns. Secondly, these data demonstrate the difficulties of overcoming the effects of inadequate material resources in the home and of poor income through the conventional type of health service aided by social security, however desirable the two are. Part of the difficulty lies in the way health systems and medical education are organised. In spite of increasing historical evidence concerning the role of the environment on health, the mechanistic view has prevailed wherein the human body is likened

Table 7.4 Neonatal mortality rates per 1000 legitimate live births by father's social class, England and Wales

Father's social class	Neonatal deaths						
	*1911**	*1921**	*1930–2**	*1939**	*1949–50**	*1970–72†*	*Decrease from 1911 (%)*
I—Professional	26.8	23.4	21.7	18.9	13.5	17.4	35.1
II—Intermediate	34.8	28.3	27.3	23.4	16.0	19.8	43.1
III—Skilled workers	39.6	{33.7	29.4	25.4	17.8	21.2	46.5
IV—Partly skilled workers		{36.7	31.9	27.7	19.9	25.7	35.1
V—Unskilled workers	42.5	36.9	32.5	30.1	21.9	35.17	17.25
Per cent excess V/I	58.6	57.7	49.8	59.3	62.2	101	

* *Source:* Morris, J. N. and Hendy, J. A. *Lancet* (1955) i: p. 554.
† *Source:* Office of Population Censuses and Surveys. *Occupational Mortality. The Registrar General's Decennial Supplement for England & Wales 1970–72.* HMSO, London, 1978. p. 157.

Table 7.5 Mortality rates per 100 000 by occupational class

Social class	Age (years)	Men				Women			
		1949–53	1959–63	1970–72	Decrease, 1949–53 (%)	1949–53	1959–63	1970–72	Decrease, 1949–53 (%)
I & II	25–34	124	81	72	41.9	85	51	42	50.6
III		148	100	90	39.2	114	64	51	55.3
IV & V		180	143	141	21.7	141	77	68	51.8
I & II	45–54	712	544	554	22.2	427	323	337	21.1
III		812	708	733	9.7	480	402	431	10.2
IV & V		895	842	894	—	513	455	510	—
I & II	55–64	2097	1804	1710	18.5	1098	818	837	23.8
III		2396	2218	2213	7.63	1202	1001	1059	11.9
IV & V		2339	2433	2409	—	1226	1129	1131	7.7

to a machine, and disease to malfunctioning of it to be corrected by therapeutics or surgery. According to this view, the 'fault' for the occurrence of disease lies with the individual, and by implication the socio-political and economic environment is absolved from any responsibility. The cause of the problem of ill health is perceived as lying with the individual and the nature of intervention is individually oriented e.g. health education or curative/diagnostic medicine. Consequently, the main thrust of professional bodies and government policies is to encourage those health programmes which are aimed at bringing about changes in the individual rather than in the economic or political environment. Failure to control the promotion of cigarettes, baby foods or alcoholic drinks is a prime example of such attitudes.

All the signs indicate that the developing countries are moving in the same direction as discussed above and are likely to embark on creating patterns of health care which bring in little value for money. This can be avoided by making community participation itself the main objective of health planning. There will understandably be many obstacles to overcome. There is the deep-rooted conviction that the élite specialist knows the best. The urban poor are often themselves not interested on account of alienation and exclusion from the mainstream of urban life. National planners resist the idea because of their fear of countless delays, arguments, even at times confrontation and subversion. Nations with socialist ideologies and governmental processes have found it easier to involve communities in the planning of their own health programmes, e.g. Tanzania, Cuba and China. Those with political ideologies to the extreme right have largely opted for token participation. Thus, depending on political ideology and maturation of democratic processes in the nation concerned, the following modes of people participation can be identified:

(1) 'Solid citizen' group appointed from amongst the squatters by outside authorities.
(2) Appointed local leaders in the government bureaucracy.

These two modes make use of the community development approach. Social workers organise community councils to channel the flow of services and materials from the larger society into the squatter community. Income generation activities, creation of credit facilities and training programmes are planned as part of self-help. People are only minimally involved in decision making. Instead, programmes planned by outside agencies are legitimised and implemented by local appointed leaders.

(3) Planners come to consult and discuss programmes with the people prior to implementation.
(4) Planners consult with people from the beginning of plan formulation.

People get a share in decision making depending upon the stage at which plans are discussed with them. Depending upon the incorporation of people's views into the final plans, the participation may vary from token to full. However, planners still control the process.

(5) People have representatives, varying from one or two to a clear majority, on the planning board.

This is true grass-root planning with significant participation by the people and a major share in decision making.

Conclusion

The above description of hyperurbanisation considers the importance of health as part of the main issue of providing basic needs for squatter settlements. The experience of some of the major industrial cities of the developed world provides useful leads to explore. Environmental improvement is considered far more rewarding than the provision of conventional curative services. Within such a framework improvement of nutrition and control of infection are stressed as the main objectives, especially for the vulnerable groups like pregnant and lactating women, and children. Ways of organising the health facilities and other resources are considered by means of a number of case studies of several urban connurbations of the developing world. The importance of community participation in the improvement of their environment is self-evident. An integrated approach is suggested wherein income generation activities, training and education programmes, welfare and social services together with community organisation help to strengthen the impact of health services and make health care more meaningful.

Further reading

Basta, S. (1977). Nutrition and health in low income urban areas of the Third World. *Ecol. Food Nutr.* **6**: 115.

Berg, A. (1972). Industry's struggle with world malnutrition. *Harvard Business Rev.* **50**: 135.

Carreon, G. G. (1981). The role of the hospital in promoting and providing primary health care. *World Hosp.* **17**: 9–12.

Chatley, A. (1979). *The Baby Killer Scandal.* War on Want, London.

Coombs, P. H. (ed.) (1980). *Meeting the Basic Needs of the Rural Poor.* Pergamon Press, New York and Oxford.

Cousins, W. J. (1978). Urban Community Development in Hyderabad. In de Souze, A. (ed.) *The Indian City: Poverty, Ecology and Urban Development.* Manohar Publications, New Delhi. pp. 171–5.

Davies, K. (1973). *Introduction in Cities, Their Origin, Growth and Human Impact. Readings from Scientific American*. W. H. Freeman & Co., San Francisco.

Department of International Economic and Social Affairs (1980). *Patterns of Urban and Rural Population Growth*. Population Studies No. 68. United Nations, New York. ST/ESA/SERA/68.

Desai, A. R. and Pillai, S. D. (1972). *A Profile of an Indian Slum*. Bombay University Press. Bombay.

Dobbing, J. (1981). The later development of the brain and its vulnerability. In Davies, J. A. and Dobbing, J. (eds). *Scientific Foundations of Paediatrics*. 2nd edn. Heinemann, London. p. 744.

Hollnsteiner, M. R. (1977). People Power: community participation in the planning of human settlements. *Assign. Child.* **40**: 11–47.

Jelliffe, E. F. P. (1975). The impact of the food industry on the nutritional status of infants and preschool children in developing countries. In *Priorities in Child Nutrition in Developing Countries*. Vol. II. Harvard University School of Public Health. p. 265.

Lappe, F. M. and Collins, J. (1977). *Food First*. Houghton Mifflin, Boston. p. 307.

Menefa Singh, A. (1978). Women and the family: coping with poverty in the *Bastis* of Delhi. In D'Souza, A. (ed.) *The Indian City: Poverty, Ecology and Urban Development*. Manohar, New Delhi.

Paterson, E. H. (1980). An Urban community health project. *Br. Med. J.* **285**: 29–31.

Report of a Study Group (1981). *Primary Health Care in Inner London*. London Health Planning Consortium, Mimeo.

Situación Socio-económica y Nutricional de las Familias de Ingresos Minimos en Lima Metropolitana (1980). Grados, Miranda y Mores.

The Tamil Nadu Nutrition Study. Vol. 1 (1973). Sidney M. Canter Associates, Haverford.

Index